EMERGING
HOPE

A Strategy for Reaching
Postmodern Generations

JIMMY LONG

IVP Books

An imprint of InterVarsity Press
Downers Grove, Illinois

InterVarsity Press
P.O. Box 1400, Downers Grove, IL 60515-1426
World Wide Web: www.ivpress.com
E-mail: email@ivpress.com

Second edition ©2004 by Jimmy Long. First edition, published under the title Generating Hope, *©1997 by Jimmy Long.*

InterVarsity Press® is the book-publishing division of InterVarsity Christian Fellowship/USA®, a student movement active on campus at hundreds of universities, colleges and schools of nursing in the United States of America, and a member movement of the International Fellowship of Evangelical Students. For information about local and regional activities, write Public Relations Dept., InterVarsity Christian Fellowship/USA, 6400 Schroeder Rd., P.O. Box 7895, Madison, WI 53707-7895, or visit the IVCF website at <www.intervarsity.org>.

Cover design: Cindy Kiple

Cover images: Digital Vision

ISBN 978-0-8308-3217-0

Printed in the United States of America ∞

Library of Congress Cataloging-in-Publication Data

Long, Jimmy.
 Emerging hope: a strategy for reaching the postmodern generations
 / Jimmy Long.
  p. cm.
 Rev. and expanded ed. of: Generating hope. c1997.
 Includes bibliographical references and index.
 ISBN 0-8308-3217-3 (pbk.: alk. paper)
 1. Church work with young adults. 2. Church work with adults. 3.
Evangelistic work—United States. 4. Generation X. 5.
Postmodernism—Religious aspects—Christianity. 6. United
States—Civilization—1970- 7. United States—Religion—1960- I.
Long, Jimmy, Generating hope. II. Title
BV4446.L66 2004
269'.2—dc22

                                                              2004009781

P	21	20	19	18	17	16	15	14	13	12	11	10	9	8	7	6	5	4
Y	22	21	20	19	18	17	16	15	14	13	12	11	10	09	08	07		

To the present

and former staff

and students in

InterVarsity's

Blue Ridge Region,

partners in ministry

for the last thirty years

Contents

Acknowledgments

This book is the work of many people. Having never expected to write the first edition, *Generating Hope,* I was pleasantly surprised when InterVarsity Press asked me to rewrite the book as part of the Emerging Culture Project. As it has been ten years since I wrote *Generating Hope,* I was honored to be asked to update the book. I continue to enjoy working with Cindy Bunch, an editor at InterVarsity Press. She has made some helpful suggestions in the rewriting process.

I want to thank the Blue Ridge regional staff, and especially Joe Moore, for giving me the needed time these last few months to concentrate on completing the Emerging Culture Curriculum, including *Emerging Hope.*

Six years ago Steve Hayner, then president of InterVarsity Christian Fellowship, gave his encouragement and blessing, with the approval of InterVarsity's board of directors, for me to head a team of InterVarsity staff in the Emerging Culture Project. The goal of the project was to help us within InterVarsity and within the church as a whole to have a better understanding of how to minister in the emerging twenty-first-century culture.

Gary Jennings of InterVarsity's Advance Department led the process of raising funds for this project. Gary and I were humbled and overwhelmed by how enthusiastically supportive each of the four foundations and one church were when we asked them to give to this venture. I want to thank the Maclellan Foundation and the other three foundations, plus my home church, the Chapel Hill Bible Church, and InterVarsity's board for being financially committed to this project.

I also want to thank the Emerging Culture Project InterVarsity staff team—Brian Housman, Rachelle (Smith) McClintock, Tony Warner, Brian Parks, Rick Richardson, Rick Mattson, Scott Anderson and Bora Reed—for their commitment and partnership in this project.

Most of all I want to thank my wife, Betsy, who has not only allowed me to invade our house with many more books on emerging culture but also has freely encouraged me to be away from home to share what I am learning with others. Furthermore, she, along with our two grown children, Andrew and Tiffany, have listened intently as I have shared with them more about the emerging culture than they probably ever wanted to know. I am truly fortunate to have such a loving family.

Introduction: *Ten Years Later*

M y have times changed! Ten years ago, when I began writing *Generating Hope,* I felt vulnerable and out there on my own. Along with a handful of other people, I was encouraging the church to begin asking the question of what ministry should look like in a postmodern culture. On the one hand, most people had never even heard of postmodernity, much less thought about ministry in a postmodern context. The few people in the church who had heard the term thought the use of the word *postmodern* would be passé within a couple of years.

In the mid-1990s most growing churches and Christian organizations were trying to emulate megachurches like Willow Creek. They did not want to hear that there might be a need to develop a new ministry strategy and methodology in the coming years. The churches and organizations that did see the need for new strategies were enamored with "generational" ministry.

What encouraged me during the last ten years were the scores of people who contacted me to tell me they thought I was describing them in the book. They were thankful that I had written about what they were feeling and had helped them to make sense of what was happening to them. My writing put into words what they were feeling. I have also had many parents and some grandparents who have told me that this book helped them to understand their children.

I also have been encouraged by young church leaders who have told me that my book *Generating Hope* was the first book they read on ministry in a postmodern context. It was the beginning of a journey for them, a journey they are continuing today.

Now, ten years later, there is growing recognition (though certainly not one that is universally accepted) that postmodern culture is with us for many years to come and that we need to develop new strategies to minister in this cultural context. Instead of just a handful of articles and books talking about postmodern ministry, there are numerous written resources and many emerging church experiments.

I have two audiences in mind as I write this updated book, *Emerging Hope.* My main audience is comprised of the people in most of our churches who recognize that ministry needs to change but do not understand the emerging culture, much less know what strategies to implement for it. To these people I say: I understand your uncertainty. I hope this book helps you not only understand the emerging culture but also embrace new opportunities to minister.

The other audience I am writing to is made up of the young postmoderns who have jumped headlong into ministry and have little patience with people who are struggling in this new ministry. I hope in the book to not only help you understand the historical and theological context for your ministry, giving you suggestions for ministry, but also help you be patient with some of the people who work alongside you and who are still struggling with emerging-culture ministry.

For the first twenty years of my ministry, I had a vision to prepare our InterVarsity students for the church. For the last ten years and the coming ten years, my vision is to prepare the church for our "emerging postmodern students" and help churches not only welcome these young people but eventually give over leadership of the church to them in the next ten to twenty years.

I hope this book helps you and others to have a heart for people—including yourself, no matter what your age—who are living in the emerging culture and to develop strategies to implement the type of ministry God desires for you and others to have in your local context.

This book is also part of a larger curriculum, *Emerging Culture: Ministry Resources for a Changing World,* published by InterVarsity Press. This curriculum includes a twelve- to eighteen-hour PowerPoint presentation on CD-ROM, a leader's guide, participant's guides and *Emerging Hope*. The purpose of the curriculum is to help churches and other ministries understand the cultural changes and develop new ministry strategies for the emerging culture.

You may also want to check out <emergingculture.com>, an InterVarsity website that will provide continual dialogue and resources on ministry in the emerging culture. You may also contact me at emerginghope@aol.com with your thoughts and ideas.

PART ONE

THE TIMES THEY ARE A-CHANGING

A Cultural Snapshot

A Simple Question, a Complex Journey

It was a simple question. I asked it merely to pass the time before the meeting began that early December evening in 1989. Little did I imagine the journey I would begin with that simple question.

The question I asked Joan, a young student sitting next to me, was "Are you going home for Christmas?" Since it was only a few weeks before Christmas, I thought I would get a simple answer, yes or no. Was I surprised when Joan burst into tears! I asked myself, *What in the world have I done?*

At that moment the meeting began, and in a few minutes I was introduced as the speaker and had to proceed to the lectern to begin my talk. I do not remember anything I said during the whole talk. All I could think about was Joan sitting in the corner with tears flowing down her cheeks. Immediately after the meeting I went over to Joan and said, "I am so sorry! Joan, obviously I touched a nerve that I did not mean to touch."

As Joan slowly pulled herself together, she told me that it was okay and then went on to say, "I don't know where my home is. You see, when I was ten years old, my parents got a divorce. Now, ten years later, each parent has gotten a second divorce, and both have remarried again. I don't know where my home is!"

Who were her parents? Where was her home? Frederick Buechner, in his book *The Longing for Home,* defines home as "the place where, if you have to go there, they have to take you in."[1] Joan realized that cold December evening that she was not sure where her home was or who would take her in.

That December evening in the waning days of the 1980s, I realized that how I began doing ministry in the early 1970s might not work in the 1990s and certainly not in the twenty-first century. Like Dorothy in *The Wizard of Oz,* I slowly began to realize that we were not in Kansas anymore.[2] It took me a few years of crying out to God before I heard God say to me, like he said to Habakkuk,

> Look at the nations and watch—
>   and be utterly amazed.
> For I am going to do something in your days
>   that you would not believe,
>   even if you were told. (Hab 1:5)

At that time God did not tell Habakkuk that the Israelites were going into captivity in Babylon. I think God recognized that Habakkuk could not have dealt with that much change. God was also gracious to me in the following years because I did not realize at the time all the change my ministry would go through in the following years.

It is ironic that for the last fifteen years I have been involved in bringing about change in ministry, because I do not like change. I initially did not want to change the way I did ministry, having been successful in doing it the old way. I had helped build a campus ministry with InterVarsity at UNC-Chapel Hill from two hundred to seven hundred students in six years. I had helped develop a regional campus ministry of close to four thousand students while building a staff team of sixty. At the same time I was a leader in my church, helping it to grow from two hundred to around twelve hundred participants.

Even in the midst of success, I realized there were two good times to change how we do ministry. Certainly we need to seriously consider changing how we do ministry when the ministry is floundering. That is obvious! However, the other time we need to reconsider how we do ministry is when our ministry is thriving. Why? Because when our ministry is thriving, it can withstand the shock that change inevitably brings. Too often, though, this is the time when we are least open to change. We think, *Why rock the boat?*

As I began my complex journey of change in the early 1990s, I first needed to be willing to change how I did ministry, if that is where God was leading me. I had to be like Habakkuk, who even though he did not understand fully—or even *partly* understand—what God was doing, had to finally say,

> LORD, I have heard of your fame;
> I stand in awe of your deeds, O LORD.
> Renew them in our day,
> in our time make them known. (Hab 3:2)

In some ways it was like relearning how to walk, ride a bike or drive a car.

As a youngster growing up in Columbia, South Carolina, I found Five Points to be one of the most intriguing spots in town. I was fascinated by this conjunction of five roads. When I began driving as a teenager, my fascination with Five Points turned to terror. I was terrified of approaching the center of Five Points and having to figure out which of the five roads to take. Later, during my seminary days at Gordon-Conwell on the north shore of Boston, I learned that other states dealt with multiple road mergers through the use of circles, or rotaries, which can be just as frightening as Five Points was in Columbia.

Whenever we approach a new rotary or Five Points as we are driving, we become anxious and tend to look for something familiar. Most of us find it hard to strike out into uncharted territory, because we fear the unknown. We are suspicious or fearful of anything new. We tend to stay where we are most comfortable. Once we actually make a turn at Five Points, it is hard to undo our decision, since we have set ourselves in a direction from which we cannot easily return. Making the right decision the first time is crucial.

As I began to develop some answers about how ministry needed changing, I wrestled with the question of who I was to share my thoughts of what ministry should look like in the emerging culture. I am neither a Gen Xer nor a Millennial. I am a Boomer. To be honest, I am more modern than postmodern. Also, for most of my life, I have been more involved in campus ministry than in church ministry. Furthermore, I do not even have a type-A personality. And remember, I do not like change!

However, I began to realize that as one who, through God's graciousness, has begun to understand these changes, I do have something to share with others. By continuing to work with college students and young campus staff, I have developed a multigenerational and multicultural perspective. Although I am a Boomer and modern by definition, I work with Gen Xers and Millennials who are becoming more postmodern as each year passes. Also, I have further realized that what we face in ministry on the college campus hits the church with force about five to ten years later as these former students become more and more the heart of the local church. In some ways we in InterVarsity are the advance scouts for the church. The church can learn from both our mistakes and our successes. Finally, as a leader in a campus-oriented church, I have been in the midst of how our church is successfully—and unsuccessfully—dealing with these changes.

The church today is at a critical juncture in regard to two major societal changes. The first societal change is the generational transition from the Baby Boom generation to Generation X and the Millennial generation. For the last twenty-five years, the Baby Boomers (people born between 1946 and 1964) have been the dominant decision-making group in the United States. This is changing as members of Generation X (people born between 1964 and 1984) come into positions of leadership and power. The Millennial generation (born between 1984 and 2000) is not far behind. The second change is a cultural shift that is occurring in Western

> *Every few hundred years in Western history there occurs a sharp transformation. Within a few short decades, society rearranges itself—its world view; its basic values; its social and political structures; its arts; its key institutions.*
>
> *Fifty years later there is a new world. And the people born then cannot even imagine the world in which their grandparents lived and into which their parents were born. We are currently living through just such a transition.*
>
> PETER DRUCKER,
> *POST-CAPITALIST SOCIETY*

society as the prevailing culture moves from the Enlightenment/modern era to the emerging/postmodern era. How the church responds to these generational changes and—even more importantly—to these cultural changes will determine how faithful and successful the church will be in the twenty-first century in accomplishing God's mission for the church.

The church today is at its own Five Points. As it moves from a ministry primarily focused on Baby Boomers to a ministry primarily focused on Gen Xers and Millennials, and more importantly, as it moves out of the Enlightenment/ modern era into the emerging/post-modern era, the church stands at a critical juncture. It needs to make sure it has enough information about these societal changes to make an informed correction in ministry. The church also needs to exercise enough faith to make a decision that might take it out of its present comfort zone. The decisions that the church is making today about how it will relate to society will influence the church's mission for the next fifty to one hundred years.

> *We finally have developed arguments that work really well in the modern age and that makes us feel comfortable among moderns. So some religious institutions already are showing signs of entrenchment preparing to defend themselves against postmodernity. But all they can effectively accomplish through resistance is to linger in modernity. . . . This results in devastating losses for the church in society.*
>
> CHUCK SMITH, *THE END OF THE WORLD . . . AS WE KNOW IT*

HISTORICAL PERSPECTIVE

Throughout its history, the church has had to make choices about how it will relate to the surrounding culture, from the Roman catacombs to Constantine's inner court, from monasteries to King Richard III, from Calvin's Geneva to the Anabaptists. The church in the United States has had to make similar choices. Many Christians came and settled in this new land because of difficulties they experienced in their European cultures. Christians and

Our experiences from the past are to give us the confidence to face the challenges of tomorrow. We are not to build monuments but to join the movement. Sometimes we choose instead to build monasteries. Too often the church becomes our secure place; our haven from the outside world. . . . The church was never intended to be a monastery. In fact God intends there to be no place where we can hide, except in his presence. When the church becomes our shelter from a radically changing world, we fail to turn to God and make him our hiding place and our shelter. . . . When the church becomes a movement and not a monastery, she becomes a place of transformation for the very culture from which we run in fear.

ERWIN MCMANUS, *AN UNSTOPPABLE FORCE*

others tried different experiments in the colonies to determine how the church and the culture would relate to each other. As the United States was founded in the 1770s and 1780s, there was much discussion of the relationship between church and culture. In the intervening years, as other immigrant groups from Africa, Asia and Latin America have entered into American culture, the church has continued to wrestle with how it should relate to society.

American Christians continue to discuss how church and culture should relate to each other. In the early 1950s, H. Richard Niebuhr wrote a seminal book, *Christ and Culture,* in which he described five models of how the church of Jesus Christ related to the culture. He categorized these five options as (1) Christ of culture, (2) Christ and culture in paradox, (3) Christ above culture, (4) Christ against culture and (5) Christ the transformer of culture.[3]

In the last fifty years, both the church in the United States and the American culture as a whole have changed dramatically. While I am concentrating on the United States, these changes and the church's response to these changes are also occurring in similar ways in other countries.

As we have entered the twenty-first century, I would like to describe six models that depict how the church is responding to a changing culture. The contemporary church responds to the changing American culture from one of these six perspectives.

How the Church Has Responded to the Changing Culture

MODERN CULTURE RESPONSES	EMERGING CULTURE RESPONSES
Unchanging Tradition	Fortress Mentality
Developmental Phase	Prophetic Voice
Generational Transition	Missional Opportunity

The three responses from the modern perspective actually ignore or dismiss the fact that any major cultural change is taking place. The three emerging-culture responses acknowledge that there is major cultural change taking place but differ radically about how the church should respond to that change. Examining each perspective will offer understanding about which model (or models) might help the church as it responds to a changing culture.

UNCHANGING TRADITION

The unchanging church ignores culture. It views the church as having nothing to do with present culture. The church is above and beyond culture. People in this camp see tradition as paramount, and many of the people in this camp believe there is never a need to change. The unchanging tradition can primarily, but not exclusively, be found in independent, rural, fundamentalist churches.

Years ago I overheard a discussion between two Christians over whether the King James Bible should still be used. One of the Christians in the discussion exclaimed in all seriousness that if the King James Version was good enough for Jesus, it was good enough for him. The King James Bible was not written until the early 1600s.

The unchanging tradition tries to hold on to its own traditions by rising above culture. Christians in the unchanging church try to equate their own traditions, as exemplified in the above story, with Jesus' blessings. They have no idea that many of their traditions did not begin with Jesus but started much later. Some of my friends in high school came from these traditions. One of them responded to me during a discussion on dating with his church's convictions on the subject. "I don't drink, I don't chew [tobacco], I don't go out with girls that do."

Many Anabaptist traditions fit into the unchanging tradition model. Some Mennonite, Amish and Quaker communities fall into this pattern of relating to the culture. Parts of the Catholic Church also fall under this model. What they all have in common is the tightness with which they hold on to their cherished traditions and the conviction that these traditions are all biblical. G. K. Chesterton once stated, "Tradition is the living faith of those now dead. Traditionalism is the dead faith of those now living."

> If the tensions created by these conflicting worldviews are significant for Christians engaging in mission within the Western world, they are even more so in many parts of Asia, Japan and South Korea that have experienced the successive waves of modernity and postmodernity pounding over the ancient cultures within a much shorter time period.
>
> EDDIE GIBBS, CHURCHNEXT

The strength of this model is its stability. It endures from one generation to the next without major change. The weakness of this model is that although the culture and the people within the culture do change, the church does not change to meet people where they are. As the culture continues to change, the unchanging church becomes more and more marginalized and exerts less and less impact on society.

This sort of marginalization occurs frequently in the business world. In 1879 the marketing concept of the F. W. Woolworth Company was amazingly successful. But by the 1990s almost half the remaining eight hundred stores had closed. Woolworth's major problem was that it had not been able to let go of its past.[4] This unwillingness to change led to its downfall.

The unchanging tradition will be unable to draw in new members and will continue to lose its youth, who feel the church has no answers for their struggles. The result for many of these churches will be extinction by the time the postmodern generations come into maturity.

DEVELOPMENTAL PHASE

Many societal and church leaders remember their childhood and adolescent years during the 1950s and 1960s when they were the rebels—beatniks, hippies. They cried out for change and were heralded as the initiators of major cultural change. However, when they grew up and came to their senses, they became like their parents before them. They had just gone through a phase—prolonged adolescence. So now, as they see young people crying out for cultural change, these present leaders think the young people are going

---

Pastors today seem driven to do something about the culture. Perhaps the best thing they could do is withdraw from it and develop a holy community, a congregation of people oriented to the reality not the unreality of the world. . . . We're not supposed to be dealing with the culture. We're supposed to be dealing with God. . . . The historical period most analogous to ours might be the time after the fall of Rome. Society fell apart, the culture shattered. The people who recovered Christian identity, Christian community and Christian culture amid that chaos were the monks. In a sense, they withdrew from the chaos to shape community and some of the gospel.

EUGENE PETERSON, "RETURN TO THE TIMELESS"

---

through a developmental phase. When they "grow up," these young people will become like "one of us."

When Willow Creek began Axis, its alternative ministry to young people, they planned that as these young people grew older they would "graduate" into their mainstream services. Many churches in the 1990s and into the twenty-first century have developed similar models. The alternative ministries in many churches are just holding patterns—like airplanes circling above airports until they are ready to land—until the young people mature into adulthood and become involved in the mainstream ministry of the church.

Certainly, there is great validity to the suggestion that we all progress through developmental stages of life. We move through infancy to child-hood to adolescence to early adulthood to mature adulthood and finally to senior adulthood. However, if people in this category are wrong in seeing that most of the changes in young people are just part of the normal devel-opmental phase, they may wake up one day, five to ten years from now, see-ing that their church, organization or business has become marginalized.

GENERATIONAL TRANSITION

In the early 1990s two authors, Neil Howe and William Strauss, wrote a book titled *13th Gen* that had and still has a dramatic, though waning, impact on how our society understands the changes that are happening all around. Al-though the terms Baby Boomer and Baby Buster were in use before the early 1990s, these two authors captured the business and church world's attention with how they described the societal changes that were occurring.

Basically, Howe and Strauss have developed a theory that between the writing of the United States Constitution in 1786 and the present day there have been fifteen generations. The most recent generations are commonly called Millennial and Post-Millennial. Howe and Strauss go on to say that these generations are cyclical. Every generation cycles back and demon-strates similar traits as the fifth generation before it.

Twentieth-Century Generations

Name	Birth Dates
G.I.	1901-1924
Silent	1925-1945
Boomers	1946-1964
Xers	1964-1984
Millennials	1984-2000

In the 1990s, and up until the present day, many businesses and churches have viewed this generational transition as the primary way to understand

In 1995 a few friends and I were explaining the phenomenon of "Generation X" to Jorge Atiencia, a prominent Latin American preacher and theologian. He initially seemed confused, until he finally said, "Ah! You are using the word generation to mean people born at a certain time; but in Spanish generacion customarily means everyone alive on earth at a given moment." It wasn't until recently that I noticed that Atencia's comment about Spanish applied equally to the words of Jesus in the New Testament. "To what will I compare this generation?" Jesus asks in Matthew 11:16—and he's not talking about forty to fifty-five year olds. One can't help noticing that Jesus almost always uses generation with an adjective like "faithless" or "adulterous," but he is referring to a historical moment, not to people in a specific demographic group. Jesus and his contemporaries understood, better than we moderns, that the spirit of the age affects people of all ages.

ANDY CROUCH, *RE:GENERATION QUARTERLY*

the societal changes. As we will see in the next chapter, generational transition is a helpful way to understand minor changes in society and gives us a chance to fine-tune our ministry from one generation to another.

However, there are a couple of significant weaknesses to this way of describing major societal changes. First, generational theory is based upon a cyclical view of history championed by certain early twentieth-century historians. Instead of history moving to a conclusion, history repeats itself every fifth generation. As Christians, we should have problems with this understanding of history. We see history as moving to a certain conclusion, not just repeating itself. Also, generational theory is very American. Few other countries even understand what we are describing with this theory. Generational theory does not describe all the cultural changes that are occurring, only a limited few.

EMERGING CULTURE: FORTRESS MENTALITY

Numerous Christians today are consciously becoming distinct from the culture. While they recognize that there are major cultural changes occurring, they see these changes as toxic. When they look around at the emerging culture, all they see is moral corruption and decay. For the last forty years, they have observed the rise of the dysfunctional family, the breakdown of the educational system and the disintegration of common moral values. Many Christians have responded to these changes with a sense of hopelessness and a desire for protection. "All of this is beyond my understanding and control. I can't make any difference in the world. Sin is awful and powerful. My best strategy is to build a wall around myself and my family to keep out the changes and evil."[5] This worldview represents a dualistic approach to society that sees the church as good and the culture as bad.

Many well-respected Christian leaders seem to endorse this desire to establish a protective cocoon for our families and for the church. As Charles Colson states in his book *Against the Night: Living in the New Dark Ages,* "I believe that we do face a crisis in Western culture, and that it presents the greatest threat to civilization since the barbarians invaded Rome. I believe that today in the West, and particularly in America, the new barbarians are all around us."[6] Carl Henry, in his book *Gods of This Age or God of the Ages,* cries out with an even greater warning. "Nightfall for Western Civilization is close at hand. Let me leave no doubt then about my deep conviction. As I see it, the believing church is the West's last and only real bastion against barbarism."[7]

Many Christians who nod along with Colson's pessimistic analysis of today's culture, and Henry's dire predictions for the future, are not coming to terms with culture or making any attempt to change the culture. Rather, they are boycotting the culture and setting up a parallel culture.[8] In the 1990s this Christian isolation-and-protection movement spread like wildfire. Christians today have their own Christian schools, home schools, colleges, bookstores and novels, entertainment and recreational industry, with church gyms and exercise classes, and their own nationwide media. One Christian businessman from Columbia, South Carolina, explained that he felt the need to "cleanse himself" after watching the network news. The only news he watches now is on *The 700 Club,* which is part of a Christian television network headed by Pat Robertson.

Many people in the church today see the present culture as beyond saving. Adopting a bunker mentality, they advocate establishing communities similar to the monasteries of the Dark Ages as the only hope for themselves, their families and the church. Even the well-known Alasdair MacIntyre, in his book *After Virtue,* suggests that in order to preserve virtue it might be necessary to project new forms of community, as the church had to do to weather the raging storm of the barbarian invasion.[9]

The fall of the West Roman Empire in A.D. 476 inaugurated the Dark Ages, which lasted until around the year 1000. The Western world was thrown into a state of confusion and instability. Like Jerome, a leading Roman Christian scholar, many saw the barbarian invaders as the enemies of Rome and of Christ. It was a time when learning and culture were at a minimum and instability and insecurity were at a maximum. The church developed a survivalist and protectionist mentality.[10] Society was corrupt and seductive. For the church to survive intact, it had to escape from the presence and control of the barbarian culture. Monasteries were established as places to flee from the barbarian-controlled world.[11] Historian Norman Cantor describes the Benedictine monastic community as a "completely self-contained community, economically as well as spiritually, and was not to rely upon the world for anything."[12] The monastic movement began as a protective society, and many in the movement never moved beyond the view that they were the protectors of the church, which was teetering on the brink of extinction.

But not all Christians who lived during the Dark Ages saw the barbarian invasion as a threat to the church. Augustine, for one, saw it as an opportunity. Augustine viewed the invaders as citizens-to-be in the city of God. He was remarkably optimistic, even though he was surrounded by a decaying civilization and a threatened church.[13]

Although the monastic movement began as a defensive reaction to the barbarian invasion, God did not allow it to remain so. While it took several hundred years to fully emerge from its protective cocoon, the monastic movement ended as a reforming and mission-minded movement. By the beginning of the medieval period (1000-1300), the church, after several hundred years of primarily trying to survive, began to have a tangible impact on the culture around it. Monasteries began providing moral order to the towns and villages around them. Monks were busy planting and harvesting crops as well as preserving the Scriptures and classical literature. They became caring and mission-minded communities. The later monasteries became a visible sign of God's love for the world.

This tension, generated by uncertainty over whether to be a protected, closed community or a mission-minded, open community is the same tension we face today. The culture around the church is decaying. We in the church feel vulnerable, afraid and hopeless. However, we need to identify our primary problem: is it the secularist culture around us, or is it our lack of faith in a sovereign God? Has the doctrine of the providence of God, which claims that God controls all that happens in this world, been forgotten by Christians today? Many of us are behaving like the Christian fundamentalist of the 1920s who was characterized as someone who "talks of standing on the rock of ages, but acts as if he were clinging to the last piece of driftwood."[14]

While the church might think it is going into a protective mode for pure motives and with a known effect (a pure church), it needs to recognize that it has been influenced by postmodern culture. Although we will look at postmodern culture in much more detail in chapter three, for now let me point out that one of the characteristics of postmodern society is the existence of tribal groups. Tribalism is the bonding together of like-minded people for protection from the rest of society. These groups are a means of survival in a drifting culture. While the fortress-mentality church thinks it can hide itself from cultural influence, it cannot. By becoming a protective community (tribal group), it has actually become a product of postmodern society.

Those Christians with a fortress mentality seem to have little faith in God's sovereignty. Did not Jesus say, "I will build my church, and the gates of Hades will not overcome it" (Mt 16:18)? Furthermore, as I hope the reader will discover in the rest of this book, although the culture around us may be decaying, the church, instead of being on the brink of extinction, may be on the verge of a great revival. If we are able to understand the changes that are occurring in our culture and are willing to adapt to these changes, we can become vital witnesses of Jesus Christ in the midst of these changes. As we shall see in coming chapters, there is a great deal of confusion and uncertainty in society because of these changes. It is during times of uncertainty that people can be more open to change. Instead of trying to protect ourselves, we in the church should overcome our uncertainty through trusting in God's faithfulness. Then we can be agents of hope in the midst of these changes.

EMERGING CULTURE: PROPHETIC VOICE

While the unchanging-tradition church is mostly oblivious to its possible extinction, the prophetic church is fighting back with all the weapons it can get its hands on. There is a wide continuum of people in the church who would describe their orientation to the emerging culture as prophetic. Many in the prophetic church have a great fear that life as they know it in this culture is hanging by a thread. They believe that God has ordained them to fight the last battle so that the culture (and the church along with the culture) does not disintegrate. Their prophetic voice is primarily pointed not to the church but to the culture. The recent battles over the display of the Ten Commandments in certain governmental buildings, or use of the phrase "one nation under God" in the Pledge of Allegiance, are prime examples of the prophetic-voice movement in the midst of these cultural changes.

How did we get into this culture war, and why has it become so important to the prophetic church? James Davison Hunter, in his insightful book *Culture Wars: The Struggle to Define America*, defines cultural conflict as "political and social hostility rooted in different systems of moral understanding. The end to which these hostilities tend is the domination of one cultural and moral ethos over all others."[15] The root of this cultural conflict is opposing worldviews and opposing views of moral authority. The diametrically opposed

> *If Christians are not involved as salt and light in our culture, we will one day wake up to find our freedom to live as Christians gone. The barbarians will be at the church door and we won't be able to have our separatist, pietist meetings. Our society will become increasingly corrupt, godless and hostile until people finally break down the doors of the church and haul Christians away.*
>
> JAMES KENNEDY,
> "FLEX THE MUSCLE"

views cause deep suspicion, deep division and deep antagonism between the two sides.

The stakes are high for Christians in the prophetic church. In the minds of the leaders in the prophetic church, the battle is not only between two opposing worldviews; it is a cosmic battle. James Dobson states, "The heated dispute over values in Western nations is simply a continuation of the age-

---

Forget about what's happened;

don't keep going over old history.

Be alert, be present. I'm about to do something brand-new.

It's bursting out! Don't you see it?

There it is! I'm making a road through the desert,

rivers in the badlands. (Is 43:18-19 The Message)

The past can become an idealized world (the "good old days") into which we retreat when the future becomes too frightening to face, or it can be a springboard from which we launch ourselves into the future with new strength. Isaiah does not want Israel to retreat into the past. . . . They can be the witnesses God has created them to be only by going forward with God by grasping the new thing he has for them.

BARRY WEBB, *THE MESSAGE OF ISAIAH*

---

old struggle between the principles of righteousness and the kingdom of darkness and someday soon I believe a winner will emerge and the loser will fade from memory."[16]

The Christians in the prophetic church are committed and serious about the battle they are waging. They see the battle lines as clearly drawn between the "good guys" and the "bad guys." For them, not fighting this battle would be disobeying God. Many Christians in the prophetic church see themselves as the "true church" and the only ones following God's will in this area.

This worldview starts with an entirely correct idea that Jesus Christ is King of all kings. However, the arrogance of many in the prophetic-voice category, in claiming to speak for all committed Christians, has already hampered the spread of the gospel among the emerging generations. As we will see in the next chapter, these emerging generations are not drawn to the political arena but to community. They seek compromise, not confrontation, and are repelled by any group arrogantly claiming to have all the answers.

While it is important for us in the church to listen to the prophets among us, most biblical prophets were primarily speaking to God's people in the community of faith to bring about spiritual renewal and justice, not to society to bring about religious domination. Both camps—fortress mentality and prophetic voice—have little understanding that God as Creator of the universe might actually be orchestrating some of these cultural changes to renew the church (Israel's exile to Babylon) in Christ's image and prepare postmodern people to embrace the gospel.

EMERGING CULTURE: MISSIONAL OPPORTUNITY

Instead of seeing the culture as a battlefield and Christians as warriors, those in the missional church see the world as a mission field and Christians as missionaries. John Woodbridge described the situation in a *Christianity Today* article. "If we follow Christ's example of compassion, we will see America more as a mission field of people who need a shepherd rather than as a culture war battlefield needing more political generals. In short, we will love rather than hate our enemies, pray for them rather than seek to destroy them."[17]

This question of whether to view our culture as a battlefield or a mission field has pitted evangelical Christians against one other. James Dobson responded angrily to Woodbridge's characterization of the prophetic church. Dobson requested the following of those in the church that choose not to join the battle:

> May I ask you to extend a little charity and grace to those of us who feel called to this cause? We are often outgunned and undermanned. We don't have all the answers. We, like you, are simply trying to serve the Lord to the best of our ability, and sometimes we do it poorly.

Sometimes in our zeal we may fail to show the love of Christ, which is central to everything we believe. You are justified in criticizing us when that occurs. But while you're there on the sidelines, I ask that you not make our task any more difficult than it already is.[18]

Jesus prayed in John 17 that the Father would keep the disciples in the world, but that they would not become of the world. So we are to be "in" not "of" and not "out of" either. I want to be in touch but not in tune with the culture. I am an indigenous missionary to this culture, which means I live and look and act as part of this culture, though it's not my home. I'm not going to anchor in this culture. I'm going to anchor in God's Spirit and in God's Word.

LEONARD SWEET,
"TARGET THE TRENDS"

Those in the missional church would see themselves as befriending individuals in the culture with the gospel. They are dialoguing over differences in order to influence change. The missional church understands that at Pentecost "God created a new community through which God intends to reach people and redeem the world."[19]

The missional church sees itself as intimately involved in the culture. Redemption does not change the fact that missional people are involved in the culture, but it changes them and the character of their involvement. They become a people who share God's love for those who do not yet follow God. They see the neighborhood and the local school as mission fields, not battlegrounds. Far from being military bunkers, their homes are "havens of hospitality" with the welcome sign displayed out front.[20]

The gospel message will be powerful only through showing love to neighbors and living lives of integrity. Members of the missional church see the fortress-mentality and prophetic churches persecuting their enemies instead of loving them. This persecution is polarizing our culture between those who are Christians and those who are not Christians. This polarization is leaving little room for influence or the voice of prophecy.

The missional church is asking whether lasting cultural change comes through battling society or through influencing it. Those in the missional church see others as people created by God and in need of God, not as the enemies of God. So their strategy is twofold. First, they seek to have influence and engage in dialogue outside the church. Second, they desire to speak prophetically within the church by calling the church to embody the gospel in the community, not to either retreat from the community or lash out at people in the community.

Instead of drawing battle lines, the missional church is opening up lines of dialogue. Christians need to be involved in secular life rather than merely "shooting from the sidelines at secular people."[21] As we will see in the coming chapters, postmodern generations need love and not war, hope and not despair. What would Jesus have us do? I am convinced that Jesus desires for us to provide people in this emerging culture with hope and not cultural war. From Tom Sine's perspective, our decision over whether to view our culture as a mission field or a battlefield will determine our witness for decades to come.[22]

IMPLICATIONS FOR MINISTRY

As a church, we have a critical decision ahead of us. We can choose the unchanging-tradition road and face cultural extinction. We can take the developmental-phase road and wake up one day to see that the culture has passed us by. We can take the generational-transition road and see that we might make a difference in people around us but have no chance of changing the culture. If we take the fortress-mentality road, we might save ourselves but will have lost any chance to save people in the world. If we take the prophetic-voice road, we might end up only critiquing the church or the world but not making any changes in either church or culture. Or we can take the missional road and provide hope for people in the emerging culture.

Emerging-culture people will most likely not even know the unchanging-tradition church exists, or if they do know it exists, they will see the church as irrelevant. People in the developmental-phase church will wonder why so few emerging-culture people are responding to its ministry. People in the emerging culture will wonder why the developmental-phase church cannot see the lifelong changes, not just the developmental changes, they are facing.

While the generational-transition church will have some surface success, emerging-culture people will wonder why the church does not understand their deeper cultural needs, not just their surface generational needs. People in the emerging culture will dismiss the fortress-mentality church because they will see that the church cares more about avoiding being tainted by the culture than about reaching out to them. The prophetic church will seem like an intolerant church, always critiquing and never giving to people in the emerging culture. We can primarily win emerging-culture people over through being missional—by befriending them, providing them a place to belong and offering hope to counter their despair.

Any church can determine whether or not it will survive the next twenty years by estimating how many people are involved in it between the ages of fifteen and thirty-five. Most children under the age of fifteen come to church because their parents bring them. People in their midthirties and beyond have not felt the full force of this emerging postmodern culture. A church needs at least 25 percent of its participants in the eighteen to thirty-five age group, or its future may be in doubt. We must minister faithfully and effectively to members of this age group if we are going to be ministering well into the twenty-first century. Even some of our "seeker sensitive" churches are in trouble because they have learned how to minister to Boomers but not to the emerging postmodern generations, with Xers and Millennials being the first purely postmodern generations.

To build a framework for ministry in the twenty-first century, we need a more complete understanding of both the postmodern generations (Gen X and Millennial) and the emerging postmodern culture. We will try to develop this understanding in the next two chapters.

2

The Adaptive Generations

Ａt a Harvard graduation ceremony a number of years ago, one of the student speakers summarized the feeling shared by many of his fellow students with the following words:

> I believe that there is one idea, one sentiment, which we have all acquired at some point in our Harvard careers, and that ladies and gentlemen is in a word, confusion. . . . They tell us that it is heresy to suggest the superiority of some value, fantasy to believe in moral argument, slavery to submit to a judgment sounder than your own. The freedom of our day is the freedom to devote ourselves to any values we please, on the mere condition that we do not believe them to be true.[1]

Steven Gibbs, a member of Generation X, expressed a similar viewpoint in his book *Twenty-Something, Floundering and Off the Yuppie Track.* When asked to comment on their twenties, the people he interviewed said that they were so out of it, so lost, that they did not feel like saying anything. These Xers marveled at how they managed at all. Even the primary term used to describe this generation, "Generation X," is confusing. If we in the church are going to minister effectively to Generation X and the Millennials, we need to gain a better perspective of these generations. For many, these generations are an enigma.

Some of my fellow Boomers think these younger generations have little drive or commitment. They worry about our society's future. For some, the X supposedly represents how they are unfocused, random, uncommitted and so on.

For others, the letter X symbolizes the algebraic term meaning "times," which signifies unlimited possibilities and opportunities. The sky is the limit, as the same word can take on vastly different meanings. If you think this issue is confusing to those of us outside these younger generations, just try to put yourself in their place. Confusion is a major force in the lives of the younger generations. The following cartoon typifies this state of confusion.[2]

SOME DAYS IT TOOK *HOURS* TO GET DRESSED . . .

Today's young people are receiving mixed messages about life that throw them, consciously or subconsciously, into a state of confusion. One of the most common responses to a difficult question from these generations is "Whatever." Life can offer too many choices, none of which represents an ideal option.

When the sky is the limit, we can lose touch with our foundation. Our culture is going through a major paradigm shift, which will require us to become adaptive. Xers and Millennials might be the best hope to lead us through this massive societal shift. These generations have been forced to feel their way through the confusion that surrounds them and to adapt to new situations. For example, these younger generations have had to adapt in their relationship with the Baby Boom generation, in the new economic world, in their interactions with their families, in their interactions with society and in their understanding of themselves within these frameworks.

ADAPTING TO THE BABY BOOMERS

As Xers and Millennials look back at my generation, the Baby Boomers, they wonder what went wrong with us. We had an outlook on life that differed dramatically from our parents' outlook. (See table 1.) As part of the post-World War II generation, we benefited from our parents' desire for stability and homogeneity in life, in the wake of the Depression in the 1930s and World War II in the 1940s. We had a safe and child-centered home life. At the same time we were not as confined as our parents were. As one Boomer puts it, "We were brought up thinking that if we don't want to do something we don't have to and we don't want to feel guilty about it. We want more self-fulfillment instead of satisfying others' needs."[3]

As the Baby Boom generation went about trying to fulfill its needs, it dismantled the very institutions that made our childhoods secure. It moved from a sense of stability and security into the realm of change and choice. We in the Baby Boom generation have been seduced by the idea of choice. George Barna, a leading pollster, describes Boomers as those who "believed that the future was waiting to be created. We were optimistic about the future. We were anx-

Table 1. Generational Outlook

	Boomers	Xers	Millennials
Defining Moment	JFK Assassination	Shuttle Explosion	Columbine Shootings
View of Authority	Challenge Leaders	Ignore Leaders	Indifference to Leaders
Authority Saying	No Problem	No Fear	Whatever

Taken from "The View from 30,000 Feet," Mike Woodruff, *The Ivy Jungle Report*, Fall 2000, pp. 10-11.

ious to experiment with innovative approaches. Part of the joy of life was to take risks and see what would happen."[4] We in the Boomer generation sometimes do not understand why the future generations do not share our dreams.

Members of the newer generations are trying to help us understand that times have changed. One Xer put it this way for us:

> It's different now than it was back then. You have to remember that each generation is living in a time that isn't the same as before. You were an idealist in your time, the 60s; and I guess I'm trying to be an idealist in the 90s and it is hard sometimes for you to understand how it is changed, the way we think. We don't have the big ambitions you and your roommates had to make the whole world better by going into political action, standing up to the far-off sheriffs and police chiefs. We're trying to connect with people who live right nearby.[5]

The three generations do not seem to know how to communicate with each other. Market analyst Karen Ritchie describes Boomers as "idealistic, manipulative, flashy and headstrong" and Xers as "streetwise, pragmatic and suspicious."[7] Millennials are described as jaded, self-confident and searching. While we Boomers are optimistic and want to change the world, and Xers are realistic and want to survive the changes in the world, Millennials want to enjoy and diversify not the world but their communities. The key skill for Xers and Millennials is not innovation but adaptation.[6] If these three generations are going to get along and work together, each needs to appreciate the other. The following chart is intended to help us understand the differences among these three generations.

Table 2. Generational Characteristics

Boomers	Xers	Millennials
Defiant	Coasting	Searching
Conquer	Connect	Confident
Get ahead	Get along	Get on a team
Conquest	Community	Collaboration
Product	Process	Progress
Live to work	Work to live	Work and live

My generation (Boomers) has needed for a number of years to understand that times have changed. For a long time we had trouble admitting that the younger generations were facing a situation that was vastly different from the one we faced. Much of that changed on September 11, 2001. All three generations went through September 11 together. As Robert Webber stated, "The world will never be the same. The ideals of prosperity and the hopes of a pre-September 11 world of peace will never happen. The rise of terror by militant fundamentalists is marking this world and creating an ideological battle of religions."[7]

While most of the rest of the world has had to live with upheaval and terror for many years, it is new for the Boomer, Xer and Millennial generations in the United States. We need to take advantage of this new reality to develop understanding among the generations. Tim Celek and Dieter Zander describe what is needed: "In the context of relationships, new understanding takes place, acceptance flourishes and personal value is communicated from one generation to another."[8]

ADAPTING TO THE ECONOMY

Generation X and the Millennial generation have seen their economic future change before their eyes. As school students in the late seventies and eighties, Xers saw unlimited future economic potential for themselves. But their hopes were dimmed by the economic crash of 1987 and the dotcom crash in the late 1990s. Now the worldwide downsizing economic realities of the early twenty-first century have dashed almost all of that hope, resulting in confusion and leading to adaptation. The confusion comes from many Xers and Millennials who, although admitting that there is a new economic world out there, do not see that it will burst their plans. A survey asked, "How optimistic are you about your career and financial prospects for the year?" Eighty-nine percent of Xers stated that they were personally optimistic. When asked how optimistic they were for the United States' economic prospects, only 45 percent said they were optimistic.[9] Many members of these younger generations have absorbed society's increasingly fatalistic attitude and see themselves riding on an ocean liner—the *Titanic*. They believe that although society will sink, they will go down in first class.[10]

Most Xers and Millennials believe themselves to be facing a bleak economic future. As one Xer exclaimed, "We watched as baby boomers went to college, got great jobs, crashed the economy and left nothing but McJobs for us."[11] "Compared with your parents, how easy will it be for you to achieve financial security?" Twenty-four percent said easier, 54 percent said harder and 22 percent said the same. This new economic reality is worldwide. A number of years ago one of Tokyo's more prestigious colleges placed 98 percent of its graduates in jobs. In 1995 it was able to place only 60 percent, with estimates that the jobless rate for many Japanese graduates would approach 20 percent.[12] The jobless rate and economic pessimism remain high today. Many Xers and Millennials are already adapting to this new reality. While many people in my generation during the sixties were dropping drugs, protesting and participating in the sexual revolution, students today are going to work. Some high school and college students in my generation had jobs, but many more do today.

As college graduates, these younger generations are changing their expectations. They are choosing to stay close to home and hold modest jobs. One Xer, Anne McCord, describes her generation's economic viewpoint this way: "We're not trying to change things. We're trying to fix things. We are the generation that is going to renovate America. We are going to be its carpenters and janitors."[13] For some Xers a changing economic viewpoint also means a changing work ethic. Millennials, on the other hand, seem to be harder workers. Expectations are changing the types of jobs that the young are pursuing. Today more students are pursuing degrees that have job openings like the teaching and nursing professions. By accepting today's economic reality, many in the younger generations are looking beyond employment for fulfillment in life.

ADAPTING TO FAMILY

We would think that the young would look to the family for personal fulfillment. Traditionally, the family has been the place for belonging and the primary environment for generating love and transmitting values. Yet family life is breaking down. Attitudes toward parenting changed profoundly in the 1970s. Rather than doing all they could to protect and develop their children, Boomer parents began to make decisions not on "the basis of what's best for the child, but on what the child could tolerate."[14] Children languished at home as Boomer parents were out pursuing the American economic dream. As a result, young Xers grew up with incredible pain. Steve Hayner, former president of InterVarsity Christian Fellowship, describes the family situation as follows:

> This is the generation that women took pills not to have and a generation whose mothers have championed the right for abortion. Divorce rates have more than doubled in their lifetime. It's been an age where children have been devalued; where they have become latchkey kids who are expected to fend for themselves.[15]

Latchkey kids. The term "latchkey child" did not exist before Generation X was born. With the American standard of living more or less peaking in 1973, it became necessary for mothers to leave the home to work to support the American dream. By 1982, an estimated 7 million children, ages six to twelve (about one in four), were latchkey kids.[16] The term *latchkey* refers to the house keys that these children wore on strings around their necks for safekeeping. While children in my generation had to help with the household chores, Xers are the first generation who undertook these chores alone. Many Xers have had to learn how to cook, shop and care for siblings. As a result, they entered adulthood prematurely, being forced to deal with challenges that once were reserved for mature adults.

Many in the Millennial generation are benefiting from a rebirth of interest in parenting by the younger Boomer generation (born in the early 1960s) who experienced the emptiness of pursuing personal freedom and climbing the corporate ladder. These Boomers are now desiring to put in more time with their children.

The Millennial generation feels more valued and loved. Unlike Gen Xers, many Millennials see their parents investing more time with them instead of just trying to climb the corporate ladder. Even Millennials, whose parents do work long hours, see that they work out of economic necessity instead of just pursuing their own career goals and neglecting their family.

However, we are seeing many latchkey Millennial children, not because both parents are working, but because they have only one parent, through death, divorce or being born outside of marriage. The changes in the last

fifty years in these three categories is staggering. Among children living with
a single mom, here are the reasons why:

	1950	1980	1998
Widowed	34%	11%	4%
Divorced	22%	42%	34%
Never Married	2%	15%	40%[17]

Children of divorce. While not all members of the X and Millennial generations have divorced parents, they are twice as likely as people in my generation to be children of divorce. Between 1960 and 1979, the American divorce rate tripled. By 1986 the United States had the highest divorce rate in
the Western world.[18] While my generation grew up with TV shows like *Father Knows Best,* this generation has grown up with *My Two Dads* and *Will and
Grace.* Fifty percent of today's teenagers
are not living with both birth parents. An
article in *Newsweek* indicated that close
to 80 percent of African American children live without both birth parents by
age sixteen.

The dysfunctional family certainly
takes a toll on children. While 80 percent of divorced parents profess to be
happier after divorce, only 20 percent of
the children say they are happier after divorce. A study by Judith Wallerstein (director of the Center for the Family in
Transition) and Sandra Blakeslee entitled
"Second Chances: Men, Women and
Children a Decade After Divorce" found
that one-third of men and women between the ages of nineteen and twenty-
nine have little or no ambition ten years after their parents' divorce. "They
are drifting through life with no set goals, limited education and a sense of
helplessness."[19] Wallerstein goes on to show that new kinds of families have

> I think our generation grew up
> with too much marital carnage.
> . . . We spent our adolescence
> ducking and covering as
> families up and down the block
> went off like time bombs.
> We got post-traumatic stress
> symptoms just going home for
> Thanksgiving, like re-visiting a
> combat zone.
>
> ETHAN WATTERS, *URBAN TRIBES*

been created that are fragile and unreliable. Children today miss out on the nurturing and protection provided for their parents only a few decades ago. Divorce is so widespread that it is disruptive to the stability of entire generations and has helped form these generations' opinions about marriage and family. In her recent study, *The Unexpected Legacy of Divorce,* Wallerstein has found out that divorce has a cumulative impact that does not reach its full impact until adulthood. In the adult years, children of divorced parents have discovered that the divorce "affects personality, the ability to trust, expectations about relationships and ability to cope with change."[20]

Judith Wallerstein goes on to say that silently and unconsciously we have created a culture of divorce.

It is hard to grasp what it means when we say that first marriages stand a 45% chance of breaking up and that second marriages have a 60% chance of ending in divorce. What are the consequences for all of us when 25% of people today between the ages of eighteen and forty-four have parents who are divorced? . . . What can we do when we learn that married couples with children represent a mere 26% of households at the end of the 1990's?[21]

Later marriage. Widespread divorce has made both of the postmodern generations anxious, cautious and slow when it comes to marrying. As Wallerstein asserts in her study, young people who come from broken homes are much more likely to be anxious about relationships with the opposite sex. "The young women are very afraid of being betrayed. The young men are afraid that when the young lady gets to know me, she won't love me."[22] These generations are much more likely than Boomers were to remain single in their twenties and postpone marriage into their thirties or never get married.

Boomerang generation. Late marriage and the economic downturn have led to another new phenomenon affecting these generations—the boomerang effect. It is ironic that Boomer parents, who created latchkey children, have been returned the favor by their children's creation of the boomerang phenomenon—children returning home to live with their parents following college graduation. Unmarried and unemployed, many college graduates are living with their parents until they can make it on their own. This experience for many Xers and now Millennials is very hard. As one young boomerang adult stated, "I had to face the thing that I dreaded most—my own shame, aggravated by my ego of going home and tumbling into the past."[23]

Family values. The cumulative effects of the dysfunctional family have taken a toll on Xers and Millennials. In 1980 a leading college educator, Arthur Levine, wrote a book titled *When Dreams and Heroes Died.* In it he predicted that these cumulative effects would cause the X generation to lose some of its dreams and aspirations, to seek simpler solutions to life's problems and to adapt to these new situations.[24] Part of this simpler solution is a desire for a simpler time in family life.

As a result, Millennials and Xers are not blindly following their parents' example. Unlike their parents, both of these generations, when they do get married, put family and friends first and job second. They want to spend more time with their kids because they were neglected as children. Nevertheless, as we will see, the difficult family experience that these generations have gone through deeply affects how they view their society and themselves.

> *The sobering truth is that we have created a new kind of society that offers greater freedom and more opportunities for many adults but this welcome change carries a serious hidden cost. Many people, adult and children alike, are in fact not better off. We have created new kinds of families in which relationships are fragile and often unreliable. Children today receive far less nurturance, protection and parenting than was their lot a few decades ago.*
>
> JUDITH WALLERSTEIN, *THE UNEXPECTED LEGACY OF DIVORCE*

ADAPTING TO SOCIETY

Generation X has adopted a survival mentality in regard to society. If Xers cannot make sense of the entire world, they try to make sense of their own world. They search for simple things that will work in the midst of a complex world. One of those simple things that worked for many of them in the 1980s was Ronald Reagan. He became a real-life Mr. Rogers, dispensing reassurance to many Xers during their troubled adolescence.[25]

Millennials, on the other hand, have embraced a diversified and global view of society. J. Walker Smith of Yankelovitch's research group stated at the beginning of this century that "the single biggest influence on this generation has been the increasing diversity of America."[26] Due primarily to the Internet, the end of the Cold War and the increasing diversity of the United States, this generation is the first American generation to think of itself as global. According to the 2000 United States Census figures, Millennials are 36 percent nonwhite; 20 percent of their parents are immigrants; and 10 percent of them have at least one noncitizen parent.[27] Among Millennials, Latinos are the largest minority group (16 percent), followed by African Americans (14 percent) and other groups. In four states—Hawaii, California, New Mexico and Texas—white Millennials are a numerical minority.[28]

Trust. Xers and Millennials both have problems with trust. The Xers' survivor mentality led them to trust nothing they could not touch or experience. Because of all the promises they feel have been broken by their parents and others in the Baby Boom generation, Pamela Paul in "Getting Inside Gen Y" describes Millennials' view of authority as follows: "Today's teens no longer have an unquestioning admiration for public figures. The scandal with athletes and celebrities have made teens realize that though these people are leaders, they are also human."[29]

Both younger generations are more responsive to deeds and actions than they are to words and symbols. They have no faith in institutions and put little stock in a chain of command. Their respect is earned, not demanded. While not attacking hierarchy directly, they ignore authority or work around it because in their youth they learned to survive by avoiding conflict. They want to be appreciated for what they have to offer.

Truth. Both generations are mistrustful of truth as well as authority. (We will examine their understanding of truth more deeply in chapter three.) For them, truth is not so much stated as experienced. These generations need to have truth lived out before them, not stated to them. Words, in and of themselves, mean little to them; image means everything. For these generations, the concept of linear thinking—one idea leading sequentially to another—is losing its hold. The new concept is image thinking.[30] This type of thinking

is expressed on MTV, with its fast-cut video images, and in channel surfing—watching two or three shows at a time by switching back and forth.
Image thinking is a kind of mental juggling act. If people in my generation
are going to be able to communicate with the younger generations, we will
need to be able to communicate not just linearly but also with images.

Caring. While image thinking is becoming more important to these generations, social image has become less important. Only about 25 percent of
today's younger generations would say that popularity and recognition are
very important to them.[31] Instead of valuing society's view of them, they
value what their friends and peers think of them. This viewpoint has freed
many in these generations to act on what they feel is right, not just what
somebody has told them is right. This freedom has generated a renewed
sense of caring and volunteerism. These generations are adapting to a new,
socially conscious reality with the phrase "Think globally, act locally." Deborah Hirsch, a college educator, depicts this adaptation in the following way:

> This new generation of college students is redefining social conscious-
> ness in a way that focuses on practical and rational responses to the
> social issues of the day. Their involvement is different from the radical
> social movements of the 1960s generation. It is the immediate, one-
> on-one reaching out to help fill a specific need and address a real com-
> munity issue. . . . Our individual efforts are far from grand, but taken
> collectively more of us are beginning to believe that we may change
> the nation.[32]

Areas of interest among these generations include cleaning up the environment, rehabilitating housing, and tutoring and befriending younger children. Having grown up in a socially divided environment, and being the victims of broken families, they tend to be peacemakers who avoid the hate and
the intolerance they witnessed as they grew up.

Inner city. One area in which the peacemakers of these generations have
not won is the inner city. Elijah Anderson, an African American, paints the
following picture:

> A vicious cycle has been formed. The hopelessness and alienation
> many young inner-city black men and women feel, largely as a result

of endemic joblessness and persistent racism, fuels the violence they engage in. This violence serves to confirm the negative feelings many whites and some middle class blacks harbor toward the ghetto poor, further legitimating the oppositional culture and the code of the streets in the eyes of many poor young blacks. Unless this cycle is broken, attitudes of both sides will become increasingly entrenched, and the violence, which claims victims, black and white, poor and affluent, will only escalate.[33]

The issues of the inner city will not be won primarily on the national level. They will be won on the local level by people working together. These generations, with their desire to avoid the hate and intolerance of preceding generations and their commitment to local action, have a chance to adapt to new strategies and work toward change in the inner city.

Sexuality. The free-love movement of the 1960s turned into herpes in the 1970s and AIDS in the 1980s and 1990s. In 1991, 63 percent of young people had sex before entering college, compared to 52 percent in 1981 and 40 percent in 1971.[34] We should be thankful to see that among the Millennials this number has dropped. While changing societal attitudes toward sex have certainly contributed to the increased sexual activity of these generations, it also stems partly from the lack of intimacy at home and the poor self-image held by many Xers and Millennials.

ADAPTING TO SELF

Both these generations bear painful scars from their childhoods. There are many reasons for this pain. Born in the era of political assassinations in the 1960s, of Watergate in the 1970s or the school shootings of the 1990s and the terrorist acts of the early 2000s, they have little faith in society as a whole helping them. Xers have grown up being called the aborted generation and the latchkey generation, while Millennials have been labeled the divorced-parents generation and the abused generation. A third of all Xers were physically or sexually abused during childhood. We will probably find out that the Millennial generation will have an even higher percentage. This family pain has left deep scars. On the whole, these generations put more trust in their friends than in their families.

Pain. This pain is expressed in many different ways. It has led some to drink. There has been a tremendous increase in those who drink to get drunk, especially among women. From 1977 to 1994, the number of young women who drank to get drunk rose from 12 percent to 35 percent, while in men the jump was from 20 percent to 40 percent.[35] Some Xers and Millennials choose suicide to end the emotional pain. Suicide is the second leading cause of death for college-age people, as reported on the website of the National Mental Health Association.

Stress. Both of these generations are particularly vulnerable to stress because they lack moorings and live in a state of fluidity. This fluidity can bring about a sense of liberation, but it can also bring about a feeling of being cast adrift. This uncertainty causes stress. Professor Chet Lesnick, who teaches at Colby College in Maine, conducts a yearly survey that asks each student to describe a personal problem. Over 90 percent identify stress as their number-one problem. Lesnick is amazed at the pain these students have encountered so early in life, the divorces and death they have had to face. David Cannon, a generational researcher in Toronto, claims this stress is a result of the thick walls these generations have built around themselves. He goes on to say that "no other generation in the past has had so many vivid images brought to them by the brutality of the world. . . . They have lived through bitter divorces that left them feeling abandoned. They've built walls because they are human beings . . . but inside the wall is a little house of bricks."[36]

Stress is not limited to American generations. British Xers and Millennials also identify stress as a critical issue.

> ERIC: There's too much pressure from outside. Life gets pretty complicated when you have to think carefully about everything you do; deciding for yourself whether it's right or wrong. In the end there can be so many conflicts going on inside of you that you can't do anything, it becomes impossible to be happy with what you think at any point.

> LOUISE: It's hard to know what to do with a feeling like that. That is partly what dance music is about—an escape.[37]

Alienation. While some in these generations deal with their stress and pain through means of escape like computer games, drinking, suicide or even dance music, others turn inward. In their book *A Generation Alone,* William Mahedy and Janet Bernardi describe the pain as alienation, a state of deprivation. They go on to describe the pain this way: "To be an alien means to be a stranger in a foreign land. The tragedy of alienated youth is that they are strangers in their own land made so by their elders who denied them the deep and abiding affection that is the birthright of all children."[38]

This pain in family life creates an aloneness that is different from loneliness. Loneliness is a state of emptiness, whereas aloneness can occur amid a plethora of activities, even dancing. Aloneness causes and is caused by a distrust of people that stems from a fear of being hurt one more time. At the root of it is a fear of being neglected or abandoned that leads to alienation from people, sometimes even one's closest friends. While aloneness is a survival technique, it can come across as independence.[39]

Essentially, aloneness is a state of the soul. We can be surrounded by people but still be alone. Aloneness can only be healed by being part of a community—ultimately the community of God. Without consciously realizing it, many young people today are adapting to their aloneness by seeking community. As we will see in chapter four, God has created within each of us a yearning for community and a yearning for God. Young people in these generations prove their adaptive ability yet again as they see their need for community. For them, community replaces the vacuum left by their family's abandonment of them.

YEARNING FOR COMMUNITY

Gen Xers and Millennials are helping to form a new, extended American family. Within this new family are found close friends, stepparents, adopted siblings, half-siblings, spouses and even live-in lovers. They are turning more and more to their friends as a new family. This phenomenon even has a name, coined by Ethan Watters in his book: *Urban Tribes.* In the next chapter we will see how the new community of these generations is part of the shift into the emerging postmodern culture.

"Friends don't let friends drink and drive." This slogan and parodies of it (such as "Friends don't let friends go to Duke") became immensely popular in the 1990s. Why does the phrase include the word *friends* but not the word *family?* Or why is it that from the mid-1990s to the middle of this decade the most popular and most copied TV program is *Friends?* In the 1950s we were immersed in family TV shows like *Father Knows Best, Ozzie and Harriet* and *Leave It to Beaver.* Today the themes of many shows center on friends, not family.

A new type of family, one that is composed of friends, is being established today. These communities of friends are trying to reestablish the trust that went out of the family during the last twenty to thirty years. While my generation (Boomers) was obsessed by the search for freedom, these generations are searching for "roots, stability, order and identity."[40] This relational drive is partly a result of my generation's failure to provide a safe, stable family unit for the nurture of our children.

These generations' legacy to our culture just may be a turning of the tide away from individualism toward community, something no generation has been able to do in the last four hundred years. Even the traditional date—a couple having dinner and seeing a movie—has changed to group dating. Instead of going out as a pair, a young person might choose to go out with that special someone and ten of their best friends. Will these generations be the ones to bring us back to biblical concepts of loving our neighbor and caring for each other's burdens?[41]

YEARNING FOR GOD

A stable community can be a place for hearing God's subtle call. Douglas Coupland, the author who coined the phrase "Generation X," shares his own yearning for God in his third book, *Life After God.* "My secret is that I need God—that I am sick and can no longer make it alone. I need God to help me give, because I no longer seem capable of giving, to help me be kind, as I no longer seem capable of kindness; to help me love, as I seem beyond being able to love."[42]

With few spiritual or absolute moorings, these generations act as if pulled in a thousand directions. Too many choices and a lack of stability in their lives pose the danger of fragmentation. In the song "Losing My Religion," R.E.M. describes this feeling: "Every whisper, every waking hour; I'm choosing my confessions, trying to keep up with you and I don't know if I can do it." For long periods of time, many emerging-culture people go through life without having to ponder the spiritual dimensions of life. However, when something in life hits them over the head, they are forced to deal with God. One Xer describes his life situation with these words: "I don't need God, we tell ourselves. I've got more important things to think about, like the economy. Then someone commits suicide and we scratch around in the ashes for a reason. Sometimes there is a reason, but more often we are lost."[43] This lostness, with all its pain, can lead to a yearning for God. As one author portrays these generations, "They are torn by dreams for the future and ridiculed by failures of the past. They are torn by the longing to get life right and the nagging suspicion that they are fatally flawed, and they are torn absolutely apart by the craving to be loved and the terrified fear of being known."[44]

Thankfully, many Millennials are more open to religious influence than Xers. They have been characterized as searching and religious. I think part of that willingness to search comes from viewing the unhealthy choices made by the two generations before them. Both generations need to recognize that there is a way out of feeling torn and hopeless—an eschatological hope, which we will look at more closely in chapter six. This journey out of hopelessness leads to a Christian community of hope and ultimately to community with God. As Mahedy characterizes the journey, "Along the way, the voyagers find healing of broken spirits, deeper relationships, ways to change the world and finally, ways to encounter the God who is the giver of these gifts."[45]

For all the bad press that Generation X and the Millennial generation have received, they are both generations that place a high value on community over against individualism, and they have a yearning for spirituality over against reason alone. Where does this desire for community and this yearning for spirituality come from? As we will see in the next chapter, the shift from the Baby Boom generation to Generation X and the Millennial generation is part of a larger shift from the Enlightenment to a postmodern culture. To understand these generations more completely, and thus be able to minister among these generations more effectively, we need to understand postmodernism and postmodern culture.

As we will see more fully in the next chapter, we are at a turning point in history. Generation X and the Millennial generation are the first purely postmodern generations. We in the church must ask ourselves, are we going to discredit them or are we going to care for them?

Has God, like so many Christians who are part of the fortress-mentality church, given up on these generations? While many Christians view these generations as a hopeless cause, I think that the opportunity for revival is greater today than it has been in the last forty years. Over the last four decades people have been trying to obtain salvation through the stable family of the 1950s, the societal changes of the 1960s, the "me generation" of the 1970s and the good life of the 1980s. In the 1990s and the first decade of the twenty-first century, Generation X and now the Millennial generation are just trying to suffer through the pain of feeling marginalized and hopeless. I think that they are more ready than any recent generation to receive God's hope, the gospel of Jesus Christ. God has not given up on these generations or on this coming postmodern culture. As we will see in the next chapter, God is laying the groundwork to send forth the gospel in a new way.

IMPLICATIONS FOR MINISTRY

To minister effectively among these younger generations, we must understand and truly appreciate the distinctives of these generations and the diversity of people within them. Members of my generation will have to leave our comfort zone and devote ourselves to understanding and appreciating these first postmodern generations. Take some time to immerse yourself in the culture, whether that means watching television shows like *Friends* or reality TV, reading the novels of Douglas Coupland, attending an Alanis Morissette concert, or watching MTV. More importantly, listen to these young people. Let them tell you their stories about their family or friends or their economic future or their view of religion. Trust is developed by listening to and then caring for Xers and Millennials as people who have deep longings and considerable pain.

Trust takes time to develop. Come as a friend in the journey of life, not as a rescuer. Invite people into your home. Many people in these generations do not know what a family is supposed to look like. Our church, which is located near the UNC-Chapel Hill campus, has an adopt-a-student ministry. The purpose is to link families and college students with one another. When our family had our two students over for dinner for the first time, we spent the time letting them share their stories. They began to feel comfortable with us as we showed them that we cared about them. As we hear people's stories, we will probably gain their permission to enter into their pain. If we ourselves are part of Generation X or the Millennial generation, we can probably identify with some of their pain. If we are older, then we can share our own points of pain. We can also provide the wisdom or perspective that only age brings. These generations, which have few healthy models, are crying out for wisdom and mentoring.

They also need a community to belong to and call home. Although chapters four and seven will explore community further, I cannot overemphasize the necessity for community as the foundation for any faithful ministry to these emerging generations. Formal or informal small groups should be at the core of ministry among these generations.

Finally, we should not underestimate the yearning for God among these generations. This yearning may be expressed in different and unorthodox ways, but it is real. Some Christian leaders see these generations as a lost cause. Maybe our traditional methods of ministry are losing the cause for us. If we are going to faithfully minister among these generations, we need to change our perspectives and methods. The rest of this book identifies some of the perspectives and methods that we need to change.

Emerging Postmodern Culture

When I entered Florida State University in the fall of 1968, I wanted to major in meteorology, with an emphasis in tropical meteorology. It was my dream to be one of the scientists who fly into the eye of a hurricane to collect data that meteorologists need to predict the hurricane's movement and eventually "tame" it. But rather than flying airplanes into hurricanes, I was led into campus ministry, which can be as stormy as any hurricane.

A hurricane is an intricate weather system. One of the intricacies involves the two wind patterns that are connected within the hurricane. One pattern is the counterclockwise wind that swirls around the eye of the hurricane. It produces the spontaneous feeder bands of rain and the devastating tornadoes that occur close to the eye of the storm.

The second wind pattern is the steering current of the hurricane. It is not as easily identified. The steering current determines where the hurricane is heading next. Predicting where the steering current is going to take the hurricane is tricky. Although it is not immediately obvious, the two wind patterns are intertwined, and that affects the movement of each wind pattern.

Public concern usually focuses on either the feeder band winds or the steering current winds, but not both. The people who are in the midst of the hurricane do not really care where the hurricane is headed, but they want to know the wind speed and the possibility of tornadoes. People who do not

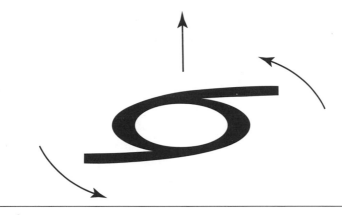

Figure 3.

live in the immediate vicinity of the storm are more interested in the storm's direction and the potential for damage.

Understanding and predicting a hurricane requires knowledge of both feeder bands and steering currents. The two wind patterns are complex and interconnected. Looking at one without looking at the other would skew the data and prevent accurate forecasting. We need to look at both the wind patterns and the relationship between them in order to assess the storm's potential for damage. Let me give you an example of what happens when we do not look more closely at the steering currents.

A number of years ago Hurricane Fran hit the coast of North Carolina. I had just put my wife on a plane to Florida to visit her parents. I reassured her that the brewing storm was not going to hit us, because we were in the middle of the state and away from the coast and the forecasted hurricane path. My daughter and I watched the news coverage as Hurricane Fran hit the coast. We were familiar with the place it was hitting and wondered what the damage would be along the coast. We went to bed confident that the storm would follow the coastline north and then go out to sea.

At about 1 a.m. my daughter woke me and suggested that we move to the downstairs bedrooms. I asked why and then realized I was hearing strong winds blasting our house. The hurricane was coming our way! Instead of following the coast, the storm had come straight across the state toward Raleigh, Durham and Chapel Hill. It hit us hard. When we went outside at daybreak, we were amazed at the destruction all around, including a large new lake at the bottom of our street, due to massive flooding.

We had failed to consider that the second wind pattern, the steering mechanism, could hurt us, because we were so far away from the coast. We thought we were insulated from the impact of the hurricane. Were we ever wrong!

I think many people in my generation think they are isolated from the impact of the emerging culture. They are too far removed from its impact, they think. As my family fooled ourselves into thinking Hurricane Fran could not affect us, so many people today think they can ignore postmodern culture.

> *The profound cultural changes that have shaped the mindset of today's spiritual seekers have less to do with their being Generation X than with society as a whole. The postmodern mind is real and here to stay.*
>
> JAMES EMERY WHITE, "GATEWAY COUNTRY"

I am convinced that we are in the midst of a societal hurricane. Over the last thirty years as a campus minister with InterVarsity Christian Fellowship, I have seen thousands of students go through their college years. When I started this ministry reexamination journey fifteen years ago after asking Joan that simple question "Are you going home for Christmas?" I was content to focus on Generation X. My goal was to study the characteristics of this generation, compare it with my Baby Boomer generation and make some suggestions for ministering to this generation. The more I studied, the more I began to feel, and then to think, that I did not have the whole picture. Something was missing. I became more and more convinced that something more than the generational transition from Boomers to Xers was affecting this student generation.

Although I did not realize it at the time, what I was looking at—Generation X and now the Millennial Generation—constituted only the feeder bands of the hurricane that we call societal change. The literature I was consulting did nothing to broaden the horizon of my thinking. Everything I read and heard was focusing on the transition from the Baby Boomer generation to Generation X. I began to search for a steering mechanism in this transition.

I found the clue I needed in David Bosch's seminal work *Transforming Mission,* in which he describes six major societal paradigm shifts. While reading his work in the early 1990s, I began to recognize a link between the transition from the Baby Boom generation to Generation X and the transition from the Enlightenment/modern era to the emerging/postmodern era.

For a while, though no longer, I felt alone in making this connection. Howe and Strauss never mentioned postmodern culture as an influence in this transition from Baby Boomers to the Xer and Millennial generations. People who are studying the movement from the Enlightenment to post-

---

The most formidable challenge currently facing evangelicals is the shift from a modern to a postmodern worldview. . . . Transitions from one paradigm to another are complex and include the breakdown of the old and the development of new ideas that eventually culminate in a new paradigm. Western history is now in a time of transition from the modern to an uncertain postmodern period. Indications of a postmodern worldview suggest that mystery, with its emphasis on complexity and ambiguity, community with its emphasis on the interrelationship of all things and symbolic forms of communication, with an emphasis on the visual, are all central to the new way of thinking.

ROBERT WEBBER, *ANCIENT-FUTURE FAITH*

---

modern culture have by and large failed to see that the Xer and Millennial generations can provide a transitional case study for the movement into postmodern culture. This generational study looks at the immediate consequences of cultural change. It is like a snapshot of change. The emerging/postmodern culture, on the other hand, can be thought of as the steering current of societal change (see figure 3). It is the driving force behind long-term societal change. It is like an in-depth video of change. The shift into postmodern culture takes time.

THE STRIKE ZONE: A SHIFTING STORY

One of my fondest childhood memories is of sitting next to my dad on the couch on Saturday afternoon and watching the major league baseball game of the week. One of my favorite players was pitcher Ryan Duren, the Yankees' closer in the 1950s and 1960s. There are several things you need to know about Ryan Duren. He was fast, wild and nearsighted. While on the mound, he would often take his glasses off, look at the batter, put his glasses back on and then throw his first pitch. Inevitably that first pitch would either fly behind the batter or come so close in front of him that he would have to jump clear to avoid being knocked down. At that time players who were brushed back from the plate did not rush the mound. Ryan Duren could throw a baseball faster than anybody at that time and probably faster than anybody today. He was known to throw the ball over one hundred miles per hour. Keep in mind that the helmets those players wore were not as protective as modern ones. Time and time again, Ryan would throw the first ball inside and then throw the second pitch tight along the knees on the outside of the plate. The third pitch would be a high fastball right across the letters of the uniform, where the strike zone began. Usually the batters would not even swing. After this third strike, they would just sit down, filled with disgust.

There have been several changes in baseball in the last fifty years, including the definition of the strike zone. The rule book still states that the strike zone extends from the letters of the jersey to the top of the knees. Although today some are trying to restore the high strike, from the 1970s until today any pitch above the belt has been called a ball. Sometime in the late 1960s or early 1970s (we don't know exactly when), the strike zone descended from the letters to the belt. Umpires are the ones who brought about this change.

Umpires are a strange lot. A number of years ago, I heard a story about a group of umpires who got together and compared notes on how they decided to call a strike or a ball. The first umpire said, "I call them as they are." The second umpire disagreed and said, "I call them as I see them." The third umpire told the other two, "You are both wrong; they ain't nothing until I call them."[1] And so the strike zone slid down.

Baseball's shifting strike zone is analogous to a major paradigm shift that is occurring in society at this time. This societal shift may be likened to the three umpires. The first umpire represents the *naive realist,* to whom it is obvious that things are exactly what they appear to be on the surface and provide all the information anyone needs to act properly. The naive realist does not need any help from other people to understand what is real and true. He represents the autonomous self of the Enlightenment era. The second umpire is more of a *subjective realist.* He admits that his view of the strike zone will vary from day to day, depending on how he is feeling. He is a twentieth-century relativist. A lot of baseball players today think that all umpires live under subjective reality—and even change their minds between innings! The third umpire lives in what we would call *virtual reality.* There is no truth or falsehood, only choices. The third umpire represents the transition into postmodern culture.[2]

THE STUDENT SHIFT: A TALE OF THREE STUDENTS

I began to see students change around fifteen to twenty years ago. They were beginning to make decisions like the ones made by the three umpires. Let me share the stories of three students.

The first student I will call Randy. One evening I was speaking at his InterVarsity large-group meeting on the topic of sexuality. I described some of the struggles that men and women face in this area. I suggested that if this group was typical, at least one or two students were probably struggling with homosexuality. I agreed that too often we in the church do not know how to minister to homosexuals and often keep them at arm's length. I went on to share that we need to help them in their struggle. After this meeting, Randy approached me and said he wanted to get together and talk.

The next day Randy told me about his struggles with homosexuality. I would call Randy a naive realist because he not only knew what was right and wrong but also knew what he should do. He felt he could do the right thing by himself. But without recognizing it, Randy was already living in the postmodern era, and the pull of community was strong in his life. Like many other students, he did not have a good relationship with his family. Randy was being pulled by both the Christian community and the gay campus community.

Although Randy stayed involved with InterVarsity for a while, he was not willing to share his struggles with other people in the InterVarsity group. He wanted to overcome his struggles on his own. About a year and a half later, Randy eased out of InterVarsity. By then he was meeting with me only occasionally and was becoming more involved in the gay community. I lost touch with Randy while he was in law school.

My heart aches when I think of Randy. He thought knowing what was right and wrong was all he needed. He tried to deal with the struggle alone instead of relying on the Christian community for help. Ultimately it was not knowing right from wrong but the pull of two conflicting communities that was the battleground for Randy.

I will call the second student Don. He was a small-group leader with InterVarsity. Somehow it became known that Don and his girlfriend, who was also in InterVarsity, were having sexual intercourse on a regular basis. Two members of the student leadership team talked with Don, but he was unwilling to change his behavior. Then another InterVarsity staff worker and I met with Don, but we could not change his mind either.

At one point in the conversation Don blurted out, "If you want to believe that it is wrong for us to sleep together, that is okay with me. However, it's my understanding of God and Christianity that if we love each other, it's okay." Don was like the second umpire, defining his own subjective reality. What Scripture said made no difference to him. Consequently we asked Don to step down as a small-group leader. He did not cooperate and had to be forced to step down. Don left the InterVarsity group, taking about twenty students with him, all of whom held a subjective understanding of reality. They thought we were being too harsh on him and his girlfriend.

Tim was the third student. He was zealous for God and everything else in life. He was compassionate and was one of our best evangelists. Needless to say, I was shocked to receive a phone call from Tim's best friend informing me that Tim had been charged by the student honor court with falsifying a term paper. When I went to talk to Tim, he was adamant that he had done nothing wrong. He exclaimed, "I don't know what this religion professor has against me, but I did not cheat." For a while his friends and I believed him. However, I knew from students who had formerly served on the honor court that overwhelming evidence was necessary for charges to be brought at all.

During the proceedings, I was called to be a character witness for Tim. It came out in the proceedings that Tim had copied an InterVarsity booklet, *Jewishness & Jesus,* verbatim. When Tim was found guilty, his friends were devastated. Yet Tim continued to proclaim his innocence. Nevertheless he was expelled from school and never came back. Like the third umpire, Tim lived in virtual reality, claiming that what was fiction was true. He would not admit that he was living a lie. Virtual reality is mixing truth and fiction.

These situations exemplify the struggles that young people experience today. Sometimes neither they nor the people working alongside them have any understanding of the overall picture. In order to minister in the gap we need to gain a fuller understanding of the forces acting on our world.

A SOCIETAL CHANGE: ENLIGHTENMENT TO POSTMODERNISM

Just as few baseball fans in the midst of the strike-zone shift understood what was occurring, so (up until recently) few people understood that we are in the midst of a societal shift. Some people still deny we are in this major cultural shift. Actually we are going through two societal shifts. One shift is the generational shift that we examined in chapter two. The other shift, which ultimately will have more lasting and far-reaching consequences, is the philosophical shift from the Enlightenment era to the postmodern era. The Baby Boom generation was the last one to grow up in the Enlightenment, or modern, era. Generation X and the Millennial generation are the first purely postmodern generations. In this chapter we will explore the characteristics of postmodern culture and then look more closely at the link between the Xer and Millennial generations and the emerging postmodern era.

Theologian Diogenes Allen suggests that this shift is as dramatic as the shift from the Middle Ages to the Renaissance.[3] It will have ramifications for us for at least the next one hundred years. It is vital that we understand as much as we can about this shift because it will affect the way we do ministry in the coming years. In the Western world there have been four major cultural paradigm shifts (transitions) since the death of Christ. The last two transitions have not only impacted the Western world but also have influenced cultures in the Two-Thirds World. Due to increasing globalization, this emerging culture will have even more of an impact throughout the world.

Major Cultural Paradigm Shifts
1. Hellenistic/Roman (A.D. 300-600)
2. Medieval (A.D. 600-1500)
3. Enlightenment/Modern (A.D. 1500-2000)
4. Postmodern/Emerging (1968-?)

Paradigms give us a lens through which we can view life, and they provide us with boundaries and structure. Paradigm shifts are major changes in culture that are caused by dramatic events and forces. They themselves cause major, enduring changes in society. While we call these phenomena "paradigm shifts," we should probably call them "paradigm changes" because instead of occurring rapidly (like the shifting of car gears), they take place over the course of years (like changes in climate).

These paradigm changes have their own distinctives. The Hellenistic/Roman period was characterized by evangelistic zeal on the part of Christians. During the years of the medieval paradigm, the church was in survival mode and was drawing people into the Christian community. Then the Enlightenment/modern paradigm shifted from faith in God to faith in human reasoning. In the current transition to the postmodern world, the emphasis is changing from self and reason to community and feeling.

Others simplify the six paradigms to three: premodern (up to 1500), modern (1500-1960) and postmodern (1960-). The premodern period was characterized by faith in God and knowledge based in authoritative traditions.[4] Anselm captured the period with his phrase "I believe in order that I may understand." Revelation preceded and served as the foundation for understanding. In the modern paradigm, the emphasis was changed from faith in God to human reasoning. Descartes summed up the era with his phrase "I think, therefore I am." Divine revelation was replaced by human reason, and people searched for certainty. In the postmodern period, as we will see, we are moving away from reason by the autonomous self and moving toward relationship. If the postmodern era has a catch phrase, it may be "I belong, therefore I am."[5] How are we moving from the modern, or Enlightenment, period to the emerging/postmodern period?

The Enlightenment was an intellectual movement that began in the 1600s and lasted until around 1800. The Enlightenment was preceded by the Renaissance (1400-1600) and was followed by romanticism (1800-1850) and modernism (1850-1960). For the sake of simplicity, I am going to use the terms *Enlightenment* and *modern* to refer to all the societal shifts between the 1500s and the 1960s.

The premodern, or medieval, paradigm went into decline by the late 1400s. The medieval way of life was shattered by events associated with Columbus, Copernicus and Luther. In the words of Albert Borgmann,

> The medieval world was like all pre-modern cultures, a locally bounded, cosmically centered, and divinely constituted world. The Columbian discovery of the New World ruptured the familiar and surveyable geography of the Middle Ages. The Copernican solar system decentered the earth from its privileged position in the universe. The Lutheran reformation, in making the Bible and the believer the final authorities of Christianity, fatally weakened the communal power of divinity.[6]

In the beginning the Enlightenment was an attempt to achieve certainty about God, not an attempt to get rid of God. The early Enlightenment era was typified by René Descartes, a Christian who desired to be more certain about his belief in God, his own existence and the reality of the external world. To accomplish this task, Descartes developed the principle of doubt through the use of human reason. From this beginning he coined the phrase "I think, therefore I am." He believed that self-knowledge was the foundation on which all knowledge could be built. As a result, human reason usurped God as the basis for all knowledge. What I think, not what God reveals, becomes the measure of truth. Thus began the Enlightenment.

Descartes led us to view human reason as king. God was gradually dropped from the picture or at least marginalized. Human reason was all that was necessary to make sense of life.

The queen of the Enlightenment was the autonomous self, sovereign and self-sufficient. John Locke, in the important *Second Treatise of Civil Government* (1690), initiated the "celebration of the individual, the unencumbered autonomous human being."[7] Cut off from community, the self must seek meaning alone.[8] Individuals did not necessarily need other people.

The princess of the Enlightenment was the process of scientific discovery, as we learn in Descartes's *Discourse in Method* (1637). People achieve understanding through the process of trial and error, by cause and effect. God's revelation was no longer needed or desired, because human beings, not God, were in control of the learning process.

Finally, human progress was the prince of the Enlightenment. Francis Bacon, in his *New Atlantis* (1627), turned society away from the fatalistic medieval view of life to the possibility of progress through the domination of nature.[9] Society was understood to be evolving, always getting better. Like a solid European fortress, the Enlightenment seemed unassailable. One commentator

---

As the modern secular version of the ancient Tower of Babel, modernity began to crumble and topple when it became increasingly evident that the technological advances created as many problems as they were solving. There was a growing realization that human progress bore within it the prospect of self-destruction. There were unseen consequences that threatened to render the planet uninhabitable as a consequence of nuclear, chemical and biological warfare; industrial pollution of the atmosphere and rivers, lakes and oceans; and deforestation. New technologies designed to free the human spirit and remove physical drudgery created new dependencies and enslavement.

EDDIE GIBBS, *CHURCHNEXT*

---

described the Enlightenment as a "quest to build from earth to heaven and to transform earthly chaos into heavenly peace through human effort."[10]

In the early 1900s the fortress of the Enlightenment/modern period began to crack, and by the 1960s it was crumbling all around the base. Coming years will witness its final collapse. The original goal of the Enlightenment was to liberate humanity from dependence on a divinely ordered universe. The universe was understood as being ruled by human reason and being committed to human freedom. It was moving toward a utopian climax.[11]

The age that began with "the bright expectations of the Enlightenment and the energies of the scientific, industrial and political revolutions has devolved to the horror, vacuity and mediocrity of the Twentieth Century."[12]

SOCIETAL FORCES CAUSING THE CHANGE

Historical forces. Events of the twentieth century, including World War I, the Great Depression and World War II, were devastating to Enlightenment thought. Faith in human reason—the belief that human beings can solve all problems unaided by God—lost validity in the face of overwhelming death and devastation. The whole European intellectual structure was mortified at the destruction wrought by the two world wars and began to doubt itself. This doubt intensified in the 1960s. As David Wells says of the Enlightenment, "It had made extravagant promises about life, liberty and happiness, but in the modern world it had become increasingly difficult to see where those promises were being realized."[13]

Although historical evidence for the breakdown of the Enlightenment was mounting, the decade of the sixties began as one last attempt to keep the Enlightenment, or modernism, intact. Robert Ellwood, in *The Sixties Spiritual Awakening,* depicts the beginning of the 1960s as follows:

> At first the Sixties were like an ultimate expression of modernism. There was an accelerating drive to complete the progressive agenda. Civil Rights, the Great Society and even the Vietnam War were seen as expressing a universal commitment to American-style democracy. The modernist scientific agenda was displayed in the no less significant race, at fabulous expense, for the moon. John F. Kennedy and Martin Luther King were the essence of progressivist schoolbook history centered on great men or heroes devoted to high ideals.[14]

John F. Kennedy's inaugural address typified this last attempt of humankind at progress when he declared that "the world is very different now. For man holds in his mortal hands the power to abolish all forms of human poverty."[15]

Even the death-of-God theological movement in the midsixties was an attempt to keep humankind at the center of life by proclaiming that God was dead. Others saw this theological movement as showing the ultimate absurdity of Enlightenment ideals and goals.

Another sixties movement leading to the postmodern era was the coun-tercultural movement, which began to question the purposes of modern civ-ilization, including technology, the upwardly mobile path to progress and the isolation of the individual. The hippies wanted to be free from traditional moral and rational boundaries. This movement continued to gain momen-tum and influence throughout the 1960s.

The year 1968 marked the year of no return in the transition from the En-lightenment/modern era to the postmodern era. Before 1968 it was univer-sally agreed that the United States and the Soviet Union were the major pow-

---

Even in the flattest landscape there are passes where the road climbs to a peak and then descends into a new valley. Most of these passes are only topography with little or no difference in climate, language, or culture between the valleys on either side. But some passes are different. They are true divides. They often are neither high nor spectacular. The Brenner Pass is the lowest and gentlest of the passes across the Alps. Yet from earliest times it has marked the border between Mediterranean and Nordic cultures.

History too knows such divides. They also tend to be unspectacular and are rarely noticed at the time. But once these divides have been crossed, the social and political landscape changes. Social and political climate is different and so is social and political language. There are new realities.

Some time between 1965 and 1973 we passed over such a divide and entered the "new century." We passed out of creeds, commitments and alignments that had shaped politics for a century or two. We are in political terra incognita with few familiar landmarks to guide us.

PETER DRUCKER, *THE NEW REALITIES*

---

ers that controlled two conflicting but parallel economic, political and philosophical commitments to human reason—capitalism and communism. In 1968 the two world powers began to falter. For the United States, the triggering events were the Vietnam War and two political assassinations. In January 1968 the United States suffered a major political setback during the Tet Offensive in Vietnam as mounting American and Vietnamese casualties caused American public support for the war to nosedive. The My Lai massacre, which occurred later in 1968, caused the American people to begin to realize that we were not the good guys anymore. It took the United States another four or five years to extricate itself from the war, but the belief that the United States was no longer the savior of the free world or the bastion of human reason took root in January 1968 during the Tet Offensive.

The Tet Offensive was followed a few months later by the loss of Martin Luther King Jr. and Robert F. Kennedy to assassination. Lance Morrow, in *Time* magazine's twentieth-anniversary commemoration issue of 1968, portrays the nation's mood following the assassinations:

> What died with Martin Luther King Jr., and later in great finality with Robert Kennedy, was a moral trajectory, a style of aspiration. King embodied a nobility and hope that all but vanished. With King and Kennedy, a species of idealism died—the idealism that hoped to put America back together again, to reconcile it to itself. In the nervous breakdown of 1968, the word idealism became almost a term of derogation. Idealism eventually tribalized into aggressive special interests doing battle in a long war of constituencies.[16]

Morrow characterizes 1968 as the "mystery of all the possibilities that vanished into death and nothingness."[17] The United States, which had begun the decade on a note of optimism and unity, was ending with nothingness and tribalism.

Neither was 1968 a good year for the Soviet Union. In the summer of that year the Soviet Union began to lose its position as the bastion of the communist world. In August 1968 Soviet tanks invaded the streets of Prague, Czechoslovakia, to topple the reform-minded Dubček regime. The tanks rolled in to crush freedom—for the Prague intelligentsia or anyone else in Czechoslovakia. Although the Soviet Union won the battle in the streets of

Prague in 1968, it lost the war to save communism. Communists themselves saw the Soviet Union no longer as liberators but as imperialists. The slow but steady downfall of communism can be traced from 1968 to 1989, when the Berlin Wall was torn down.

The year 1968 represents the entire decade of the 1960s in microcosm. It was a tragedy of events, a struggle between generations, and a war between the past and the future. It was the "cultural and political harbinger of the subsequent turn to postmodernism."[18] It was in 1968 that one graduate student in Paris, following the Paris student riots, abandoned all hope of a social revolution. From revolution, he shifted his focus to the subject of "difference." This shift ended with the publication of *The Postmodern Condition* in 1979. The student was Jean-François Lyotard, who is one of the pivotal leaders in the shift into the postmodern era.[19]

It is ironic that the year 1968, which brought about the beginning of the end of the Enlightenment, culminated with the Enlightenment's greatest achievement—a manned spacecraft circling the moon on Christmas Eve. Ultimately, however, the 1960s exploded the belief in progress, linear thinking and moral clarity.

Philosophical forces. Philosophy was the second force involved in bringing about the change from the Enlightenment to the postmodern era. In the Enlightenment the autonomous self was the center of philosophical thought, culminating in Friedrich Nietzsche's superman. In the twentieth century two of Nietzsche's supermen ascended to power—Joseph Stalin and Adolf Hitler. These two men did what they wanted to do and made up the rules as they went along. Philosophically, no one could challenge them because they were taking the autonomous self to its logical conclusion. After seeing the devastation these two men brought, people began to realize the necessity for a community that can hold individuals accountable.

Scientific forces. A scientific revolution—quantum physics—was the third force involved in bringing about the collapse of the Enlightenment. Albert Einstein, with his theory of relativity, began to understand that there was no universal cause-and-effect principle. The scientific method could no longer be the measure of deciding truth from falsehood. The world began to be seen as a place that we do not fully understand.

Thomas Kuhn in 1962 wrote a book titled *The Structure of Scientific Rev-*

olutions. In it he describes a major paradigm shift in the scientific community that does away with the Enlightenment's primacy of scientific discovery as a basis of knowledge. He depicts the revolutionary transition as follows:

> The transition from a paradigm in crisis to a new one from which a new tradition of normal science can emerge is far from a cumulative process, one achieved by an articulation or extension of the old paradigm. Rather, it is a reconstruction of the field from new fundamentals, a reconstruction that changes some of the field's most elementary theoretical generalizations as well as many of its paradigm methods and applications. During the transition period there will be a large but never complete overlap between the problems that can be solved by the old and by the new paradigm. But there will also be a decisive difference in the modes of solution. When the transition is complete, the profession will have changed its view of the field, its methods, and its goals.[20]

Economic forces. The fourth major factor contributing to the demise of the Enlightenment was the Great Depression, which seemed to contradict the Enlightenment view of human progress. In the midtwentieth century, economic struggles in Africa, Asia and other places came to the fore. Apparently not everybody could have a piece of the economic pie. As Gene Edward Veith writes, "In our own time, it has become clear that reason, science and technology have not solved all of our problems. Poverty, crime and despair defy our attempts at social engineering."[21] Thus the Enlightenment, the European fortress, was replaced by the sandcastle we call postmodernism.

THE SANDCASTLE OF POSTMODERNISM: A DESCRIPTION

If you have ever built a sandcastle at the beach, you know that when you return to it the next day, it looks very different. Either the tides have come in and washed it away or the wind has reshaped it. This picture describes present-day postmodernism. It is never the same from one day to the next. Different people have different viewpoints as they define postmodernism. You can look at the sandcastle from one side and see it from one perspective. But then you can go around to the other side and see it from a totally different perspective. As the sandcastle is continually reshaped by the restless tides or the changing winds, so too is postmodernism in a continuous state of flux.

Václav Havel, a leader of the Prague intelligentsia in 1968 and later a leader in the Czech Republic, described our current state of flux as follows:

> Today we find ourselves in a paradoxical situation. We enjoy all the achievements of modern civilization that have made our physical existence on this Earth easier in so many important ways. Yet, we do not know exactly what to do with ourselves, where to turn. In short, we live in the postmodern world, where everything is possible and almost nothing is certain. The abyss between the rational and the spiritual, the external and the internal, the objective and the subjective, the technical and the moral, the universal and the unique, constantly grows deeper.[22]

The state of continual change that characterizes the postmodern era should be expected if we actually are in a major transition, as Thomas Kuhn and others say we are. It is going to take scores of years, not just a few years, to bring about this transition. A time of transition entails confusion, differences of opinion and uncertainty, not stability.[23]

Some people today react to these changes by trying to hold on to the Enlightenment paradigm in spite of the signs that changes are coming. Instead of holding on to the passing paradigm, we need to be like Aleksandr Solzhenitsyn. In a speech delivered at Harvard University he stated, "The world has reached a major watershed in its history, equal in importance to the turn from the Middle Ages to the Renaissance. It will demand from us a spiritual blaze; we shall have to rise to a new height

Table 3.

Enlightenment	Postmodernism
Objective truth	Subjective truth (Preferences)
Individual	Community
Scientific discovery	Virtual reality
Metanarrative (Societal progress)	Micronarrative (Societal cynicism)

of vision, to a new level of life."[24] Contrary to what many evangelicals are saying, I hope that the postmodern era will prove to be a better environment than the modern era for the gospel to be received, believed and obeyed.

What does this sandcastle we call postmodernism look like? Each of the four primary traits of the Enlightenment has a parallel in postmodernism.

SUBJECTIVE TRUTH (PREFERENCES)

Instead of human reason that leads to truth, postmodernism posits multiple truths that lead only to preferences. The search to find the central theme of life or to distinguish the grand narrative has given way to multiple alternatives and competing viewpoints.[25] Richard Rorty, a prominent postmodern thinker, defines objectivity as agreement among everyone who is in the room at the present time.[26] Truth is not so much found as created. What is true is what one believes to be true.

The saying "To each his own" could be the motto of postmodern culture. People act out this motto every day. An editorial in the University of North Carolina's student newspaper *Daily Tar Heel* demonstrated deconstruction in full force. Writing in support of Gay Awareness Week, editor Holly Ryan proclaimed that "there will be a welcome change to the doom and destruction typically preached in the Pit today. It's National Coming Out Day (NCOD) and the only thing that B-Glad members will be preaching is acceptance and honesty. . . . There's information there for everyone, homosexual and heterosexual alike. And the only preaching you'll hear is *to be true to yourself*."[27] This editorial is preaching that no individual and no group has a hold on the truth, that there are only preferences or subjective truth, not objective truth.

Deconstruction is the uncentering of modern life that leaves us with multiple possibilities and the equal validity of all interpretations. MTV is an excellent example of deconstruction. The images in any given video are constantly changing and redefining reality. Taken together, the images suggest that there is no objective reality, only preferences. Kenneth Gergen suggests that "rock videos represent a full breakdown in the sense of a rationally coherent world. Few videos offer a linear narrative, most will jolt the viewer with a rapid succession of images which have little obvious relation to each other."[28] The Gen Xer and Millennial world is defined by MTV. There is no grand theme to life. We are left with fleeting images, and it is up to us to define reality as we choose.

This local definition of reality is consistent with the view of Jean-François Lyotard that the grand story, or metanarrative, is dead. Only local narratives exist. The question being asked is "What do I believe?" or "What does my community believe?" not "What is objectively true?" Today only 28 percent of Americans believe in absolute truth.[29] (It is ironic that the statement "There is no absolute truth" has become an absolute truth with its demand that everyone needs to agree with this statement.)[30] Consequently, distinctions between right and wrong or between good and bad lose their relevancy.[31] Since this postmodern society cannot find its center in objective truth, it has moved to finding or defining its center in its community.

> *The Oprah Winfrey Show is a good example of postmodernism expressed through popular media. When someone from the audience says "the bible says" Oprah will nod and smile but say something like, "That may be true for you but who are we to judge as long as people are happy and are not hurting anyone else."*
>
> ED STETZER, *PLANTING NEW CHURCHES IN A POSTMODERN AGE*

COMMUNITY

The autonomous self of the Enlightenment has been replaced by tribalism. The community decides what is true. *The Real World* on MTV, *Survivor* on

CBS and *American Idol* on Fox all depict tribalism at work. These "reality" shows are showing up on TV all over the world, including England and Colombia. These shows and all the other "reality" shows are composed of a group of six or more people who are selected by the producers. The selection process is elaborate. The daily experiences of this diverse group living in community are captured on video. In a period of weeks or months, as they live together, the diverse people in this group become a community, the members of which share many more similar viewpoints than they did when the group first came together. They have a new sense of truth, which the community has helped to shape.

By a 3-1 margin (64% vs. 22%) adults said truth is always relative to the person and their situation. The perspective was even more lopsided among teenagers, 83% of whom said moral truth depends on the circumstances, and only 6% of whom said moral truth is absolute. . . . While six out of ten people 36 and older embraced moral relativism, 75% of the adults 18-35 did so. Thus it appears that relativism is gaining ground. . . . Among adults, 32% of those who were born again said they believe in moral absolutes, compared to just half as many (15%) among the non-born again contingent. Among teenagers there was still a 2-1 ratio evident, but the numbers were much less impressive: only 9% of born again teens believe in moral absolutes versus 4% of the non-born again teens.

GEORGE BARNA, *BARNA RESEARCH ONLINE*

Although relativism has been with us for many years, it takes on new dimensions in the emerging world. Stanley Grenz spells out this difference in *A Primer on Postmodernism:*

> Relativism and pluralism are not new. But the postmodern variety differs from the older forms. The relativistic pluralism of late modernity

was highly individualistic; it elevated personal taste and personal choice as the be-all and end-all. Its maxims were "To each his/her own" and "Everyone has a right to his/her own opinion." . . . Postmodernism beliefs are held to be true within the context of the communities that espouse them.[32]

Only those within our own community or tribe have the right to comment or criticize our truth. Postmodernist thought divides people into conflicting groups wherein the individual can become lost and power can become the controlling factor. From Rwanda to Bosnia to the Middle East, we see the formation of this new tribalism. In our own country we see this fragmentation as issue after issue causes us to split into our different groups. Whether it was Vietnam or Watergate in the past or abortion, the environment or the war on terror today, we have become fragmented. We now live in many different Americas, eating at different restaurants, shopping at different malls, watching different cable channels.

While television, with shows like *I Love Lucy* and *Ozzie and Harriet,* brought America together in the 1950s, cable television today, with its emphasis on market segmentation, divides audiences. The result is that national consensus or community becomes more difficult to maintain. The breakdown of the family has contributed to the loss of national identity. It is hard for young people, especially, to develop a sense of connection when their own families have little if any stability. As Edward Veith says, "Whereas traditional communities (families, villages, churches) gave a sense of belonging and permanence, the contemporary social scene is characterized by impermanence."[33] With the breakdown of the family and the loss of any national consensus, we are becoming a culture of homeless people who search continually for a place to belong.

Richard Middleton and Brian Walsh, in their book *Truth Is Stranger Than It Used to Be,* help us to see that this sense of postmodern tribalism, which can degenerate into a feeling of homelessness, might be the very place where God can meet us.

Our modernist dreams have become nightmares, and it feels like our Western inheritance of world leadership, progress, economic growth, moral superiority and a well controlled, safe environment has been stripped away, leaving us as homeless nomads in a postmodern desert, exiled from the only home we have known.

It is precisely when we experience ourselves as exiles, displaced and uprooted, that the biblical story can speak most eloquently to us of being at home in a secure creation. The most powerful biblical language of coming home is in the context of either wilderness wanderings or exile. Such language speaks words of healing and hope in a postmodern age.[34]

It was during the exile that God led the Israelites to a new vision that created a hope for the Messiah and provided a way that would help the community of faith survive. In many ways, Generation X and the Millennial generation are like bands of exiles who have been kidnapped from their homes and transported to a strange land. They may feel that they have nowhere either to look back to or to look forward to that offers hope for a better tomorrow.[35] During this time of transition into postmodern culture, the church needs a new vision and new strategies to faithfully minister to these emerging postmodern generations. As we will see in later chapters, a vibrant Christian community can provide a critical dimension in reaching the emerging postmodern world with the gospel and in caring for new Christians after they have made a commitment to the gospel.

> *The transition from modernity to postmodernity represents a seismic shift that can result in churches becoming paralyzed in the midst of the shock waves. The changes are deep-rooted, comprehensive, complex, unpredictable and global in their ramifications.*
>
> EDDIE GIBBS, *CHURCHNEXT*

VIRTUAL REALITY

Instead of the scientific discovery of the Enlightenment, we now have virtual reality. Technically, virtual reality is "an experience that is real in effect but not in fact."[36] As the Enlightenment tried to free the Western world from biblical authority, so postmodernism is trying to free the West from scientific authority, which came about through the scientific method of determining truth.[37] Virtual reality teaches us to trust only what our senses can verify. Since our senses perceive the world differently, each individual's view of reality will be unique. Virtual reality leads us to mix fact and fiction. How did it happen that Dan Quayle, the vice president of the United States, became embroiled in 1992 in a dispute with Murphy Brown, a fictional character on a television show? The ensuing debate, over a fictional out-of-wedlock baby, muddled the distinction between reality and fiction. Another example of the mixing of fact and fiction was the chad controversy in Florida in the 2000 presidential election. Few people could distinguish between hanging and dimpled chads. Fact and fiction became ambiguous. Movies like *Groundhog Day*, in which a man keeps reliving the same day over and over, and *Field of Dreams, The Matrix* and *Lord of the Rings*, which mix the present and the past, are centered around virtual reality and the blurring of boundaries in time and space.

> *During the Enlightenment, the idea of progress resulted in an optimistic view of history. Church leaders were characterized by an enormous confidence in the future. The twentieth century was to be the Christian century. The church was going to permeate the world with its message of love, society was to become one family under the reign of God; nations would cease their warring against each other; disease and poverty would be practically unknown.*
>
> ROBERT WEBBER, *ANCIENT-FUTURE FAITH*

Pop culture today is full of virtual reality. Stars like Michael Jackson, Britney Spears and Madonna demonstrate multiple identities and personality transformations. Madonna, the queen of postmodernism, has blurred the boundaries between reality and fiction. Richard Lints writes that "Madonna is in many ways a perfect personification of the postmodern reality; sensation without substance, motion without purpose, a self-centered persona undergoing perpetual change for its own sake."[38]

Our world today finds it harder and harder to distinguish fact from fiction.

This confusion, as we will see in coming chapters, is causing many young people to search for stability in the midst of the quicksand of confusion.

MICRONARRATIVE (SOCIETAL CYNICISM)

The fourth parallel between the Enlightenment and postmodernism sees the metanarrative of societal progress change to the micronarratives of societal cynicism. The Enlightenment's promises of continued human progress were shattered in the twentieth century. Two world wars, one poisoned by mustard gas and the other by Zyklon B, shattered any faith in human progress. The protracted war in Vietnam and the civil unrest at home put the final nail in America's dream of a future characterized by human progress and Enlightenment ideals. Instead of ever-increasing wealth and prosperity, we are left with societal cynicism, whether it is about starvation in Rwanda or AIDS in Kenya. Even the celebrity atmosphere of the O. J. Simpson trial and the Kobe Bryant criminal case was surrounded by societal cynicism.

The war on terror in response to the attacks of September 11, 2001, initially led some in the United States to believe we were returning to a unified national metanarrative. However, that short-lived unity quickly reverted to numerous micronarratives based on societal cynicism. This cynicism leaves people desperately looking for something to give them meaning. Lacking a common thread to hold us together, we grope

Rather than mimic the trends of the postmodern world, we do better to figure out what those trends say about the needs and desires of our culture, and then use those insights to strengthen the incarnational nature of our ministries. . . . As church leaders we would do well to study the various characteristics of postmodern culture. But our goal is not to uncritically adopt the trends. It is to understand what the people pursuing the trends are actually hungering for. What people are really hungering for is community, authenticity and genuine faith.

SOONG-CHAN RAH, "NAVIGATING CULTURAL CURRENTS"

around in the dark. "The optimism of the modern era and the 'hope in God' of the pre-modern era has been forsaken in the postmodern era."[39] Instead of optimism, there is now suspicion and mistrust. Instead of hope, there is insecurity and instability.

WHY IT MATTERS

Subjective truth (preferences), community, virtual reality and micronarratives (societal cynicism) are the four primary characteristics of postmodern culture. Why do we need to recognize the traits of postmodern culture or understand the transition from the Enlightenment? Responding to an article in *Christianity Today,* one reader proclaimed that his church did not need all of this analysis because it was called to "present the gospel and the whole counsel of God in all its eternal and existential relevance and leave the results up to God."[40] Such people fail to perceive that, even though the gospel does not change, the world does, and the strategies that we use to reach the world also must change over time. As we move into the twenty-first century, many Christians continue to minister as if they were living in the nineteenth century, convinced that they are ministering as Jesus did. God calls us to be like the "men of Issachar, who understood the times and knew what Israel should do" (1 Chron 12:32).

Underlying this book is the realization that the key issues of the next thirty or forty years—maybe even further out—have already been largely defined by the events of the last half-century. The key lesson this book tries to get across is that decision-makers—in government, in the universities, in business, in the labor unions, in churches— need to factor into their present-day decision the future that has already happened. For this, they need to know what events have already occurred that do not fit their present-day assumptions, and thereby create new realities.

PETER DRUCKER, *THE NEW REALITIES*

God is preparing people in the world to respond to the gospel, and we need to understand how he is doing this. We need to understand not only the gospel message but also the cultural reality of these generations. Karl Barth, the Swiss theologian, once said that we need to live our lives with the Scriptures in one hand and the newspaper in the other hand in order to minister to the people God brings before us. The apostle Paul would wholeheartedly agree with Barth.

As he went about his missionary journeys, Paul first tried to meet people in their own reality. In Athens (Acts 17) Paul went first into the synagogues, following his normal practice. However, instead of teaching and preaching there as he did in Jewish communities, Paul "reasoned" or "argued" with the Athenian Jews, as was their custom. When Paul went to the Areopagus, he again followed the local custom and began to dialogue with those in attendance. After seeing the statue they had erected to the unknown god, Paul acknowledged that the Athenians were a religious people. He went on to identify this unknown god as Yahweh, the God of the Jews. Paul understood the gospel and was able to share it with the Athenians more compellingly because he also understood the Athenian culture.

Only as we understand Generation X and the Millennial generation, along with the postmodern culture they share, will we be able to reach these generations and coming generations with the gospel. Baby Boomers need to be prepared to enter into a crosscultural experience, moving from the modern into a postmodern culture.

SUMMARY

Now that we have looked at both the two newest generations and postmodern culture, let me describe the link between them. If Neil Howe and William Strauss are correct in their book *Generations,* history is cyclical and what we have in Generation X and the Millennial generation is no more than just a reaction and correction to the Baby Boom generation. David Bosch and most other theologians would disagree with them because they see history as linear, not cyclical. History is moving toward a climax. Certainly within both these generations we have a reaction to the excesses of the Baby Boom generation. Their emphases on relationships versus careers and surviving versus striving are certainly reactions to the Baby Boomers. However, in addition to these incremental changes, some major changes are occurring within all generations and the whole culture, and these cannot be explained away as a reaction or a correction to the Baby Boom generation. These changes can best be explained by the transition to an emerging culture.

Within both these generations and culture as a whole there is a major shift in how truth is viewed. Objective truth has become less important. When these young people are pushed with logical argument, they often respond, "Whatever." Truth is less essential to these generations than relationships. Their understanding of truth is greatly influenced by the community in which they are involved. In the 1960s the autonomous individual, such as John Wayne in the movies or David Jansen in *The Fugitive* TV show or Art Garfunkel in the song "I Am a Rock," was the epitome of life for my generation. But today's younger generations see community as essential, as shown in top-rated TV shows like *Friends*.

Another dramatic change within these generations is their outlook on life. Almost all generations of Americans preceding Generation X had an optimistic outlook on life, even during the Great Depression. Faith in human progress reigned then, but no longer. Societal cynicism shapes our outlook on the future. This outlook represents a major societal change of view, not just a reaction to the Baby Boom generation.

Ultimately we must observe the Millennial generation as well as the generations that follow in order to determine if Generation X is only reacting to the generation before it or if it really is the first postmodern generation, thus setting the tone for future generations. But we cannot wait twenty years to see if these changes will be enduring. If we do, we evangelicals will lose touch with this emerging culture. We will be reacting to rather than anticipating cultural changes. I think that the observable evidence points to Generation X as the first postmodern generation, the first generation of a new era. If I am right, then we need to rethink how we are going to do ministry in the future.

We need to focus less on the smaller generational transitions from Boomers to Xers to Millennials while focusing more on the larger transition from the Enlightenment/modern era to the emerging/postmodern era. The transition from the Baby Boom generation to Generation X is a foreshadowing of the larger transition to postmodern culture. Let me employ a meteorological analogy to explain what I mean.

The East Coast of the United States occasionally experiences nor'easters, storms that develop off the shore of the Carolinas and move up along the coast, devastating the New England shore. But the storm may also start out as a low-pressure area moving up the western side of the Appalachian Mountains, a couple hundred miles from the coast. However, as the storm moves north along the mountains, its energy may be transferred to the Carolina coast and turn into a nor'easter while the storm moving along the mountains diminishes in intensity. If we were only observing the storm in the mountains, we could easily miss the development of the nor'easter. Then people living along the New England shore would not have enough time to prepare for the damaging winds and blizzard conditions. Generation X and the Millennial generation are like the storm along the mountains. It is a foreshadowing of the larger "nor'easter" (postmodern) culture. If we focus narrowly on generational ministry, we will not be prepared for the greater and enduring consequences of postmodern culture.

I am convinced that God is preparing the people of this postmodern culture to hear God in new ways. In the following sections of this book I want to suggest foundational theological concepts and new strategies that are both biblical and vital to ministry in the emerging postmodern world.

IMPLICATIONS FOR MINISTRY

Persons who move from one place to another temporarily lose their sense of identity. Do I belong to the place I came from, or do I belong to this new place that seems so foreign? This period of transition is confusing. We are now moving into a postmodern culture, and we are experiencing the trauma of moving. We do not know where we belong. But if we continue to deny that we are moving into a new city, we will never be able to become settled or productive in it.

To effectively minister in a postmodern culture, we first have to admit that we are in a new city and not waste time longing for our former city, the Enlightenment/modern era. Although the emerging culture is continuing to define itself, we need to learn as much about it as we can, even as we would learn as much as we could about a new city to which we had moved.

One of the first lessons for us to learn is that fewer people believe in absolute truth. What effect does that fact have on our ministry? As we will see in later chapters, our apologetic strategies need to change. We will need to emphasize embodying the truth in our lives versus only talking about the truth with our words. The lives of Christians will become more important to seekers as evidence to use in deciding whether or not to follow Christ.

Similarly, young Christians will grow in their Christian lives more by observing how other Christians live than by listening to what other Christians say. Modeling is becoming more crucial for Christian development. How do our ministries need to change to allow this modeling to take place? Teaching that stresses cognitive learning but does not also include relational learning will be less effective with people in a postmodern culture.

As we will see later, community life, not individual life, will form the center of Christian ministry. How will that change affect our ministry? Is community presently the core of our ministry in our church or Christian organization? The care of the community will be vital for Christian growth.

These communities will need to be places where the hurting—those living in cynicism or despair—can belong and be comforted and reassured. Do our ministries allow people to share their hurts and receive consolation? If we are going to be faithful in our ministry to postmodern generations, we will need to create places where people can mature and find comfort. Where do those places exist in your church or ministry?

One final question: What should be the Christian response to each of these cultural changes? We will be answering this question for the rest of the book. The framework below gives an overview of the answer.

MODERN CULTURE	EMERGING CULTURE	CHRISTIAN RESPONSE
Individual	Community	Christian Community
Objective Truth	Subjective Truth	Embodied Apologetics
Word	Image	Word & Image
Metanarrative	Micronarrative	God's Kingdom Story

The first line of the table highlights that we as Christians should rejoice that the culture is moving away from the individual and moving toward community. God created us to live in community. However, what we see in the culture today is not true Christian community but tribal-like groupings that tend to be separate from other groups. Christians need to enter into true Christian community, caring for each other and reaching out to others outside the community.

The second line of the table addresses the difficulty of operating in a culture that says there is no objective truth, only preferences based on experience and opinion. The church needs to allow people to experience the gospel through the lives of Christians. The best apologetic will be to show seekers how the gospel changes our lives, not just our vocabulary. As they see the truth lived out in our lives, they become more open to hear and accept the truth themselves.

In a culture that is fascinated by television and movies, the power of image (the third line of the table) is easy to see. And yet the gospel, to the non-Christian, appears stuck in the realm of tolerable (but hardly attractive) words. The emerging culture wants to see and experience, not read someone else's description. We need to use both words and images to communicate the power and relevance of the gospel.

The final line of the table explores how we communicate in a society that is fragmented into racial and generational and religious groups, with no single, unifying story of human history. Instead each group has its own version of history that it claims to be the correct history. In this chaos the gospel is frequently unwelcome because it does not match a particular person's history. We must seek to display the unifying nature of the gospel, showing that it is in fact intended for every person and ethnic group and not a separate history in and of itself.

PART TWO

LONGING
TO BELONG

A Theological Foundation

Created for Community

Friends endured for years as one of the top five most-watched TV shows. It is easily the most emulated show, with close to ten other shows using the same concept—a group of friends trying to make sense of life together. The show's popularity was due to the fact that these six friends (Chandler, Joey, Monica, Phoebe, Rachel and Ross) became a community of people who cared for each other. They became the family they all lacked growing up.

In the 1950s and 1960s most popular TV shows were built around the traditional family, such as *Ozzie and Harriet* and *Father Knows Best*. Why have the emerging generations become so caught up with friends and community rather than the traditional family? The traditional family is not meeting the need for belonging that is such a part of people in the emerging culture.

As Christians, we should be sad about the breakdown of the traditional family. At the same time, though, we should applaud and take advantage of the change we are observing among people as they reject the autonomous self of the Enlightenment era and embrace the tribalism of postmodern culture. At least they are moving in the right direction. We should be embracing this change because tribalism is much more closely aligned than the autonomous self to God's intention of how we should function in relationships. God created us to live in community. The key theological concept in building a framework for ministry in the postmodern world is biblical community. What is biblical community?

THE GENESIS STORY

In Genesis 1 we discover that humans alone, out of all creation, were created in the image of God (Gen 1:27). Furthermore, we were given a responsibility to oversee the rest of creation as a result of our special relationship with God (Gen 1:28).

Bearing the image of God places us in community because the triune God is himself in community among the Father, Son and Holy Spirit.[1] We see that divine community from the beginning of time (Gen 1:1-3). God the Father is the designer, or Creator, of all things. As we see in verse 2, the Spirit of God is the protector of all things. And we know from the first chapter of John that Jesus is the *Logos,* the Word of God. So when God speaks in Genesis 1:3, it is actually God the Son speaking. Thus from the beginning of creation we see the community of God relating to each other in the Trinity and to creation, especially to humankind, through community.

After creating Adam, God declared, "It is not good for the man to be alone" (Gen 2:18). Does this mean that God made a mistake in creation? Did God omit a part of Adam that would make him feel secure and not alone? The answer is an emphatic no! God from the beginning of time had planned to create all humans to need both God and other humans. He created all of humankind to live in community. The relationship between God and Adam and Eve, as well as Adam and Eve's relationship with each other, was a prototype of how God wants to relate to people and how God wants us to relate to each other.

The relationship between Adam and Eve laid the foundation for relationships between people in community. Genesis 2 demonstrates harmony and equality in community. Adam could say of Eve,

> This is now bone of my bones
> and flesh of my flesh. (Gen 2:23)

The author of Genesis could state that "the man and his wife were both naked, and they felt no shame" (Gen 2:25). They felt at home with each other and with God. There was no fear or alienation. God was present in the community, and thus Adam and Eve were content with all of life.

As loving community was the norm at creation, so God desires for us to relate with each other and with God through a loving community. Christians should demonstrate what a loving community is like to people crying out for community.

REBELLED AGAINST COMMUNITY

Eventually, Adam and Eve became discontented. Instead of staying in communion with God and in proper community with each other, they sought independence. Their rebellion alienated them from God as well as from each other. They felt shame, which caused them to throw up barriers between themselves. They also felt ashamed and afraid of God, so they tried to hide (Gen 3:7-10).

The community was shattered. Instead of contentment, there was contention. Instead of harmony, there was hatred. Instead of sharing, there was shame. As we see in Genesis 3:16, God told Eve,

Your desire will be for your husband,
and he will rule over you.

"Innocence and community have given way to self-consciousness and domination."[2] So Adam and Eve faced the dread of dissension instead of the joy of community. Their sin led to mutual alienation.

Even more important than the alienation between Adam and Eve was the alienation between them and God. For the first time in their lives, they hid from God. For us the experience of hiding is commonplace, but for them it was new and frightening. Stanley Grenz categorizes this state of fear as follows:

Sin gives birth to alienation from God. Designed to be God's friends, even God's children, our sin leads us to live as enemies of God (Romans 5:10). Rather than enjoying the presence of God we flee. We live in fear, presuming God is hostile towards us. Despite our infinite dependence, we run from the only one who can overcome our fear, brokenness and hostility, the one who can fulfill our deepest needs. Sin therefore destroys the community God intends for his creation. . . . Consequently, we are alienated from our own true selves. We simply are not who we are meant to be.[3]

The creation story moves from the loneliness of Adam to the community among Adam and Eve and God to the loss of all community. Adam and Eve hid from each other and from God. Their disordered state became the origin of dysfunctionality. The rest of human history became a struggle between humanity's continued rebellion from community on the one hand and its desperate search for that community on the other hand. That struggle continues today, as many people in the emerging culture resist commitment while longing to belong.

Jason was a student caught in the tension between wanting to belong but resisting commitment. When he arrived at college, I encouraged him to get involved in a Christian fellowship on campus and a church in the community. But he wanted to explore possibilities for community that did not have a Christian base. In essence he was rebelling against God. We got in touch periodically during his next few years of college. I prayed for him on a regular basis.

By the time he reached his senior year, Jason realized that his attempts to find secular community had not satisfied him. He realized that he had rebelled against God. Although he never did become involved in a Christian fellowship on campus, he slowly became involved in a church. The small group that he found in the church has provided the Christian community that he was unwilling to commit to while he was a student.

As God has been patient with me in my times of rebellion, so we have to be patient with Jason and others like him in the emerging culture. Commitment to a biblical community may take a long time for some of today's young people.

The first book in the Bible describes people who live in the tension of longing for, yet rebelling against, biblical community. Nowhere is this tension more evident than in Genesis 11 and 12. In Genesis 11 we see how humankind continued its rebellion against community with God by attempting to build a tower. "Come, let us build ourselves a city, with a tower that reaches to the heavens, so that we may make a name for ourselves and not be scattered over the face of the whole earth" (Gen 11:4).

This attempt at building community without God's presence was ultimately unfulfilling because God had created humankind to be in community with him as well as with each other. God was also righteously jealous of humanity's attempt to take his place by building a tower to the heavens. As a result, God interrupted the project by confusing their languages and scattering the people throughout the earth.

J. Richard Middleton and Brian J. Walsh, in their book *Truth Is Stranger Than It Used to Be,* explain the consequences of the tower of Babel. "The curse of Babel is that human community is fragmented and scattered. While this scattering is in judgment upon an autonomous attempt at establishing unity, it also enforces God's original creational intent that we multiply and fill the earth, thus diffusing an oppressive concentration of human power."[4] Without God's intervention, there is little likelihood that humankind is going to be unified in community.

RESTORED TO COMMUNITY

Although humankind rebelled against God in the past and continues to do so in the present, God has not abandoned us. After God scattered the people from Babel in Genesis 11, he gathered together a community, Abram's family, to begin a planned restoration of community in Genesis 12.

> *The church should be a reflection of the communitarian God whom we worship. And if you think about it, the church is:*
>
> • *The covenantal people of God the Father*
>
> • *The body of Christ, the Son*
>
> • *And a community born on Pentecost and constituted by the Spirit*
>
> TONY JONES, *POSTMODERN YOUTH MINISTRY*

> The LORD had said to Abram, "Leave your country, your people and your father's household and go to the land I will show you.
> "I will make you into a great nation
> and I will bless you. . . .
> All peoples on earth
> will be blessed through you." (Gen 12:1-3)

Genesis 12 establishes a pattern that continues to this day: God initiates and we respond. This pattern is the biblical concept of covenant. The biblical phrase "I will be your God, and you will be my people" is the covenant formulation for God's being in community with Israel and now with the church as the new Israel.[5] The word *covenant* comes from the word *convene*. A covenant brings together two or more people in a binding agreement. Biblical history is a history of God in covenant community with people. God's presence and God's initiative are what held the covenant community together. From the "let us confuse and scatter" in Genesis 11, God takes the initiative in Genesis 12 to "make you into a great nation."

While God first tells Abram that he wants to work through him to make a great nation and to have a covenant with that nation, God has further plans for the future. God wants not only to bring the Israelites back into community with him but also to restore community to all nations. As a sign of that future, God changes Abram's name, which means "exalted father," to Abraham, which means "father of many" (Gen 17:3-7).

We see God's commitment to keeping the covenant. He delivered the Hebrew people from bondage in Egypt to bring them together at Mount Sinai in order to establish a covenant with them as a people, not just with their leaders. The covenant community took shape during the exodus, at Mount Sinai and in the wilderness. The characteristics of the community consisted of the initiating activity of God followed by the response of the community in worshiping God as deliverer and sustainer.[6] God initiated living among the Hebrews in the tabernacle (Ex 25:8). God's house, like their houses, was a tent. The community of faith was a pilgrim community, always moving. It was oriented toward the future, expectantly waiting for God's leading. God led them into the Promised Land and resided there with them. After Solomon built the temple in Jerusalem, God resided in the innermost part of it, the holy of holies.

> *At the heart of community is the idea of God among humans.*
>
> • *God with Adam and Eve in the Garden*
>
> • *God tabernacled among the Israelites in the wilderness*
>
> • *God resided in the temple in Jerusalem*
>
> • *Jesus tabernacled among us*
>
> • *The Spirit dwells with us.*
>
> HENRY BLACKABY,
> *EXPERIENCING GOD*

The faithfulness of God is one of the messages we need to proclaim to Jason and to others in his generation. We need to share with them that God, unlike others in their lives, is faithful to them, even when they are not faithful to God. Old Testament history demonstrates that although God was faithful to the Israelite people, the Israelite people were not faithful to God. Could this dilemma ever be resolved?

RE-CREATED IN COMMUNITY

A totally new creation of humankind in community came when God sent his Son, Jesus. Jesus' mission was to re-create us in community with God and with each other. In Jesus, God became flesh and "tabernacled" among the people. "The Word became flesh and made his dwelling among us" (Jn 1:14). No longer was God residing in a tent or in the temple, as in the Old Testament. Now God

Jesus never wrote a book or established a school. Rather his legacy was a community. The greatest hermeneutic of the gospel is a community that seeks to live by it. We should not seek community but pursue love, a practice which yields community as a by-product.

BRIAN McLAREN, "AUTHENTIC COMMUNITY"

was residing in the flesh and blood of the people. As in the Old Testament, God continued to remain faithful to the covenant and to maintain a presence among the people.

Jesus chose to live most closely with a small community that he called to follow him. "Jesus went up on a mountainside and called to him those he wanted, and they came to him. He appointed twelve—designating them apostles—that they might be with him and that he might send them out to preach" (Mk 3:13-14). Gareth Icenogle characterizes the disciples' community as follows:

Jesus called out a small group of people to experience their own exodus journey together, to move from the enslavement of controlling social, political and religious patterns and to enter into the freedom of "pouring new wine into new wineskins" (Mark 2:22). . . . Jesus' mission was to demonstrate the nearness of God to alienated humanity. To do this he formed small group communities.[7]

Throughout his three years of ministry, Jesus instilled within his small-group community a commitment to himself and to each other.

The disciples gradually began to recognize Jesus' leadership in their lives. When Jesus asked Peter, "Who do you say I am?" Peter answered, "You are the Christ" (Mk 8:29). The disciples began to see that they could no longer control their own destiny. They needed to submit to Jesus' authority. They also needed to depend on each other. Slowly the Twelve became the new family of God—Jesus' family (Mk 3:34-35). They left behind everything to follow Jesus and formed a new family.

Belonging to that new family meant that the disciples needed to change their attitudes and expectations about their own roles. One day Jesus heard them arguing among themselves, so he said,

> "What were you arguing about on the road?" But they kept quiet because on the way they had argued about who was the greatest.
> Sitting down, Jesus called the Twelve and said, "If anyone wants to be first, he must be the very last, and the servant of all." (Mk 9:33-35)

Time and time again, Jesus demonstrated for the disciples what it meant to serve each other in the community. Jesus even washed the disciples' feet, a task usually performed by the lowliest servant. By doing this task, he was recreating the kind of community that existed among God and Adam and Eve before the Fall. The community that existed in perfect harmony before the Fall had vanished from human consciousness. Jesus gave people a vision of what they were created for—community with God and with each other.

We need to help people in the emerging culture contrast friends and other communities of today with Jesus' model of community. Jesus was the true servant in the community. He did not try to dominate others or get his way selfishly. We need to enlarge the concept of community for this emerging culture, even as Jesus tried to enlarge his disciples' concept of who belonged in the community. In the Old Testament era the Israelites at times assumed that the community of God was restricted to them because of their special relationship with God through the covenant. However, through his deeds and words, Jesus began to enlarge their understanding of membership in the community. He expanded the membership of his community to include tax collectors and sinners, the Samaritan woman and lepers, among others.

Jesus provided the disciples with a vision of human community. All that was left was to give them the means to re-create the community between humanity and God. He accomplished this by taking our place on the cross and suffering the punishment we deserved for our rebellion from community with God. Jesus' sacrificial death on the cross broke down the barrier that had existed between men and women and God since that first act of rebellion. That re-creation of community with God was symbolized by the removal of the curtain in the holy of holies in the temple in Jerusalem at the moment of Jesus' death. God had continued to be present with people after the Fall, but during the Israelite period, he resided in a separate place, the holy of holies, because of their sins. Jesus' atoning sacrifice on the cross, taking our deserved place, abolished the necessity of separation between God and human beings. If we admit our rebellion, and if we desire Christ to be Savior and Lord, we are able to reenter community with God and humankind.

At Pentecost the Holy Spirit came to tabernacle in the hearts of the people of God. At Pentecost the people of God were re-created in community, and the church was born. At Pentecost the Lord reversed the tower of Babel, where language was confused and people were scattered. Here at Pentecost we see the Holy Spirit gathering together a scattered people and giving them the ability to understand each other (Acts 2:5-12).

What all this means is that God wants to gather the covenant people together in a new way, establishing his church. God wants to bring them together and give them a ministry of reconciliation. This type of community is crucial to a postmodern world in which people long to belong. I am convinced that this is the type of ministry God is calling his church to model as we make the transition into a postmodern culture.

RECONCILED INTO COMMUNITY

The ministry of reconciliation is the ministry of taking people who are alienated from God and from each other and building them into a community that deeply cares for each other and allows God to care for each one. The house churches of the early church, such as the ones that met in the home of Aquila

Only in relationship—as persons in community—are we able to reflect the fullness of the divine character. And because the company of Jesus' disciples are called to be the divine imagery, the church is essentially a community characterized by love, a people who reflect in relation to one another and to all creation the character of the Creator.

STAN GRENZ, BEYOND
FOUNDATIONALISM

and Priscilla in Rome (Rom 16:3-5), were the first attempts at forming reconciling communities. The church did not consist of a building like the temple in Jerusalem or modern church buildings today. It was the people of God, and their lack of a fixed residence, that made them a pilgrim church. According to David Bosch, "The biblical archetype is that of the wandering people of God. . . . It is ekklesia, 'called out,' of the world and sent back into the world. . . . God's pilgrim people need only two things, support for the road and a destination at the end of it. It has no fixed abode here; it is a paradox, a temporary residence."[8]

The early churches followed Jesus' model and became communities of love, loving each other and loving those outside the church. Jesus had told them before he departed that those outside the church would "know that you are my disciples, if you love one another" (Jn 13:35). As love had bound God the Son with God the Father, so Jesus wanted the church to be bonded by that same love. Stanley Grenz describes the purpose of the church as follows:

> To be the people in covenant with God who serves as the sign of the kingdom means to reflect the very character of God. The church reflects God's character in that it lives as a genuine community—lives in love—for as the community of love the church shows the nature of the triune God. . . . God calls the church to mirror as far as possible in the midst of the brokenness of the present that eschatological ideal community of love which derives its meaning from the divine essence.[9]

This love is acted out primarily through fellowship shown by word and deed. As Robert Banks points out, "The focal point of Paul's community is neither a book nor a rite but a set of relationships. . . . Paul's idea was to place fellowship with God and with one another at the heart of the community. The result was a unified community breaking down the cultural barriers of Jew and Gentile, men and women, master and slave (Galatians 3:28)."[10]

This love shown within the community, as well as to those outside the community, is possible only where there is reconciliation, first, between a person and God, and second, between people. As today's world becomes more and more fragmented, a ministry of reconciliation is a powerful witness. A number of years ago I had the opportunity to speak at a conference in Austria that was attended by over 150 Christian students from more than 50 countries. One of the highlights of the conference was to see students from Serbia, Croatia and Macedonia singing a song of peace as tears streamed down their faces. Although they had become reconciled with each other, they all came from countries that had been involved in a brutal war. By the end of the song, all the conference participants were weeping tears of joy and tears of sadness. Although God had used the time to bind us together in community, we were going back to countries that were locked in conflict with each other. We would be witnesses to the possibility of reconciliation.

The completion of reconciliation in community will not happen until the end times. This reconciliation is the goal of God's work. Stan Grenz describes the culmination as follows:

> Fellowship with God in community is the teleos or goal of God's activity in salvation, beginning already at creation. The biblical narrative presents fullness of community as eschatological. Rev. 21:1-3. . . . The New Testament writers declare that the future reality is the community of Christ—the community of reconciled people in fellowship with God through Christ.[11]

The mission of the church since the time of Christ is to embody this reconciled community and invite others to be reconciled and renewed by joining this community.

RENEWED IN COMMUNITY

Throughout church history, small Christian communities persisted as places of renewal in the church. The monastic movement was begun in the sixth century by the Benedictine order. At their best, monasteries helped preserve the church from the pagan takeovers that took place in Europe during the Middle Ages. In the twelfth century, small communities like the Waldensians in the Italian Alps were established to preserve the truth of the gospel from increasing corruption within the church. Small-group preservation communities continued for the next few centuries.

Following the Reformation, small-group communities sprang up once again, this time for purposes of renewal. The community that probably had the most influence, the forerunner of small-group communities today, was the Herrnhut community founded by Count Nicholas von Zinzendorf in 1727. It was divided into small groups, or choirs, that met daily. Their purpose was to foster intimate sharing, confession, prayer and discipline. Zinzendorf helped to oversee each individual's Christian growth through the leaders of the choirs. The community sent missionary teams throughout the world, establishing new communities whose purpose was to reconcile others to God and to continue renewal in community.

One of the people most influenced by Zinzendorf was John Wesley. Wesley had already been involved in a small-group community as a young Christian at Oxford University. Wesley described his community experience at the university in the following way:

> I know no other place under heaven, where I can have some [friends] always at hand, of the same judgement, and engaged in the same studies; persons who are awakened into a full conviction, that they have but one work to do upon earth; who see at a distance what that one work is, even the recovery of a single eye and a clean heart; who, in order to do this, have, according to their power, absolutely devoted themselves to God, and follow after their Lord, denying themselves, and taking up their cross daily. To have even a small number of such friends constantly watching over my soul, and administrating, as need is, reproof or advice with all plainness and gentleness, is a blessing I know no where to find in any part of the kingdom.[12]

John Wesley went on to incorporate small-group communities into his missionary work in the United States in the mid-1700s. As a result of his work, Christian small-group communities sprang up in cities and towns and at such campuses as Princeton, William and Mary, the University of Pennsylvania and Brown. Student small-group communities were a major force in the spiritual awakenings of the 1790s and mid-1800s. Small-group communities served as vehicles for ministry on the campuses of Cambridge University in England and Williams College in Massachusetts in the 1800s.

As we try to reach people in the emerging culture, community will play a vital role. A key factor to remember as we reach out and minister to the younger generations is that their understanding of family may be closer to the *oikos* pattern of the New Testament culture than that of any preceding American generation (see Gal 6:10; Eph 2:19).[13] From creation until today, God has placed his people in small communities. Although these early church communities and Christian communities have always had their problems, they have special qualities that make them a suitable model for twenty-first-century communities. We will look more closely at the specific role of small groups for ministry in the emerging postmodern world in chapter seven. However, we have the ability to minister to the one who is homesick for the home he never had and others through biblical communities. A number of years ago, Elton Trueblood defined the Christian community when he said, "The church is consciously inadequate persons who gather because they are weak and scatter to serve because unity with each other and Christ has made them bold."[14]

IMPLICATIONS FOR MINISTRY

Jesus' relationship with his disciples in community is an excellent place for us to observe what a healthy, loving, biblical community might look like today. Too often we have studied the doctrinal sections of Paul's letters to discover what the Christian faith should look like. Although such studies provide a strong doctrinal foundation for the Christian life, they do not always give us a model of how we are to relate in community. In the coming years we need to look more to the Gospels as a model of how we are to relate to each other in community. Jesus' model for relationships provides rich material from which we can learn.

Because many young people in the emerging culture have not had healthy models in their families to show them how to develop a loving community, our churches and ministries need to model healthy relationships. We need to have patience with one another as we work to create an environment where sharing pain can take place and where trust can develop. For such openness to occur, the leaders of the community need to model openness and vulnerability by sharing their pain with the group.

As God created Eve to be a companion to Adam, so God has created men and women to be friends with each other. In Christian communities women and men can come together to develop mutual friendships that are not sexually charged. We need to make sure our Christian communities develop a climate that supports friendship. Whether in small groups or in larger groupings of people, we need to be careful that we do not isolate women and men from each other. These younger generations especially need to learn to relate across gender lines.

Finally we need to be careful that Christians in our churches or organizations do not fall into either of two societal patterns—consumerism or tribalism. Numerous Christians are "double dipping." Instead of becoming part of one Christian community, they attend two or more churches in a quest to have personal needs met. Thus they remain spectators or consumers in each church. We need to help Christians see that this path is not God's path. He desires us to be involved in one fellowship where we can give as well as receive.

Many Christians are succumbing to the postmodern temptation to fragment or tribalize into smaller units within the church. God does want us to be involved in smaller communities. However, when those smaller communities become tribal groups, we are in danger of fragmenting. Tribal groups are groups through which we gain identity and to which we give loyalty, even to the exclusion of the larger group. A while ago I gave a sermon at our church entitled "Postmodern Tribalism or Biblical Community?" In this sermon I named the groups in our church that seemed to be in tension with each other—contemporary versus traditional worship, public versus home school, spiritual versus cognitive, and programmatic versus relational. I challenged the groups to try to understand each other and to try to unite in biblical community rather confront each other from their tribal groups.

The ministry of reconciliation is the key to helping communities within our churches become united rather than fragmented. Jesus, once again, is our model for what it means to be involved in a ministry of reconciliation, not fragmentation. As a church, we should continually be in prayer that God will unite us in one body with Christ only as its head.

Freed from Guilt and Shame

Let me return to Joan, the young person I mentioned in chapter one of whom I asked the simple question, "Are you going home for Christmas?" As Joan and I continued talking in the new year, she began to explain that something was missing in her Christian life. Although she knew in her mind that she was free from her guilt and justified before God, she did not feel close to God and consequently did not feel close to her brothers and sisters in Christ. I would like to suggest that Joan and many other postmodern Christians are correct to feel that something is missing from their Christian lives. Many of us who grew up in the modern era cannot even recognize that something is missing. What is missing is a critical element of salvation, the relational side.

While Joan realized in her head that she was "saved," she did not feel worthy of God's love because she had never been loved before. Many of us do not recognize this deficiency, because for the last three to four hundred years, whether we admit it or not, Christianity has been influenced by the Enlightenment, which affirmed the autonomous self and rational thought. We emphasized guilt and justification at the expense of shame and adoption. Christians in the emerging culture are beginning to see that we need to reemphasize the relational side of salvation along with the objective side.

JUSTIFIED FROM GUILT AND CALLED OUT FROM SHAME

In discussing salvation, we rightfully state that we are guilty before God and need to be justified. Jesus Christ took all our guilt upon himself through his death on the cross, and if we confess our guilt, God forgives us and sees us as if we had never sinned. Paul summed up this process: "All have sinned and fall short of the glory of God, and are justified freely by his grace through the redemption that came by Christ Jesus. God presented him as a sacrifice of atonement, through faith in his blood" (Rom 3:23-25). If we admit our guilt and appropriate salvation by faith through the grace that comes about through justification, we are no longer condemned. Paul described this process in Romans 1—7 and concluded with the summary statement in Romans 8:1-2: "Therefore, there is now no condemnation for those who are in Christ Jesus, because through Christ Jesus the law of the Spirit of life set me free from the law of sin and death." However, that is only part of the story. Not only are we free from guilt, but we should also be free from shame.

Like guilt, shame cannot be fully understood apart from a biblical perspective. From creation to the Fall to the wilderness to Jesus to the early church, shame and the consequences of shame have comprised a vital part of the salvation process. Before the Fall, shame and guilt were absent from the drama. Adam and Eve could stand before each other and before God and feel no shame. "The man and his wife were both naked, and they felt no shame" (Gen 2:25). Nakedness, exposure and vulnerability presented no threat in creation.[1] Harmony reigned between God and the human pair, between Adam and Eve, and within the hearts of Adam and Eve. They had no desire to hide from each other.

When Adam and Eve sinned, however, "the eyes of both of them were opened, and they realized they were naked; so they sewed fig leaves together and made coverings for themselves" (Gen 3:7). The sense of nakedness that Adam and Eve felt was linked to sin. Their awareness of their nakedness symbolized their awareness of their sinful state.[2] Adam and Eve were now ashamed. They were ashamed of their loss of unity with God and with each other, which was a vital part of who they were as complete persons.

Adam and Eve felt remorse and guilt because they were at fault, and they felt shame because they now lacked something—their perfect relationship with God, with each other and within themselves.[3] This shame made Adam and Eve feel exposed and vulnerable, so they attempted to cover their nakedness. Not only did they try to cover themselves from each other but they also tried to hide from God (Gen 3:8). It was their shame, not their guilt, that caused them to try to hide from God.[4]

It is important to note that it was Adam and Eve who did the hiding and it was God who did the searching. "The LORD God called to the man, 'Where are you?' " (Gen 3:9). The rest of the Bible depicts the shamed as wanting to hide and God as going to find them. The shamed want to die, but the godly seek them out. God is calling to his community of believers in the postmodern world to seek after those who feel ashamed, to offer them hospitality and to invite them into our Christian community. This type of caring and welcoming is what Joan and others in the emerging culture so desperately need. They need us to reach out to them, invite them in and provide a safe place where they can share "where they are."

The sin of Adam and Eve separated them from God. This separation is like a wall that God built to shield his holy character from our guilt. We build a second wall when our shame causes us to feel unworthy of God's presence. We try to cover ourselves and hide from God. We may then take this one step further and arrogantly refuse to allow God to see us. Thus we create the dilemma that we still face today. Being created for community with God and with other humans, we long for the kind of intimate relationships that the human pair experienced before the Fall. But because of our sin state, we are ashamed to let God, others and even ourselves have a look at us. We hesitate to reveal ourselves.[5]

Adam and Eve tried to get rid of their guilt first by denying their sin and then by blaming others (Gen 3:11-13). The shame they felt caused them to resort to concealment.[6] People still try to deal with their sin through denial and concealment. But this strategy did not work for Adam and Eve, and it does not work today. For many years Joan concealed her pain. Then a simple question, "Are you going home for Christmas?" opened up a flood of emotions within her. I am glad I did not leave her alone.

We can give thanks that God did not leave Adam and Eve wallowing in their denial and concealment. After punishing their sin, God gave Adam and

Eve hope—a foretaste of how he was going to provide an ultimate solution to sin in the future. At the end of Genesis 3 God shows compassion. He "made garments of skin for Adam and his wife and clothed them" (Gen 3:21). James Boice describes the significance of God's act of compassion. "In Genesis 3 we gain a foretaste of God's provision. We find God taking animals, killing them in what was the first sacrifice for sin, and then clothing Adam and Eve with their skins."[7]

This incident foreshadowed the coming future salvation in which God covered our sin through the death of his Son, Jesus Christ, on the cross. In the meantime humankind had to exist behind walls that separated them from God and from themselves. This separation was evident on numerous occasions throughout the Old Testament period. For example, during the wilderness sojourn, God traveled with his people while remaining separated from them, dwelling behind the curtain in the tabernacle (Ex 26:31-33).

Once the temple in Jerusalem was constructed under the guidance of King Solomon, God resided in the holy of holies. Only the chief priest could enter this area, and he only once a year. The curtain that hung before the holy of holies symbolized the separation between God and humankind that began in the Garden of Eden.

Then Jesus came. His mission was to take our sins upon himself as a guilt offering of redemption and to remove our shame by restoring us to a right relationship with God the Father, thus tearing down the wall of separation. In order for Jesus to accomplish his mission, he had to face his own shame as he approached his death on the cross. While today we sanitize and idealize the cross, in Jesus' time the experience of the cross was shameful.[8] Norman Kraus reminds us of the cross:

> We must recall that the cross was designed above all to be an instrument of contempt and public ridicule. Crucifixion was the most shameful execution imaginable. The victim died naked, in bloody sweat, helpless to control body excretions or to brush away the swarming flies. Thus exposed to the jeering crowd, the criminal died a spectacle of disgrace. By Roman law no citizen could be so dishonorably executed. The cross was reserved for foreigners and slaves.[9]

The movie *The Passion of the Christ* vividly portrays the horror of crucifixion. The author of Hebrews reminds us that Jesus recognized the shame of the cross but did not allow that shame to prevent him from fulfilling his mission. "Let us fix our eyes on Jesus, the author and perfecter of our faith, who for the joy set before him endured the cross, scorning its shame" (Heb 12:2). Jesus experienced shame on the cross and in the events leading up to the cross. He felt shame when his disciples betrayed him (Judas), denied him (Peter) and abandoned him (the rest of the disciples). He felt shame when the soldiers stripped him, mocked him and spit on him (Mt 27:28-30). He felt shame when religious leaders and others surrounding the cross mocked him and hurled insults at him. Probably Jesus endured the most shameful moment when he cried out, " *'Eloi, Eloi, lama sabachthani?'*—which means, 'My God, my God, why have you forsaken me?' " (Mt 27:46). At that moment Jesus felt the guilt of sin and the shame of separation from God that humankind has felt since the Fall. At that moment Jesus not only received our guilt by taking all our sins upon himself but also experienced our shame, our feeling of separation from God, which Joan and so many people feel today.

The cross shows God's identification with the shame-based person (Lk 23:35-39; Heb 12:2). Robert Albers declares, "The cross as God's shame-bearing symbol is a word of good news for the shame-based person. It celebrates the incarnational identification which God in Christ has with the shame-based person."[10]

Jesus' experience on the cross was both different from our experiences and similar to it. It was different in that, while we are guilty and deserve punishment, Jesus was guiltless and did not deserve to die. His experience was similar to ours in that he shares with us the feeling of shame and the "sense of failure, the dejection of defeat, and the realization that one cannot remedy failure."[11]

Jesus considered valueless the shame that his crucifixion earned him in the eyes of the world. He was more concerned about what God the Father thought. In the book of Hebrews we see that Jesus was vindicated, because after the experience on the cross was over, he "sat down at the right hand of the throne of God" (Heb 12:2). Jesus was disgraced in the eyes of the public, but God found him worthy of the highest honor.[12] Our guilt and shame were overcome, redeeming us before God the Judge and restoring us to God the Father.

Jesus' resurrection is assurance that what Jesus accomplished on the cross is everlasting. The shame of the cross turns into the glory of the resurrection. The resurrection elevates the shame of the crucifixion by giving people hope in their future.[13]

Joan's problem was that she was still ashamed of her past and herself and did not feel that God accepted her as his child and desired to be her Father. Accepting Christ removed one wall—guilt. Joan needed to see that Jesus' sacrifice on the cross also removed another wall—shame. This allowed Joan to experience the joy of being God's child once again. The cross creates the possibility of a community of people who are "no longer afraid of being defined and destroyed by shame and can admit their failures and allow their neediness."[14] A community of Christians reached out to Joan when she returned to school from the Christmas holidays. As Joan saw how this small-group community cared for each other and cared for her, she slowly began to experience the glory of the resurrection. Through experiencing the love of the Christians around her, she began to understand God's unconditional love for her. Her wall of shame slowly began to come down.

Part of that restoration for Joan and others can occur now. But part of it will have to wait until the end of time when Christ returns. Paul described this now-but-not-yet process in 2 Corinthians 5:1-5:

> We know that if the earthly tent we live in is destroyed, we have a building from God, an eternal house in heaven, not built by human hands. Meanwhile we groan, longing to be clothed with our heavenly dwelling, because when we are clothed, we will not be found naked. For while we are in this tent, we groan and are burdened, because we do not wish to be unclothed but to be clothed with our heavenly dwelling, so that what is mortal may be swallowed up by life. Now it is God who has made us for this very purpose and has given us the Spirit as a deposit, guaranteeing what is to come.

While we have to wait until Christ comes again to fully realize the benefits of a restoration with God the Father, much can be accomplished in the here and now. The Holy Spirit's role in this process is to bring us back into relationship with the Father. While Christ died to reconcile God to humanity, the role of the Holy Spirit is to reconcile humanity to God. Christ's role is to enable God to be a Father to us, while the Holy Spirit's role is to allow us to again be children of God.[15] The Holy Spirit helps us deal with shame, which prevents us from restoring our relationship with God as our Father.

STATE OF SHAME

Because the Baby Boom generation grew up primarily under the influence of the Enlightenment, it tends to be guilt based. The younger generations, having grown up mainly under the influence of postmodernism, can be characterized as shame based. They feel badly not so much about what they have or have not done but about who they are.[16] Guilt is based on the violation of an objective standard. Guilt says, "I have done something wrong."[17] Guilt can be absolved when the penalty for the wrong has been satisfied. Then the perpetrator of the wrongful act can be pardoned for the wrong and forgiven for the act.[18] Shame says, "There is something wrong with me." Shame has less to do with actions and status and more to do with a loss of identity and being.[19] Shame cannot be removed as easily as guilt. It is easier for us to change our actions than to change our being.

Psychological shame is the primary cause of emotional distress in our time. It has its roots in the theological shame that comes from our separation from God. Psychological shame is a byproduct of the social changes and the dysfunctional families of our day.[20] Shame attacks the core of the self by exposing it to others, which leads to physical and emotional isolation. Shame causes diminished self-esteem. The result is a heightened self-consciousness and a sense of personal unworthiness, a sense of being left wanting as human beings. We feel that we can never be good enough. We feel like failures.[21]

A few years ago I was talking to David, a college student who was going through some difficult times. He described what he was experiencing as depression. This mood caused him to say some things and do some things that he later regretted because his friends thought less of him owing to his behavior. He felt out of control and exposed in front of people and as a result isolated himself from his friends. He was having a hard time forgiving himself for his actions and his emotions.

People try to overcome shame in all sorts of ways. John Bradshaw tells a story of someone trying to overcome shame by doing. "I tried all my life to heal my shame with doing. I was president of the class. I was editor of the paper. I was on the baseball team. I was number six academically. People came to me with all their questions about life. And I was one of the sickest kids in the school. . . . I'd become a human doing. I wasn't a human being."[22]

Shame that is based on not being able to live up to the expectations of others can never be overcome by trying to do more, because more is never enough. However, shame can be healed. But first we must be willing to come together in community and admit that we are hurting and that we are vulnerable. In the Christian community the whole group needs to agree on universal shame. We are all sinners who are unworthy of God's love. We are all equal in God's eyes. Far from isolating those who feel shame, admitting the universality of sin can actually bind the community together rather than isolate those who feel shame.[23]

Whereas shame isolates, recovery from shame restores people to relationships. Their sin caused Adam and Eve to isolate themselves from God and from each other. They tried to cover their shame by covering their bodies and then by blaming someone else for their sin. As part of recovery from shame, we need to accept responsibility for our actions and then allow God to cover us through the blood of Jesus that was spilled on our behalf (Rev 1:5).

Shame needs to be covered. The etymological root of the word *shame* means "to cover."[24] However, we cannot cover our shame through our own actions. God desires to remove our shame as well as forgive our guilt. Norman Kraus has written,

> The intention of forgiveness is to nullify shame and guilt so that reconciliation and a new beginning become possible. The shamed person must find new identity and personal worth. . . . Only a forgiveness which covers the past and a genuine restoration of relationship can banish shame. . . . Reconciliation and restoration of mutual intimate relationships through a loving exchange is the only way to heal resentment and restore lost self-esteem.[25]

Jerry was a college student who seemed to have his act together. In high school he had tried to meet people's expectations for him, especially his father's. His father was a successful businessman who expected his son to be successful in everything he did. Although the son usually succeeded, he could never do enough to please his dad. He felt sad because he let his dad

down and feared him at the same time. As a result Jerry became profoundly disappointed in himself. When Jerry arrived at college, he began to question the way he felt about himself. Slowly he began to share with a couple of friends his doubts about himself, as well as the struggles he had with his dad.

As these caring friends affirmed Jerry as a person and challenged some of his thinking, he gradually started to see the light. His burden of shame lifted during a retreat of silence on a mission trip. Over a period of time he and his dad, who is now a Christian, have been able to talk about how they related in the past. Slowly their relationship has begun to heal, and a healthy love has developed between them. The love that Jerry's father feels for him has changed from a tough love to a tender love.

As I talked with Jerry, I asked him how his sense of shame affected his relationship with God. He admitted thinking that God, like his father, was not pleased with him. No matter what he did for God, it was not enough. During that retreat of silence, and through the encouragement of a few friends, Jerry began to realize that God viewed him as a worthy son, not an unworthy servant. Jerry had developed a new hope in life.

> *Nothing, apparently, defends against the internal ravages of shame more than the security gained from parental love, especially the sort of sensitive love that sees and appreciates the child for what he or she is and is respectful of the child's feelings, differences, and peculiarities. Nothing seems to cut more deeply than the lack of that love.*
>
> ROBERT KAREN, *ATLANTIC MONTHLY*

IMPLICATIONS FOR MINISTRY

Anything to do with reason becomes suspect in postmodern culture because truth is not allowed, only preferences. People now believe only what they feel or experience. This change from rational reasoning to experience as the basis for determining validity causes much concern within Christian circles. Nevertheless, these changes have brought some needed correctives to our understanding of belief. The Greek word *pisteuo,* which we translate "believe," means "to rely on or trust in." The Gospel of John was written that "you may believe that Jesus is the Christ, the Son of God and that by believing [trusting in him] you may have life in his name" (Jn 20:31). During the Enlightenment, the word *belief* lost its original meaning (trusting in) and came to refer to intellectual assent. This change came about partly because the Enlightenment began to discount feelings and experience as being subjective and unreliable.

For the sake of our witness and for the sake of Christian formation, we need to reclaim the original meaning of the word *believe*.[26] We need to call people to trust in Jesus, not just nod in intellectual assent. Also, in our Christian journey we need to realize that Jesus is not just calling us to agree intellectually that he is the Son of God. Rather, he is calling us to trust in him as Savior and Lord. It is because the meaning of the word *belief* changed to indicate intellectual assent that we have so many nominal Christians today.

Nominal means "in name only."[27] Is the phrase "nominal Christian" an oxymoron? Are some people who call themselves Christians actually pagans masquerading as believers?[28] According to the 1980 Lausanne Congress in Thailand, a nominal Christian is "one who, within the Protestant tradition, would call himself a Christian, or be so regarded by others, but who has no authentic commitment to Christ based on personal faith."[29] Nominal Christianity flourished during the Enlightenment era because too many people confused belief as intellectual assent with belief as trusting in or relying on.

Christian belief focuses on the heart, or emotions, in addition to the mind. In the Old Testament the heart is the center of the self. The heart is the seat of spiritual and moral capacity as well as the place of the soul's intellectual and volitional activity.[30] For the Israelites, thinking was not solving abstract problems but grasping the totality of something.[31] It was experiential and relational.[32]

God created humankind in God's own image. Our emotions constitute part of that image. Augustine of Hippo, as well as others of his time, understood and valued the emotional dimension of the Christian life. The medieval emphasis on the affections by such people as Bernard of Clairvaux and Julian of Norwich stemmed from Augustine's recognition of the relationship between the mind and the heart. Some Reformation leaders got caught up in the foreshadowing of the Enlightenment by emphasizing the mind and reason over the emotions and feelings. Ray Anderson, among others, regrets this dichotomy between heart and mind, saying that it has "led to a distortion in our understanding of God as well as to a repression of the subjective life of the self in the faith experience."[33]

In a postmodern world where logic and reason are not givens and where the emotions are more in evidence, an approach to discipleship that emphasizes only reason will fail miserably. Both the heart and the mind have to be engaged in the spiritual journey. We need to recapture the biblical view of belief as trust in God. If we are willing to make some of these changes, and if we are able to grasp the emotional and spiritual condition of people in the emerging culture and to adopt new methods for evangelism and discipleship, then we can have a great influence on today's society. Carlyle Marney has stated that Christianity "may yet have another chance to make an impact upon our culture, not because we deserve it, but because the alternatives have defaulted. I believe that we are in the midst of a shift in cultural consciousness of major proportions."[34]

If we are going to minister faithfully within the emerging culture, our churches need to provide teaching and practical assistance to help people overcome their shame. And as we will see in the next chapter, we can also help them realize their adoption into God's family.

6

From Lonely Orphan to God's Adopted Child

The Christian faith of many is shaped by the concept of God as master and believers as servants. We are free from guilt, but too often we do not feel we are free to enjoy a relationship with a loving Father. Derek Moore-Crispin describes the difference when he writes, "The servant with hat in hand stands at a respectful distance awaiting the orders of his master, the child of God rushes into the presence of his Father, leaps into his lap and nestles in his bosom."[1]

For people like Joan, who desperately need to belong, we need to recapture the child-of-God concept. We do so by supplementing the objective (redemption) side of salvation with the relational (restoration) side of salvation through emphasizing our being adopted into God's family.

The Holy Spirit's role in this process is to bring us back into relationship with the Father. The Holy Spirit helps us to regain our role as God's child and to experience adoption into God's family. While Christ died to reconcile God to humanity, the role of the Holy Spirit is to reconcile humanity to God. Christ's role is to enable God to be a Father to us, while the Holy Spirit's role is to allow us to be again a child of God, see God as our Father and be adopted into God's family.[2]

CALLED INTO ADOPTION

Adoption is a key element in being fully restored to God. Because Joan's earthly family let her down, she desperately needed to experience being a child of God, which is what we call adoption.

In biblical times secular adoption was a legal process whereby a person became a part of a different family and perpetuated that family line.[3] But in the theological world adoption has a different meaning. Biblical adoption means being returned to our original family, not joining a new family. Humankind began as sons and daughters of God the Father, members of God's household. As we saw earlier, this original design for children of God was forfeited by the disobedience of Adam and Eve and thus was canceled by God.[4] After the Fall, humankind became "outlaw citizens of the kingdom, and banished and disinherited children of the house of God,"[5] instead of being sons and daughters of God.

Throughout the Old Testament we see God laying the foundation for the adoption process that came to fruition in the New Testament period. As God led the Israelites out of their bondage in Egypt, the Israelites were referred to as God's firstborn son. This concept of the Israelites as firstborn son continues in the book of Hosea (1:1-11): "In the place where it was said of them, 'You are not my people,' they will be called 'sons of the living God.' "[6] God hinted to David the king how this would come about.

> The LORD declares to you that the LORD himself will establish a house for you: When your days are over and you rest with your fathers, I will raise up your offspring to succeed you, who will come from your own body, and I will establish his kingdom. He is the one who will build a house for my Name, and I will establish his kingdom forever. I will be his father, and he will be my son. (2 Sam 7:11-14)

Thus the Lord declared that he would restore his people to a covenantal relationship, and he would adopt them as his children through the Messiah.[7]

Although the Old Testament gives us a foreshadowing of adoption, it is only through Christ's work on the cross that God adopts us as sons and daughters. *Adoption* is defined as "an act of God's free grace, whereby we are received into [his family] and have a right to all the principles of the sons [and daughters] of God."[8] The Greek word for adoption, *hyiothesia,* was used by Paul to express the intimate relationship between God and women and men that is inaugurated by saving grace.[9] Just as Israel was redeemed from slavery as an heir to the promises God gave to Abraham, so we as believers were redeemed and adopted as sons and daughters of God from our slavery to sin.[10] Paul in Galatians depicted the process as follows:

> When we were children, we were in slavery under the basic principles of the world. But when the time had fully come, God sent his Son, born of a woman, born under law, to redeem those under law, that we might receive the full rights of sons. Because you are sons, God sent the Spirit of his Son into our hearts, the Spirit who calls out, "*Abba,* Father." So you are no longer a slave, but a son; and since you are a son, God has made you also an heir. (Gal 4:3-7)

In this passage Paul alluded to the Israelites, who were adopted out of slavery in the exodus to become children of God. Similarly, we have been adopted out of our slavery to sin to become sons and daughters of God as well as heirs of God.

Adoption is the ultimate purpose of the incarnation and the culmination of the redemptive process.[11] Paul even described it as "the very goal of the gracious purpose of God."[12] He proclaimed that in love God "predestined us to be adopted as his sons through Jesus Christ, in accordance with his pleasure and will—to the praise of his glorious grace, which he has freely given us in the One he loves" (Eph 1:5-6). Although we rebelled, God through adoption restores us to the relationship of sons and daughters for which we were originally intended.[13]

Many young people can identify with the story from the Gospels of a prodigal son who strayed from his family, only to end up in despair and misery. Many young people, like the prodigal son, cannot imagine being restored to their place as a son or a daughter. Although an earthly family might not be willing to restore the relationship, God is eager to restore it. As in the story of the prodigal son, God wants to throw a party to celebrate the adoption. What a loving God we have! God the Father even goes further. Rather than just welcoming us back, God sends his Son, Jesus, to take our place on the cross so we can be adopted. Many people in the emerging culture will need to hear this story over and over again to believe that God would love us enough to send his own Son to look for us and restore us to God's family.

We in the church must make sure we do not stand in the way of God's love for people in the emerging culture. It is sad that in many of our churches today the members of the modern church act like the elder brother who enjoyed life before the prodigal son returned. They want everything to remain the same. They do not want to make the changes the Father wanted to make to celebrate the prodigal son's return and make the prodigal son feel at home. We need to be careful that we who have been in the church for a long time do not stand in the way of the Father, who wants to do everything possible to welcome the prodigal son home.

As we see in Galatians 4:5, the means of adoption are through Christ Jesus. Earlier in Galatians, Paul depicted Jesus as giving himself for us (Gal 2:20). Adoption begins with Christ's giving himself for us. By sending his own perfect and sinless Son to the cross to die for us, God was able to adopt us as his special children. Adoption ends with our inheritance. Although we tend to think of an inheritance as something received in the future, this inheritance has privileges from the start.

Part of our inheritance that we can enjoy from the beginning is its unconditional nature. "God choosing us as adopted children is not predicated on what we have achieved or will achieve, according to Paul. Instead, God chooses us because he loves us. There are no conditions or preconditions to this love, even though he knows everything about us—our past, present and future."[14] Adoption ultimately depends on the one who is adopting, not the one who is being adopted. Only parents, not children, can adopt. We cannot adopt God, but because of his love for us, God has adopted us. For Joan the idea that God, not just another human being, would adopt her was almost too unbelievable to be true.

Adoption brings with it a new relationship with God as Father. Instead of being slaves, who have few or no privileges, we are now sons and daughters who have the privilege of calling God *Abba,* an intimate term that means "dear Father." *Abba* occurs three times in the New Testament. First, Jesus himself cried out to his *Abba* during his prayer in Gethsemane when he was concerned about what lay ahead of him on the cross (Mk 14:36). In the other two occurrences (Rom 8:15 and Gal 4:6) *Abba* is used in reference to adoption. "Calling God *Abba* should help us in knowing that we are God's children and should cause us to act like God's children with full awareness of his love for us and our utter dependence on him as our Father."[15]

Another benefit of adoption is a new trust in God. God is our beloved Father and has set us free from slavery to sin. "It is for freedom that Christ has set us free. Stand firm, then, and do not let yourselves be burdened again by a yoke of slavery" (Gal 5:1). Because of this freedom and the love God shows us, we now obey and serve God because we desire to please him as a child wants to please his or her earthly mommy and daddy. Another basis of trust is the knowledge that God our Father will never desert us, although an earthly father or mother may. Romans 8 teaches that our adoption is assured: there is no condemnation for those in Christ Jesus (our guilt is overcome), and there is no separation for those who have been adopted as children of God (our shame is removed).

> *I'm convinced the main reason God chose to make us most like himself—conscious of who we are, longing for relationship and with a desire to know the Truth—is so all of us would grow up with this mysterious yearning or longing inside to find our Creator and to enjoy an intimate relationship with him.*
>
> KEN FONG, *SECURE IN GOD'S EMBRACE*

Let us return again to Joan. Over a period of time, as she came to see her small group's care for her, she began to realize that God cared for her. Joan began to feel that she was a child of God. She began to sense that God had truly adopted her and would never leave her or desert her, as her earthly mother and father had. She was able to begin calling God *Abba*.

There are thousands of Joans in our churches. They have a difficult time answering the simple question "Are you going home for Christmas?" People like Joan need to be shown that their ultimate home is where Jesus is. They desperately need to be restored to God as their dear Father who has adopted them as his daughters and sons. Are we willing to emphasize the salvation language of adoption, in addition to guilt and justification, in order to minister more effectively to the Joans of this emerging world? The process of people inviting people into God's family through adoption will begin to provide hope for the future.

IMPLICATIONS FOR MINISTRY

We need to emphasize different truths of Scripture for the changing times. Those of us who are more modern must not fall into the trap of ministering to our own needs rather than the needs of others. We do not want to be like the elder brother. What are the needs of people in the emerging culture?

Some of my older staff assume that because they struggled with a legalistic view of Christianity, the students they minister to must also struggle with the same issue—legalism. We need to listen to the people we minister among to hear from them the issues that are putting roadblocks in their spiritual journey.

Relational issues are crucial to young people who come from dysfunctional families and are moving away from an autonomous self to a community orientation. A critical issue for them is acceptance, by others and themselves. The church needs to make sure that these emerging generations feel welcomed as they enter our communities. We must go out of our way to make them feel comfortable and wanted. My own church, for example, has established an adopt-a-student ministry. Families and singles in the church adopt college students for the year, inviting them into their homes and welcoming them into the church.

In addition to helping postmodern people feel accepted within the church, we need to emphasize God's love for us and acceptance of us in our worship services and in our small groups. Within our talks or sermons, such passages as the parable of the prodigal son or the stories of Jesus' incarnation and death on the cross can help us learn something about God's acceptance of us and God's desire to remove our shame.

We also need to learn that we have been adopted by God into a new family—the church. Our ministry should include helping people feel that they are part of the core of the church family. In chapters eight, nine and ten we will discuss ways our churches can be more sensitive to postmodern people.

Hope in the Midst of Suffering

For over thirty years I have been a loyal fan of the Boston Red Sox. I converted to the Red Sox during my days at Gordon-Conwell Seminary, which is located on the North Shore of Boston. During the early 1970s, my wife and I, along with some friends, spent numerous hours rooting for the Red Sox from the right-field bleachers. Over the years the Red Sox have built up my hopes, only to dash them, again and again. But true Red Sox fans can never forget the suffering we went through in 1975, 1978, 1986 and now 2003. (I am writing this section of the book two days after the Red Sox lost to the Yankees in the eleventh inning in the seventh and decisive game in the American League playoffs.) Why do I remain a Red Sox fan? My team has not won the World Series in the last eighty-five years. If I am honest, I have to admit that whereas I do not really have hope, I do wish that the Red Sox would win the World Series sometime soon.

Many people today define both *hope* and *wish* as "belief in something you know not to be true," such as a Red Sox World Series victory. People in the younger generations have grown up with broken promises from parents, friends and society. If they possess hope, it is a virtual-reality hope having little if anything to do with reality. Most of us in the postmodern world are changing from belief in progress to resignation in the face of societal cynicism. We are living in a time of despair.

Arthur Levine, a college educator, wrote a book a number of years ago titled *When Dreams and Heroes Died,* which aptly describes the despair of emerging culture people. A few years ago I was meeting regularly with a young freshman named Ed. Ed came to college as a struggling Christian with many dreams and much hope. However, it did not take long for Ed to begin to lose his dreams as he began to struggle with classes and relationships. Ed also struggled with God. He had an inadequate view of God, understanding God as Judge but not as Father. He did not grasp the hope for the future that God could provide him in the midst of his struggle. He had nothing to hold on to as he drifted into a sea of despair. Sadly, he would not allow the members of a church or a campus fellowship to support him in his struggle.

> *Although the essential commitment of the believing community to the God revealed in Jesus does not change, the context in which this confession and its implications are lived out is in constant flux.*
>
> STAN GRENZ, *BEYOND FOUNDATIONALISM*

Would it have made a difference in his life if Ed had opened up to people in a church or a campus fellowship? Is the church ready today to enter into the pain and suffering younger generations feel? Is it ready to meet, minister to and give desperately needed hope to individuals like Ed? Will the church be ready to meet people in the emerging culture who have no Christian involvement or background and offer them hope?

THE CHURCH'S FUTURE PERSPECTIVE

In order to be a church that provides hope to the world, we first need to understand the hope that has been provided for us by God the Father through Jesus Christ his Son and the Holy Spirit. This means we need a correct understanding of eschatology that can aid our ministry. By "eschatology," I do not mean a focus on the end times that combines obscure verses in the Bible with present political events to try to determine when Christ will return. Eschatology needs to give us a perspective on how to live in the present, not just how to predict the future.

Jesus told us, "It is not for you to know the times or dates the Father has set by his own authority" (Acts 1:7). Rather, he called the disciples to concentrate on the present by being his witnesses "in Jerusalem, and in all Judea and Samaria, and to the ends of the earth" (Acts 1:8). The church that is overly concerned about the future will neglect the call to be Christ's witness in the midst of the pain and suffering of the present. The church that lives in the past and is overly concerned about its own traditions or about worldly contamination will lose its witness for Christ in the present society.

A promise is a pledge that proclaims a reality which is not yet at hand. . . . Rather than moving from the present to the future, our task is to look from the future to the present and to anticipate the future in the midst of our present existence.

STAN GRENZ, *BEYOND FOUNDATIONALSIM*

To reach the emerging culture we need to "live in the present from a future perspective." In part this means we need to meet people where they are in the midst of their pain and suffering. Yet more than anything else these generations need hope for the future, since at present they have no hope. Jürgen Moltmann, the theologian who wrote *Theology of Hope,* declared, "Living without hope is no longer living. Hell is hopelessness and it is not for nothing that at the entrance to Dante's hell there stand the words: 'Abandon hope, all you who enter here.' "[1] Without hope, postmodern generations will live in a present and future hell.

The Christian perspective of the future should include hope for us and an offer of hope to others. When I was growing up in the 1950s, the church, especially in the South, was accused of being "so heavenly minded that it is no earthly good." Today the church seems to be so earthly minded that it is no heavenly good. It emphasizes a gospel of the here and now: "God loves you and has a wonderful plan for your life." It overemphasizes the present blessings of the gospel, whether the health-and-wealth gospel, second-blessing experience or miraculous healing. We saw in chapter two that young people today are characterized by experience with pain and suffering. Rather than an easy way out of the suffering and pain of this life, they need hope for a better life in the future and a realistic view of the present.

THE HOPE OF THE GOSPEL

Before we are able reach emerging culture people, we in the church need to understand and appropriate the eschatological hope of the gospel. Members of the younger generations have a fairly realistic view of who they are. They need to know "who I am going to be."[2] In this chapter we will focus on eschatological hope. We also need to learn how to witness to these generations by offering hope in the midst of their misery, pain and suffering. (Chapter ten discusses how to be witnesses offering hope.)

Eschatology is the study *(logos)* of last things *(eschatos)*. Unfortunately it has become a "loosely attached appendix" that has a tendency to venture off into enigmatic tangents.[3] Instead of being seen as the last chapter in a theology textbook, eschatology should be the perspective from which all of the Christian faith is viewed—living in the present from the future perspective.[4] The future perspective is one of Christian hope.[5]

This Christian hope is not synonymous with wishing. If I say that I hope the Red Sox will win the World Series next year, I am expressing a wish that may well be a fantasy. When we talk about the Christian hope, however, we are expressing a certainty according to the Scriptures. Biblical hope assumes "unconditional certainty."[6] In the Scriptures we read confessions of hope that are preceded by phrases such as "we believe" and "I am convinced" (Rom 6:8; 8:38). Let us look more closely at how the Scriptures portray this Christian hope.

Most ancient secular philosophers viewed hope as a temporary illusion, and thus they had no hope. As they pondered death, they sensed little comfort or freedom.[7] Whatever human hope did exist for ancient thinkers depended on human concepts and attitudes. When crises arose (as they always do), human hope broke up "like that house that is built upon the sand."[8] Paul observed that those without Christ grieved because they had no hope (1 Thess 4:13). But the followers of God have had hope from the beginning of biblical times. The Hebrew word for hope means "hopeful watching."[9] The Hebrews also used another word, *shalom,* to depict God's action and vision in the future. In this shalom vision, God's desire is to reconcile us to himself, to one another and to his good creation. The result will be a new heaven and a new earth.[10]

ISRAEL: A PEOPLE OF HOPE

From the beginning of their history the Israelites were a people on a journey. This journey began when God called Abraham to leave his home. Abraham's hope was grounded in his personal relationship with God, whom he learned to trust, and on God's threefold promise to Abraham.[11] God promised to give Abraham land, to make his descendants into a great nation and to bless him (Gen 12:1-3).[12] God called Abraham to hold on to hope in God's promises, even under difficult circumstances. God called Abraham to hope for the birth of a child even when it was impossible, humanly speaking. God also promised to provide for Abraham when Abraham bound his son Isaac to offer him as a sacrifice. Just as Abraham was about to put the knife to Isaac, the angel of the Lord called him from heaven,

> "Abraham! Abraham!"
>
> "Here I am," he replied.
>
> "Do not lay a hand on the boy," he said. "Do not do anything to him. Now I know that you fear God, because you have not withheld from me your son, your only son."
>
> Abraham looked up and there in a thicket he saw a ram caught by its horns. He went over and took the ram and sacrificed it as a burnt offering instead of his son. So Abraham called that place The LORD Will Provide. And to this day it is said, "On the mountain of the LORD it will be provided." (Gen 22:11-14)

As God continued to provide for Abraham, his hope and trust in God strengthened.

A life of bondage in Egypt brought the Israelites' belief in God's promises to a halt. Yet it was on the way out of Egypt that their hope in God was solidified. What is crucial in the exodus story is God's intervention. In a seemingly hopeless situation God provided for the Israelites as he had for Abraham and Isaac. "The LORD brought us out of Egypt with a mighty hand and an outstretched arm" (Deut 26:8). The covenant relation between God and Israel was cemented in the exodus from Egypt, through the journey in the wilderness and during the conquest of Canaan. And a vision of hope for the future was opened.

At numerous times during Israelite history the covenant between God and

Israel was put to the test. One of the most critical testing times was the year 587 B.C., when Judah fell to the Babylonians and the temple was burned. The Davidic dynasty was terminated, and the leading citizens of Judah were exiled. In this time of crisis the Israelites had to give up the former world built around the king and the temple and be willing to accept from God a new world of exile that they had not chosen and did not think would work. As we today move from the Enlightenment era to a postmodern world, we, like the Israelites, have to be willing to give up the world as we have known it and be willing to wait for what God will show us for the future.[13]

The Israelites had to wait on God for over one hundred years to show them that he had not abandoned them and that he would still fulfill his promises. Even in the midst of the exile, God continued to care for the Israelites and to teach them to put their hope in him as their faithful God who keeps his promises, not despairing in the midst of adverse circumstances. Jeremiah proclaimed this faithful God to the Israelites:

> "For I know the plans I have for you," declares the LORD, "plans to prosper you and not to harm you, plans to give you hope and a future. Then you will call upon me and come and pray to me, and I will listen to you. You will seek me and find me when you seek me with all your heart. I will be found by you," declares the LORD, "and will bring you back from captivity. I will gather you from all the nations and places where I have banished you," declares the LORD, "and will bring you back to the place from which I carried you into exile." (Jer 29:11-14)

The people who thought they had been abandoned really had not been abandoned. They had abandoned God, but God had never abandoned them, even in the midst of their exile. The people who had gone into exile were now preparing for a "luxuriant homecoming."[14] The God who brought the Israelites out of Egypt is the same God who brought the Israelites out of exile. Judah, devastated by the Babylonians, now had hope once again—not by their own efforts, but through God's faithfulness.

The God who had been faithful to his people, the Israelite nation, was also laying the groundwork for a new future. This new future would include all peoples and nations and historic eras. This new future would include a new David and a new Jerusalem with a new temple and a new covenant.[15]

This future hope gives postmodern people a perspective by which to view life—a perspective that brings personal peace in the present and eternal peace in the future.

The new David, Christ Jesus, will establish a new kingdom that will last forever. In the Old Testament we already see Jesus as the coming Messiah who would be the link between the Israelites' hope and our hope today. It should comfort us to realize that long ago God was laying the groundwork for the hope we have today (2 Sam 7:11-14).

Part of that groundwork was the promise of a new Jerusalem and a new temple that will dwarf the importance of the present Jerusalem. Isaiah prophesied about this new Jerusalem and new temple over twenty-five hundred years ago.

In the last days

the mountain of the LORD's temple will be established
     as chief among the mountains;
it will be raised above the hills,
     and all nations will stream to it.

Many peoples will come and say,

"Come, let us go up to the mountain of the LORD,
     to the house of the God of Jacob.
He will teach us his ways,
     so that we may walk in his paths."
The law will go out from Zion,
     the word of the LORD from Jerusalem.
He will judge between the nations
     and will settle disputes for many peoples.
They will beat their swords into plowshares
     and their spears into pruning hooks.
Nation will not take up sword against nation,
     nor will they train for war anymore. (Is 2:2-4)

We look toward the future with this powerful promise from God. The hope it gives us is based on our faithful God, not the present world. In addition to hope for the future, we have a perspective from which to live in the present. That fulfillment of the promise is centered on Christ's death on the cross and his resurrection. The fulfillment of the future hope will be realized at Christ's second coming and the full establishment of God's kingdom.

THE HOPE OF THE CROSS

The center of hope in the New Testament is the cross. In Roman times the cross was a symbol of shame, not hope, even in the minds of the disciples. They went into hiding after Jesus died. Although the world was changed forever on the cross that Friday, neither the disciples nor anyone else realized what changes had taken place. All the disciples could see were their own pain and suffering.

Many people today are like the disciples on that Friday and Saturday after Jesus' death. They do not understand what God has done in history and in their lives. Where there should be hope, there is despair. Where there should be faith in God, there is only doubt in God and in themselves. People who live without the promise of hope are in as much despair as the disciples were from the time Jesus died on Friday till his resurrection on Sunday.

The disciples' despair lifted on Sunday when they discovered that Jesus had somehow risen from the dead. Their despair changed to hope because death had been conquered through Jesus' resurrection. The disciples' "fear and gloom had been changed to courage and joy."[16] We today should participate in the disciples' transformation. As we realize God's faithfulness, our gloom and despair should be transformed into hope. Tom Sine calls Christians today to be people of hope offering hope to others. "In a world drowning in cynicism, nihilism and polarization, people are looking for a reason for hope. And I am convinced that the people of God have no higher calling than to offer hope to the world. The only problem is that we cannot offer what we do not possess."[17]

Christians must experience the hope themselves before they can offer it to those who have no hope (see chapter nine). The first step in experiencing that hope is understanding the basis for hope in the New Testament, and the second step is understanding how Christian hope has emerged throughout Christian history.

In the New Testament hope is founded on two concepts: (1) God's defeat

of Satan through Christ's death and resurrection, and (2) the gift of the Holy
Spirit. The church could properly be called an eschatological community
that looks back to God's faithfulness in the Old Testament and Christ's death
and resurrection, lives in the present power and guidance of the Holy Spirit,
and looks forward expectantly to Christ's second coming to establish the
new heaven and the new earth.

The Holy Spirit provided a context for the experience of hope in the New
Testament church. The Holy Spirit was in one sense a down payment of the
full hope that we will experience when Christ comes again. As Paul stated in
Ephesians 1:14, the Holy Spirit is a "deposit guaranteeing our inheritance
until the redemption of those who are God's possession—to the praise of his
glory." The Holy Spirit helped the Christians have faith that the expectations
God had given them about the future will be fulfilled.[18] The Holy Spirit also
encouraged the early Christians with the word that even though their circumstances were difficult, they were to live in hope and to hold on to the
promises of God. The Holy Spirit reminds us that the God who has been
faithful in the past will be faithful in the present and the future. The Holy
Spirit, through Paul, reminded the church in Rome to remember God's faithfulness to Abraham.

> Against all hope, Abraham in hope believed and so became the father
> of many nations, just as it had been said to him, "So shall your off-
> spring be." Without weakening in his faith, he faced the fact that his
> body was as good as dead—since he was about a hundred years old—
> and that Sarah's womb was also dead. Yet he did not waver through
> unbelief regarding the promise of God, but was strengthened in his
> faith and gave glory to God, being fully persuaded that God had
> power to do what he had promised. (Rom 4:18-21)

The Holy Spirit helps us look forward to the future and the hope that has
been promised. Part of what the Holy Spirit helps us to look forward to is a
return to the kind of relationships that existed between God and the first
couple as well as between Adam and Eve before the Fall.

In this world we are continually reminded of the incompleteness of life
and of the struggles of our existence. However, God has prepared a house
for us.[19] From the beginnings of the early church until now we have strug-

gled between trying to build the house on earth and impatiently waiting for the house in heaven.

HOPE: A HISTORICAL PERSPECTIVE

Until about A.D. 300, the church occupied a marginal position in society. That changed when the Roman emperor Constantine became a Christian. For the first time the church faced the possibility of exercising great power on earth. That led many Christians to focus on what could be done in and of this world, and the church became worldly in the process.[20]

The Middle Ages began with Augustine's bringing the church back to a more accurate understanding of Christian hope.[21] The heavenly city, as opposed to the secular city, is the proper focus of Christian hope. Later in the Middle Ages, with the rise of medieval millenarianism, the church once again focused on building the heavenly dwelling on earth through the Crusades' goal of building a single empire of peace.[22]

During the Reformation, John Calvin helped focus Christian hope less on earthly possibilities and more on the church as the basis for our hope in Christ. The church needs to be built up as it prepares itself for Christ's return in glory. But Christian hope changed dramatically in the Enlightenment era with its emphasis on the autonomous self, human progress and nontranscendent truth. Not surprisingly, individual hope was emphasized instead of that of the corporate body of Christ. Ultimate future hope was relegated to a belief in immortality.[23] By the nineteenth century, under the influence of Albert Ritschl and others in the liberal Protestant church, the future kingdom of God lost all its heavenly characteristics and referred to utopian life on earth, with an emphasis on worldly optimism and human progress.[24]

By the late nineteenth century and early twentieth century, the conservative Christian church, in reaction to the liberal emphasis on human progress, emphasized the Christian hope in heaven. Conservative Christians were pessimistic about this world, only reacting to it in the sense of throwing out life preservers from the lifeboats in order to save as many people as possible.

The liberal emphasis on worldly optimism reached its heyday in the early twentieth century. The new century began with a *New York Times* editorial on January 1, 1901, proclaiming itself "optimistic enough to believe that the 20th century will meet and overcome all perils and prove to be the best this steadily improving planet has ever seen."[25] Certainly the editorialist did not foresee that the century would include two world wars, a worldwide depression, Nazism, fascism, communism, the Holocaust and the threat of mutually assured nuclear destruction for most of the second half of the century. The optimism in which the century had begun turned to despair and pessimism at the conclusion of the century. We now live in a culture of mistrust. Jean Bethke Elshtain portrays it as follows:

> All social webs that once held persons intact having disintegrated, the individual finds himself or herself isolated and impotent, exposed and unprotected. Into this power vacuum will likely move a top-heavy, ever more centralized state. Or we will hunker down in defensive "lifestyle enclaves," forbidding others entry.[26]

That mistrust has greatly multiplied since September 11, 2001. Self-interested individuals are forming groups whose membership is restricted to people of similar characteristics. The result is multiple communities that have little or nothing in common with other groups except their mutual mistrust.[27]

We as evangelical Christians can fill this vacuum. However, our track record in this regard is not good. When the country was still reeling from the Civil War, for example, evangelicals began retreating from a liberal-influenced society instead of becoming agents of reconciliation in a fragmented society. As we saw in chapter one, evangelicals today are struggling to decide how best to influence society. David Bosch, in his work *Transforming Mission,* calls the church to step into the gap and provide direction for the future.

> We should not capitulate to pessimism and despair. All around us people are looking for new meaning in life. This is the moment when the Christian church and the Christian mission may once again, humbly yet resolutely, present the vision of the reign of God not as a pie in the sky but as an eschatological reality which casts its rays into the dismal present, illuminates it and confers meaning on it.[28]

BIBLICAL HOPE IN THE POSTMODERN ERA

I am convinced that the best message we can offer society today is a biblical message of hope. People in the emerging culture are searching for something to guide them as they live in the present and look toward the future. We have a golden opportunity to proclaim God's hope. If we do not provide direction, others will. Biblical hope is not built on confidence, but it builds confidence because it is based on the character of God, not human potential or human capacity. Hope comes not from the situation but from someone outside the situation. Hope is "not a weaker form of believing and knowing, but precisely a source of confidence and strength."[29] To hope is to trust not in ourselves but in God. God is our hope.

Our world today tries, at all costs, to avoid pain and suffering. Even Christians get caught up with trying to eradicate all pain and suffering from their lives. Yet pain and suffering are here to stay. Christians need to change their perspective on suffering, first by recognizing that God never exempted us from it. As Paul reminded believers in Rome who were facing suffering, "Now if we are children, then we are heirs—heirs of God and co-heirs with Christ, if indeed we share in his sufferings in order that we may also share in his glory" (Rom 8:17-18). We are called to endure, and in the midst of our pain and suffering we have the assurance that our suffering is not in vain. Paul reminded the Romans that their suffering would ultimately end and that they were to wait for that end:

> *In the end, the object of Christian hope is not the future itself but the God of the future; not our creaturely destiny but the God who destines; not the telos of our existence but the God who is leading us toward that glorious goal. In short our hope is in the God who declares, "I am making all things new."*
>
> STAN GRENZ, *BEYOND FOUNDATIONALISM*

We know that in all things God works for the good of those who love him, who have been called according to his purpose. For those God foreknew he also predestined to be conformed to the likeness of his Son, that he might be the firstborn among many brothers. And . . . those he called, he also justified; those he justified, he also glorified. (Rom 8:28-30)

Nothing can destroy or prevent this ultimate glory. God is victorious. We have that assurance and that expectation. Expectation makes life good, for in expectation we can accept our present suffering and pain. Hope is an encouragement to Christians in the midst of suffering. Hope should also prevent believers from accepting their present circumstances as their fate. Hope causes us to wait eagerly and longingly for the day when all of God's promises will be fulfilled.[30] The book of Revelation gives us a glimpse of what is in store for us in the future when Christ returns.

> I saw a new heaven and a new earth, for the first heaven and the first earth had passed away, and there was no longer any sea. I saw the Holy City, the new Jerusalem, coming down out of heaven from God, prepared as a bride beautifully dressed for her husband. And I heard a loud voice from the throne saying, "Now the dwelling of God is with men, and he will live with them. They will be his people, and God himself will be with them and be their God. He will wipe every tear from their eyes. There will be no more death or mourning or crying or pain, for the old order of things has passed away."
>
> He who was seated on the throne said, "I am making everything new!" Then he said, "Write this down, for these words are trustworthy and true."
>
> He said to me: "It is done. I am the Alpha and the Omega, the Beginning and the End. To him who is thirsty I will give to drink without cost from the spring of the water of life. He who overcomes will inherit all this, and I will be his God and he will be my son." (Rev 21:1-7)

Hope not only points us to the future but also gives us a basis for living life in the present. We are pilgrims in this life whose permanent home is in heaven (Heb 11:13-16). Since we do not (or should not) have to spend all our time trying to preserve our lives, we can devote them to serving God. Knowing that God has secured our future, we can concentrate on serving God in the present.

Peter wrote to the church in Asia Minor to give them hope and a heavenly perspective by which they could serve God in the midst of painful, seemingly hopeless circumstances. They were mostly rural, Jewish Christians who were facing persecution and suffering at the hands of the Roman emperor Nero. From a worldly perspective, their situation was hopeless.

Peter's first letter could easily be addressed to our present situation with its despair and misery. People in the emerging culture, like the people to whom Peter was writing, feel marginalized and hopeless. And trouble was no stranger to the apostle Peter. He had made a living as a lowly fisherman until he became a follower of Jesus. In the end he betrayed Jesus, the person who had cared most for him. About Peter one commentator remarks that "when Jesus died on the cross, it was the end of all of Peter's hopes. He knew only bitter sorrow for his own denials [of Jesus]. The dawn could not bring hope; with the crowing of the cock he heard the echo of his curses against Jesus."[31]

Yet Peter went on to find hope in Jesus, who restored him after the resurrection. Thus Peter was able to write to the church in Asia Minor and offer it a message of hope. In the first chapter of 1 Peter we see three dimensions of this biblical hope—new birth, living hope and eternal inheritance. Physical birth brings us into a world that will eventually perish. Spiritual birth brings us into a world that has hope for the future.

This hope is an assured fact, not a wish. This hope is the conviction that something will happen in the future. According to 1 Peter, the basis of this hope is the mercy that God demonstrated in raising Jesus from the dead. This living hope holds the future (eternal life) in the present (a world of suffering) because it is anchored in the past (Jesus' death on the cross and resurrection from the dead).[32]

This living hope is defined as an eternal inheritance. Part of that inheritance is being part of God's family. We do not have to feel like orphans. We have a new "tribal" group that will be faithful. "You are a chosen people, a royal priesthood, a holy nation, a people belonging to God, that you may declare the praises of him who called you out of darkness into his wonderful light. Once you were not a people, but now you are the people of God; once you had not received mercy, but now you have received mercy" (1 Pet 2:9-10).

Christians today need to see life from this heavenly perspective. Hope is not so much an earthly attitude to be cultivated as a heavenly reality to be recognized. The emerging postmodern world may be ready to hear this message of Christian hope with its vision of heaven because they live in the present without any hope to sustain them in the present or in the future.

Will we be people who are willing to let hope richly dwell in our lives, willing to offer hope to those who have no hope?

IMPLICATIONS FOR MINISTRY

Today's younger generations suffer from a sense of past abandonment as well as hopelessness about the future. The church can offer these generations hope. We can perform this service in multiple ways.

First, we need to provide sermon series and classes that tell the story of God's interaction with this world, from creation to the end times. We need to place our present situation within that overall context. God is a faithful God!

Next, we need to make sure that we as a church do not keep trying to live or teach the societal progress myth. We cannot have it all now. Young people in the emerging culture know this all too well. Our hope must be in the future and not just the present.

The Old Testament stories of God's faithfulness to Israel, which might seem overly familiar to some of us, are fresh and comforting to these new generations, which feel abandoned. Providing opportunities during fellowship meetings or church services for people to share God's faithfulness to them in the midst of their pain and suffering would be comforting and inspiring to postmodern people. For example, from time to time my church provides three to five minutes to people attending the church service who wish to share with others some way God has been faithful to them. A few years ago a young couple shared what it was like to lose a baby. In the midst of their pain and suffering, they spoke of how God and others were faithful to them. Their testimony was both sobering and inspiring. Their sharing was especially helpful to other young couples, who bring many fears with them to parenthood.

We need to make sure that we create an environment in our churches and our Christian fellowships that allow people to become vulnerable enough to share their pain and struggles. We also need to make sure that in the midst of this pain we provide a framework of hope emphasizing that God was faithful in the past, is faithful in the present and will be faithful in the future.

PART THREE

AN INTIMATE
JOURNEY OF HOPE

A Framework for Ministry

Cummins A

120 E. ALDER • BOX 4
1-509-525-8212 • Natio
website: www.cum
FAX 1-5

_____

_____

_____

_____

_____

_____

_____

_____

_____

_____

_____

_____

_____

_____

_____

_____

_____

_____

Bud Waggoner • Chris Waggoner •

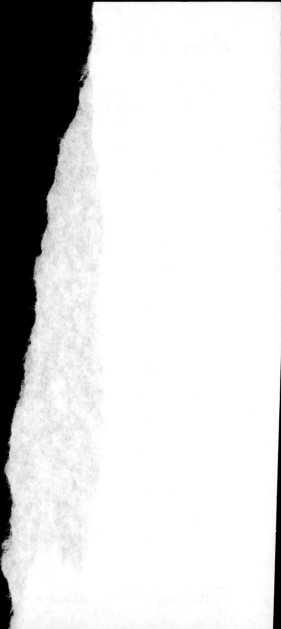

Communities of Belonging

Having established a new theological foundation that is centered on community, adoption and hope, we now need to turn our attention to the practical implications for ministry. Since we are in the midst of a major societal paradigm shift to an emerging postmodern culture, we need to adjust our ministry framework even as we establish a new theological foundation. Many of us find it difficult to change the way we do ministry after ten, twenty or thirty years in ministry. But if we are going to minister effectively in this emerging culture, we need to adapt.

AN ADAPTIVE COMMUNITY

Jenny was scared to death. For a young, single, Christian college student, the unexpected news that she was pregnant brought sadness, not joy. How could she announce her news? She thought through the options open to her and finally decided to tell two people in her small group. Still, she worried. How would her two friends react? Would they judge and reject her?

But Jenny did not need to worry. Far from rejecting her, the two friends comforted her. They grieved with her over her sin but began to care for her in her time of need. Jenny was thankful that she had gotten involved that fall in the InterVarsity small group in her all-female dorm. The group had already meant a great deal to her. And she had no way of knowing how much more the group would come to mean to her in the months ahead.

When Jenny told the rest of her small group about her pregnancy, they rallied around her as well. In the coming weeks some members of the group just listened to Jenny, showing Christ's love to her. Others made phone calls for her to the Pregnancy Care Center to see what services she might be eligible to receive. She stayed in the group for the remainder of the school year. Toward the end of the school year, the group gave Jenny a surprise baby shower, even inviting her mom and sister to come to the shower. All the members of the group chipped in to buy Jenny a car seat for the baby. Jenny was surprised and overjoyed at the love her small group showed her that night at the party. Later that summer, a number of friends from the group went to visit Jenny after the baby was born. Jenny visited the small group with her new baby when school resumed in the fall.

Through the group's love for her, Jenny experienced intimate friendships. Because the group accepted her, Jenny understood what it meant to experience God's grace and acceptance of her. The intimate friendships that she experienced with the other women in her small group in the dorm allowed her to experience a more intimate relationship with God her Father.

People bring complex personal problems with them into the church. Will we be able to care for the Jennys of the world who get pregnant, the Randys of the world who are gay, the Susans who have been molested by their fathers, the Toms who express racist attitudes? As we have already seen, we are in the midst of a major societal paradigm shift that should cause us to reevaluate our ministry patterns. Robert Wuthnow, a leading sociologist, describes this change as follows: "America at the end of the 20th century is fundamentally a society in transition. . . . It is far from clear what kind of society we will have in the next century. One thing is clear, the search for community and for the sacred will continue to characterize the American people."[1]

It is interesting that in many parts of the country the place where people are looking to belong is the church. You may be surprised to know that is especially true in urban communities. In a recent study Robert Wuthnow reports: "The most significant traditional voluntary organizations left in many urban communities are the churches. Only 15% of inner-city African Americans reported belonging to any kind of nonreligious civic organizations but 55% say they attend religious services at least monthly, 37% weekly."[2] This desire to belong is a spiritual desire for most people. We in the church need to be ready to meet this need.

In the church we think of two primary places, the large worship service and small groups, for people to belong. However, Joseph Myers in a recent book identifies four places people need and desire to belong. These four spaces are termed public spaces, social spaces, personal spaces and intimate spaces.[3]

An example of a public space in society would be one of the large sporting events where people come together with one thing in common: rooting for the same team. Whenever I wear my Boston Red Sox hat in public, inevitably some stranger will comment on the hat, usually by saying, "I am sorry" or, "I suffer with you."

In the church the large worship gatherings are our public spaces. Even though we may be a diverse congregation, when we worship together, we share a sense of belonging. I think that most people who eventually leave a church do so because they feel a disconnection in the worship service. They feel that if they cannot have a sense of belonging in this most public of church spaces, the worship service, they will have a harder time belonging in the other spaces of the church.

The social spaces are the places we most neglect in the church. Myers identifies the "front porch" as the significant social space in the community. In the past people would gather on their front porches (or in cities, on front stoops) to talk casually with their neighbors. These were important places for informal social interaction, making people feel like they were part of a larger community. As society has lost many of its "front porch" spaces, the church has neglected many of these important opportunities for people new and old to connect with each other.

In the South, the old Sunday evening potluck suppers were important social spaces in the church. The larger atriums or lobbies in many newer churches provide spaces for social gatherings. My own church, in order to build community, has established "medium community groups" as a social space for people who live further away from the church to get to know other people in their community who go to the same church. They also provide an ideal place to invite neighbors who are not Christians to come to a social gathering in the neighborhood. In campus ministries, weekly ultimate Frisbee games or Krispy Kreme doughnut runs provide social spaces for people to belong.

The small-group community is an ideal personal space. Most people who are considering their need to belong to a community will eventually look for some type of small-group community, formal or informal. Small groups do not have to be religious in nature. Recently Ethan Watters has written a book, *Urban Tribes,* in which he describes the characteristics of informal small-group communities that have sprouted in urban areas among singles in their twenties and thirties. The characteristics of these personal-space communities include intense loyalty, shared routines or rituals, defined roles and a sense of "barn raising" or caring for each other.

The intimate spaces are reserved for best friends or spouses. The intimate space is the place where you can share anything and the person will still love you. While it is appropriate to consider what to share in the other three spaces (public, social, personal), in the intimate space we can share our whole self.

This yearning for community is one of the societal forces that is behind the rise of the small-group movement.[4] The change from an emphasis on self to an emphasis on community is the primary characteristic of this emerging culture. We see this emphasis acted out in Douglas Coupland's *Microserfs.* (Coupland coined the term "Generation X" in his 1991 book *Generation X.*) In *Microserfs* he depicts the basic unit of life as an urban tribe, an informal small-group community. As the story begins, Dan, Karla, Amy, Susan, Ethan, Michael and a few others happen to work alongside each other as microserfs in the world of computer technology. By the end of the story, they have grown into a personal community. One of the characters, Amy, even defines heaven as "feeling intimate forever."[5] The novel concludes with the personal community around Dan's family pool as Dan muses on their life together. "I thought about us . . . these children who fell down life's cartoon holes . . . dreamless children, alive but not living—we emerged on the other side of the cartoon holes fully awake and discovered we were kids . . . and suddenly I realized that what's been missing for so long isn't missing anymore."[6] People are not looking for friendly churches; they are looking for friends.

Small groups characterized by close community will be a key factor in reaching people in the emerging culture. Up until now, small groups have been effective in ministering to the Baby Boom generation. The leaders of the small-group movement understand that we in the United States are living in a fluid and transitory time. Many people's lives are fragmented, which causes them to seek out community in small groups. There they regain the intimacy that they once experienced in their families when everyone remained in the same neighborhood for most of their lives.[7] However, the popularity of small groups today cannot be explained merely on the basis of the transitory nature of our society. Over 40 percent of Americans are involved in some type of small group that meets on a regular basis. They come to the groups hoping to find lasting friendships.[8] Why are so many Americans involved in small groups?

The small-group movement is part of the answer to the human longing for community. This longing is one outgrowth of the current societal transition from the Enlightenment, which served as the major paradigm for the last four hundred years, to postmodernism, which will most likely be the major paradigm for the next one hundred years.

Postmodern generations are characterized by a yearning for personal communities, as the small-group movement has witnessed. This need for belonging in a personal community has a horizontal dimension in deep friendships and a vertical dimension in yearning for the sacred or the spiritual.[9] All types of small groups, such as Bible studies, prayer fellowships, self-help groups, twelve-step groups and recovery groups, have sprung up in recent years for emotional support and spiritual growth. Some have observed that small groups are not only a way to save Christianity but also a way to save American society by turning people away from destructive, self-oriented addictions and toward caring for the needs of others.[10]

If I am correct in tying the rapid growth of the small-group movement to the transition into postmodern culture, then the need for small groups will constitute a major priority in ministry. As we have seen, the younger generations live in a state of familial, economic and societal flux. They live in the present moment, neither anchored to the past nor pointing to the future.

They desperately need a close community that can offer comfort, healing and direction. Small groups can provide stranded and lonely young people places to belong—secure environments in which to pursue their spiritual journeys. Dramatic changes, such as becoming a Christian, are more likely to occur in the more intimate small-group setting than in the large-group service. According to Tim Celek and Dieter Zander, who pastor emerging-culture people, "Large-group meetings merely lay down the groundwork, lower the drawbridge and tear down the walls so that life change can occur in more intimate settings. With a Postmodern mindset, people in this emerging culture process truth relationally."[11] As we saw in the beginning of this chapter, Jenny's small group of young women maintained a place where she could belong and an environment in which she could continue on her spiritual journey in the midst of distress.

Carl George, a Christian leader in the small-group movement, explains the importance of small groups. "I believe that the smaller group within the whole—called by dozens of terms, including the small group or the cell group—is a crucial but underdeveloped resource in most churches. It is, I contend, the most strategically significant foundation for the spiritual formation and assimilation, for evangelism and leadership development, for the most essential functions that God has called for in the church."[12] Although, as I have shown earlier in this chapter, there are numerous types of spaces people need to belong to, small-group ministry remains a critical strategy needed to provide a community for people in the emerging church.

As one of his last acts of ministry, Jesus prayed for the establishment of a reconciled community (a small group) among the disciples that would be a model for the beginning church.

> I pray for them. I am not praying for the world, but for those you have given me, for they are yours. All I have is yours, and all you have is mine. And glory has come to me through them. I will remain in the world no longer, but they are still in the world, and I am coming to you. Holy Father, protect them by the power of your name—the name you gave me—so that they may be one as we are one. (Jn 17:9-11)

After Pentecost the disciples began to fulfill Jesus' goal for them as they went about establishing reconciling communities. In one day the church in Jerusalem grew from 120 people to over 3,000 people (Acts 1:15; 2:41). How were all these new believers in Christ going to grow in their faith? How were they going to become agents of reconciliation for the gospel? They could no longer meet only in large groups.

As God directed Moses during the exodus to divide his people into small units of tens and fifties, so God also led the early church to meet in smaller units. In Acts 2:46 we see that the Jerusalem church was divided into two mutually supportive meetings—a large-group meeting that expressed the Christians' corporate unity (meeting together in the temple courts) and more intimate small-group meetings (breaking of bread in homes). The smaller units were most likely composed of individuals who lived close to one another and met together in each other's homes. In Acts 2:42-47 we catch a glimpse of the character of these small-group communities:

> They devoted themselves to the apostles' teaching and to the fellowship, to the breaking of bread and to prayer. Everyone was filled with awe, and many wonders and miraculous signs were done by the apostles. All the believers were together and had everything in common. Selling their possessions and goods, they gave to anyone as he had need. Every day they continued to meet together in the temple courts. They broke bread in their homes and ate together with glad and sincere hearts, praising God and enjoying the favor of all the people. And the Lord added to their number daily those who were being saved.

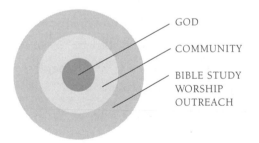

GOD

COMMUNITY

BIBLE STUDY
WORSHIP
OUTREACH

Figure 5. Components of a small group

This passage allows us to identify four characteristics of these small groups: (1) community, (2) Bible study, (3) worship and prayer, and (4) outreach. These components are as essential to emerging-culture small groups as they were to small groups in the early church.[13]

As we saw in chapter four, God's intention is for community to be the core of the church and the center of small-group life (just as it is the center of the above figure). Community has not always been the core of the church or the core of most small groups. But now we have come to identify community as the core component of small-group life, not just one of four components.

In a postmodern world, community is vital and at the heart of our ministry. In the 1960s and 1970s and into the 1980s most Christian small groups were primarily Bible studies with a bit of the other three components thrown in. The groups primarily pursued an intellectual understanding of the Christian faith and scanted the relational dimension. If the small group met for an hour, then forty-five minutes were spent in a heady Bible study that emphasized the mind over the heart. In the postmodern context the small-group emphasis is shifting to the heart.

The reason for the change is twofold. First, it stems from the emerging generations' need for a community where they are comforted, cared for and

---

Let us imagine thousands of communities whose members in an intentional fashion do the following six things:

1. Pray together

2. Share their joys and struggles

3. Study the context in which they find themselves

4. Listen for God's voice speaking through Scripture

5. Seek to discern the obedience to which they are called

6. Engage in common ministry

DIXON JUNKIN, *THE CHURCH BETWEEN GOSPEL AND CULTURE*

---

then challenged to grow. The second reason for the shift is the church's recognition (sometimes subconscious) that we have been caught up in the Enlightenment emphasis on the autonomous, rational self at the expense of God's design for us to live in community and to be a people of the heart as well as a people of the mind. We need to correct that mistake. Therefore, for most small groups today, community should be the core component.

COMMUNITY: THE CORE COMPONENT

Community is a set of personal, dependable and durable relationships that are based in the values of the community's participants.[14] A community is also a place where people find themselves sustained spiritually and emotionally.[15] The heart of today's small group is not a program ministry but a relational ministry.[16] This relational center creates a supportive environment where people can begin to share their joys, fears and vulnerabilities.

The larger a church becomes, the more need there is to have smaller communities where people can get to know each other in a personal setting. In essence, small-group community offers a place for people to tell their stories and develop intimate relationships with others.[17] The group moves at its own pace, reflecting people's spiritual journeys. How does community happen in small groups? Here are a few beginning ideas.

It takes the right attitude. People join a small group to develop community with others in the group. An open attitude is essential in this endeavor. Let me illustrate what I mean.

Thirty years ago my wife, Betsy, and I moved to Chapel Hill, North Carolina, where I had accepted a staff position with InterVarsity Christian Fellowship. The first Sunday at church we were invited to have dinner with Al and Debbie. The only problem was that Al, a former InterVarsity student leader, had not cleared the invitation with his wife, Debbie. She clearly was not excited about the prospect of entertaining us on Friday evening, so Betsy and I agreed to keep the visit short. Eight hours later

---

Characteristics of Community

1. *It will be a community of praise.*

2. *It will be a community of truth.*

3. *It will be a community that does not live for itself but is deeply involved in the concerns of its neighborhood.*

4. *It will be a community where men and women are prepared for and sustained in the exercise of the priesthood in the world.*

5. *It will be a community of mutual responsibility.*

6. *It will be a community of hope.*

LESSLIE NEWBIGIN, *THE GOSPEL IN A PLURALIST SOCIETY*

we dragged ourselves home! Obviously we all enjoyed ourselves that evening. Sometime during the first couple of hours together our attitudes changed, and a fledgling community was born among the four of us. We went on to form a small group within our church and invited others to be a part of our community. Our two couples were separated for over fifteen years when Al and Debbie moved away, but we remained close friends throughout that time. Now Al and Debbie have moved back to Chapel Hill, and we have returned to being in a small group together.

> *The larger challenge of megachurches is how to turn the "crowd" into a "congregation" and into the "committed." . . . In any large organization people's sense of loyalty, connection and identification comes from being part of a smaller team or group who spend enough time together to know and be known to one another. Joining a small group is the first essential step in being part of a megachurch rather than just attending it.*
>
> ROBERT PUTNAM, *BETTER TOGETHER*

For community to happen in today's small groups there has to be a willing attitude. People in this emerging culture desperately want a community where they can know and be known. However, they are hesitant to open up because they have been burned by broken promises many times before. The leader of the small group plays a crucial role in facilitating an experience of community in the group. The leader must come with a desire to be a part of this community. The leader needs to be willing to take the initial risk in being vulnerable and beginning to unpack her or his story.

It takes the right people. Part of the right attitude depends on how the group is formed, bringing together the right people. We did not realize it before we met, but Al, Debbie, Betsy and I had many things in common that drew us together quickly. Without understanding it at the time, we were part of the same tribal group—to use a postmodern term. Similarly, people today are more willing to come together in community if the whole group, or at least the core of the group, has some common basis. The common basis might be geography—they live in the same neighborhood or dorm. It could be the same tribal group—lawyers, athletes, close friends. The common basis could be the same task—worship team, evangelism team, soup kitchen team. The basis of the small group could be missional—evangelistic outreach or service in the community.

I am not saying that community cannot happen in a group of total strangers. Look at the twelve disciples. But some of the disciples knew each other before Jesus called them. Plus, Jesus gave them a task to do—following in his steps. Too many small groups in the past got thrown together because they could all meet on Tuesday nights or they were newcomers to the church and were looking for a small group to participate in. These groups rarely developed into true communities. Members remained together for a while, primarily for Bible study, but rarely saw each other outside the group. Postmoderns will walk away from this kind of group.

It takes time. For small groups to develop into true communities, it takes more than an hour and a half per week. Most people need time to develop trust in the group. Part of that trust can come from furnishing a variety of exercises people can do together, allowing them to open their thoughts to the group. Jenny's small group in her dorm did not create instant community. During that fall semester, the group participated in a number of icebreaker activities and only initiated deeper sharing as the group members became comfortable with each other. Becoming comfortable with each other usually does not happen if the group members see each other only at group meetings. They need to share activities outside their meetings, such as meals, movies, shopping or sports events. They should go on an extended weekend retreat together. Spending two or three days together creates lasting memories that promote group bonding. When a group goes on a retreat together in its second or third month of existence, something significant often happens. Many people go into that retreat thinking that the group belongs to the leader. But they leave with the commitment that this is "my" or "our" group. Ownership of the group is transferred from the leader to the entire group. Service projects in the community can also bind groups into a community.

Continued development of community within a small group is based not only on the group's initial activities but also on the length of time the group exists. Many Baby Boomer groups stay together for nine weeks. Youth and college small groups stay together for a semester or at most a school year. However, in the emerging culture small groups need to stay together longer. Remember that people in the younger generations tend to be reluctant to open up because of being burned in the past. Yet they desire to be in community because they long for the intimacy they have never experienced. Also, like most of us, they are not able to open up too many times in different groups. Therefore, if at all possible, small groups today need to stay together for two or more years to be able to develop the intimacy in community that they desire and need.

Being together for two or more years does not mean the group should not be open to new participants. Groups can grow over a period of time and then divide into two groups, retaining a solid core in both groups. There are many reasons for continuing to welcome new people. First, the small-group communities in the New Testament continually welcomed new people. Even the Twelve incorporated additional participants, including some women. "Jesus traveled about from one town and village to another, proclaiming the good news of the kingdom of God. The Twelve were with him, and also some women" (Lk 8:1-2).

Second, we need to keep the group open for outreach purposes. Our own small group is the perfect place to invite a friend. We will deal with the role of small groups in outreach in chapter ten. Suffice it to say here that one outreach strategy is to keep an open chair at each small-group meeting to demonstrate openness and a desire for new people to be invited to the small group.

Groups that welcome new participants continue to grow. Groups that do not open up to new members really do not understand what community is all about. Carl George shares his strong feelings regarding openness:

> Show me a nurturing group not regularly open to new life and I will guarantee that it's dying. If cells are units of redemption, then no one can button up the lifeboats and hang out a sign, "You can't come in here." The notion of group members shutting themselves off in order to accomplish discipleship is a scourge that will destroy any church's missionary mandate.[18]

A third reason to remain open is that God has created all of us with spiritual gifts to be used for the greater good of the community, which includes small groups. The group that remains closed hampers God's desire to bring different gifts into it to enhance the life of the group. This point leads us to the next dimension of community development within a small group.

IT TAKES EVERYONE'S SPIRITUAL GIFTS

Functioning fully as a community requires the involvement of every community member. God gave each of his people certain abilities or gifts. To fulfill their reconciling ministry to each other and to the world around them, the early Christians depended on each other in these small-group communities. The young house church in Ephesus saw this need for interdependence in community early on (Eph 4:11-13, 16).

In this kind of community the whole becomes greater than the sum of its parts as all the members work together. They use their gifts to help each other become reconciled to God and to each other and to promote reconciliation between God and people who are presently alienated from him.

Unlike Baby Boomers, who like to be spectators, people in the emerging culture like to be contributors. Throughout their lives they have been involved in participatory, interactive learning. They learn and belong by doing. There is an old saying that a minister ministers and the congregation congregates. For Boomers that system might be satisfying. However, small-group leaders need to get the younger generations involved in doing tasks for the group so that they feel like members of it. Tasks might include bringing refreshments, planning outings, calling people to see how they are doing and leading worship, prayer or Bible study.

IT TAKES COMMITMENT

Commitment is a puzzling issue for people living in a postmodern world. Postmodernity defies commitment to ideas because it accepts no ultimate truth. The only commitment that postmodernity does allow is to a tribal group, because it is within the tribal group that truth is experienced. Also, many people in the younger generations were never called to commitment by their parents because their parents never made any commitments to their children. They sometimes confuse demands with commitments. For many of them, commitment is a foreign concept. Thus commitment will have to be downplayed as a group begins. Julie Gorman describes the early process: "Small groups will probably have to exist with 'light' involvement, functioning with paradoxical statements, with slow maturation and fluctuating responsibility."[19]

> *Historical and sociological studies have shown repeatedly that churches with high belonging expectations are more vital, grow faster, have more counter-cultural impact and last longer than those that relax the intensity of their community life.*
>
> HOWARD SNYDER, "AUTHENTIC FELLOWSHIP"

Some who lead small groups for younger people, in trying to move slowly and sensitively on commitment, never get around to it. "Too often our failure to commit our own young people to our own cause leads to their subsequent defection. We fear that we shall risk too much if we make demands upon them, and we lose all as a consequence."[20] Without someone moving them toward commitment, they will drift in and out of small groups, based solely on whether the small group is meeting their needs. They may drift into another fellowship—or into a secular group—until they find a group that draws them in. An emerging-culture small group is responsible to point the group to Jesus, who has set the example of what it means to be committed and who is calling this generation to commitment.

People in the emerging culture desire to be in community but need help in hearing Jesus' call to community and commitment. The quality of the community becomes the context for commitment. The community's vision inspires commitment, but the relationships provide the foundation for commitment.[21] One small group described its reason for existence as follows:

Common commitment: accountability
Common vision: partnership
Common life: fellowship[22]

BIBLE STUDY: THE NEGLECTED COMPONENT

In the 1960s and 1970s (still under the influence of the Enlightenment era) the Bible study component was the essence of most small groups, to the neglect of community. Many members understood their small group as a place for them to come to study the Bible with other people so they could better understand the Christian faith. As was the case in the Enlightenment, rational understanding was the supreme focus. Community, worship, prayer and outreach were foreign concepts to many Bible studies. I am concerned that in the postmodern era the nurture component has been pushed out of many small groups altogether, leaving only the community component. As it was wrong to overly emphasize the nurture component, so it is wrong to overly emphasize the community component of a small group.

In the postmodern era the tribal group, not the autonomous self, is the essence of existence. There is no longer any concept of ultimate truth, only preferences. Postmodern culture has actually helped Christians regain the concept of biblical community as the foundation of human existence. We lost this perspective during the Enlightenment era. However, we cannot allow emerging postmodern culture to distort our perspective of ultimate truth.

Our finitude limits our ability to grasp the complex richness of the text. Our race, gender, economic status, and upbringing—all contribute to the perspective through which we encounter God's Word. We all wear "lenses" through which we read, influencing what we find or what we expect to find in the text. A modernist-scientific viewpoint denies this and asserts neutrality or objectivity.

TREMPER LONGMAN, *MARS HILL REVIEW*

Therefore, Bible study is vital for a Christian small group today. Bible study sets us apart from secular small groups. My concern for Christian ministry in the emerging world is that we are converting and developing Christians into Christian community rather than to the King of the Christian com-

Our goal for the Bible study is for the participants to encounter Jesus. This means that they not only learn the truth about Jesus as shown in the Scripture, but also experience the presence of Jesus in every element of their time gathered as a small group, from the hospitality of the leader, to the gentle and loving interaction with the other members, to how well they are listened to.

LINDSEY OLESBERG,
INTERVARSITY'S NATIONAL BIBLE
STUDY COORDINATOR

munity—God the Father, Son and Holy Spirit. If we are converting and developing people only into Christian community, they may well leave and join another community that has nothing to do with the Christian faith when they get upset with someone or disillusioned with some aspect of the community.

Although Bible study is critical for the postmodern Christian small group, it may differ from traditional Bible studies. In the modern world we thought we could come to our Bible study with total objectivity, without any of our prejudices. Also, in the past many Bible studies emphasized the intellectual dimension of the Christian faith, concentrating on the theological sections of the Bible and neglecting the narratives. Paul and the Old Testament prophets were preferred over Jesus, Acts and the Old Testament histories.

The younger generations that learned their alphabet from *Sesame Street* characters and are more attuned to the emotional side of life need to spend more time in the Gospels and the Old Testament historical books.[23] The Gospel parables and the life of Jesus are more likely to connect with postmodern people. The Gospel stories will be fresh and new for many of the postmoderns who have not grown up in Christian homes. They will be able to get to know and identify with Jesus as they study his life. The historical books will help them to see the faithfulness of God through the ages. They, for the most part, have never seen anyone keep promises that were made to them. Through Bible study they will begin to see God as someone who is always faithful.

Bible studies also need to be shorter and possibly use different methods. Since small groups today are emphasizing community, the Bible study needs to be shortened to about thirty to forty-five minutes out of a one and a half hour small-group meeting. Unfortunately, most Bible study guides that are being written today take over an hour to complete. Traditional Bible studies proceed in linear fashion and use the inductive method with its progression of observation, interpretation and application. In the postmodern era, as can be seen in such diverse fields as quantum physics, MTV and channel surfing, the linear method is no longer the primary method of study. We have been noticing a heavier emphasis on application in Bible studies than we have seen in past years. This trend is due to the change in emphasis from the mind to the heart. For postmoderns, Bible study needs to be more interactive and more free flowing. That is the way younger people learn best. We will have to continue to experiment to see what Bible study methods will be most effective for the postmodern generations and yet remain faithful to the biblical text. Let me suggest a possible new format.

INTRODUCTION (TWO MINUTES)

More and more people today have limited biblical background. Therefore, we need to make sure they understand the special biblical context for the study. Also, they will need to put the study in the overall metanarrative (context) of Scripture. Finally, they will need to have some understanding of how this study might connect to today's context.

ENTER THE TEXT (TEN MINUTES)

In the past we tried to study Scripture detached from the situation. Today people need to be more involved. So we need to give them an exercise in the beginning that would get them involved by using different senses. Some of these exercises might include having them read the passage and do one of the following:

- Describe how you would have felt if you were there.
- Draw a picture describing the situation.
- Describe how the different characters would be feeling.
- Put the Scripture in your own words.

DEVELOP QUESTIONS (TEN MINUTES)

As a group, reread the passage and write down the key questions you think need to be discussed for your group to understand what the passage says and means. Have everyone share their questions. This exercise will make sure the whole group has a say in what is critical for them to understand the passage. As the leader, arrange the key questions in some type of order. (Hopefully, you have done your own study beforehand so you can anticipate some of the key questions.)

ANSWER QUESTIONS TOGETHER (TEN MINUTES)
Using the order you developed above, proceed to answer the questions. Feel free to pursue a given theme of questions all the way through to applying what you learned from the passage and not wait to the end of the study to do the application.

SUMMARIZE (THREE MINUTES)
As the leader, summarize the study, showing the context of the passage, an understanding of the passage and an idea of how the passage fits into the larger picture of God's kingdom story. Here is your chance to do some teaching.

APPLICATION (TEN MINUTES)[24]
If you have not discussed how to apply the Scripture to your group's situation, do so now. Application can be focused on the individual or the group, inward or outward. Recognize that in the past most application was centered on the individual and was inward focused. We need to recognize the importance of the community for emerging-culture people and the need for us as Christians to be focused more on God and what he is doing and less on ourselves and what we need.

It will take time to adjust to a new method. However, I think this method helps us remain true to the text while at the same time producing a more communal experience. It also makes sure we do apply Scripture to our lives today.

WORSHIP AND PRAYER: A REASSURING COMPONENT

Worship and prayer are making a comeback in the postmodern world, since postmodernity has brought openness to the supernatural. It is recognized today that there is something more to life than the human misery we observe all around us. In *Microserfs* we see Douglas Coupland grappling with the supernatural through the relationships among Dan (the main character), Todd and Todd's religious parents.

> Right there and then, Todd and his parents fell down on their knees and prayed on the Strip, and I wondered if they had scraped their knees in their fall and I wondered what it was to pray, because it was something I have never learned to do and all I remember is falling, something I have talked about and something I was now doing.[25]

Like Dan in Coupland's novel, people in the emerging culture have a strong interest in the transcendent God. We need to recapture the idea of the transcendent God in our small groups. We can do that in two ways.

First, we can focus more on worship and prayer within the small group itself. Depending on the size of the group and the gifts within it, the group can hold its own periods of worship, including prayer. A period of intimate worship can bring the group closer together by focusing on God, who brought them together in the first place. If any members are gifted in playing instruments such as the guitar or the flute, then worship can include singing songs of praise. Certainly, any group meeting can include prayers of praise and thanksgiving, which also unify the group around the triune God.

The group can also worship together at the weekly worship service of the church or the weekly fellowship meeting of a campus Christian group or a church youth group. Sitting together as a group to worship the Lord together can provide a powerful bonding experience, as David Prior points out: "To worship God is to taste eternity, to dwell in the presence of the One who inhabits eternity (Isaiah 57:15). This high and lofty one whose name is Holy, has also placed eternity in man's heart (Ecclesiastes 3:11). Created to worship God, we need to forget time in order to allow God himself to speak and to satisfy the eternity in our hearts."[26]

People in the emerging culture are crying out for personal connection and intimacy with others and with God. We in the church need to be willing to reevaluate our priorities in ministry. Are we primarily a program-based or a person-based ministry? Do we concentrate on the individual, on small-group ministry or on corporate meetings? If we are going to minister effectively and faithfully to postmodern generations, we will need to focus our ministry around close community, which is best accomplished in a small-group ministry. These small-group communities will provide the foundation for the people in the emerging culture to find a community in which they can belong and find intimacy.

LEADERSHIP DEVELOPMENT IN POSTMODERN COMMUNITIES

Effective leadership is essential to the development of small-group communities. Any successful ministry in the emerging culture will design new philosophies and strategies of leadership development. A paradigm shift necessitates changes in various aspects of ministry, including leadership development.

If we are going to minister more and more within an emerging-culture context, we need to understand the changes in leadership style that are tak-

---

The executives who ignited the transformation from good to great did not first figure out where to drive the bus and then get people to take it there. No, they first got the right people on the bus (and the wrong people off the bus) and then figured out where to drive it.

. . . If you begin with "who" rather than "what," you can more easily adapt to a changing world. If people join the bus primarily because of where it is going, what happens if you get ten miles down the road and you need to change directions? You've got a problem. But if people are on the bus because of who else is on the bus, then it's much easier to change direction.

JIM COLLINS, *GOOD TO GREAT*

---

ing place between the modern and emerging cultures. If we are more modern ourselves, we need to become more aware of these differences so we will be willing to make needed changes as we are interacting more and more within an emerging culture. Those of us who are immersed in the emerging culture need to understand where some of the older people in leadership are coming from in our church or ministries.

Leadership in a postmodern context will look very different from leadership in a modern context (in which most Baby Boomer leadership developed). Let me compare some of these differences.

MODERN	EMERGING
Individual leader	Team leadership
Task	Community
Positional authority	Earned authority
Perfect leader	Broken leader
Building structures	Developing vision
Control	Empower
Destination	Journey
Aspire to leadership	Inspire for leadership

Although this list is not exhaustive or authoritative, it does highlight the changes that are taking place. The differences suggested above need to be taken into account in Christian churches and organizations that want to minister effectively in a postmodern context. Moving from the individual leader to team leadership and community does coincide with the biblical descriptions of the church as a community. As we go about our task, if the task is ongoing, we will need to recognize that developing the task members into a community is critical.

Most of today's discussion about leadership focuses on the "visionary" leader. It's the Moses as CEO model. Americans value the Moses style of leader. This approach is rooted in the rugged individualism that is so much a part of our culture. The frontier spirit has surely spurred growth and creativity, but it comes in our culture often at the expense of community.

PAUL FORD, "FROM MY VISION TO OUR VISION"

We also need to understand that just because a person holds a certain position, that does not mean that people will automatically follow or trust the person. Given the independent nature of the emerging culture, leaders will need to earn their trust and respect rather than command it. That trust will be earned in part as the leader comes across as less perfect and more "broken," or what Henri Nouwen describes as the "wounded healer" leader. Leaders can do this by showing themselves to be real people who have real hurts. Their compassionate leadership flows from their hurts, not from a persona of perfection. As leaders share their hurts, trust is developed. People want leaders they can identify with. Since they have been deeply wounded, they do not trust leaders who pretend they do not make mistakes or have no problems. They need leaders who can learn from mistakes rather than avoid making them altogether—leaders who can help them work through their problems. Seeing a leader making mistakes frees them to take risks.

New paradigm churches have a leadership that . . . is concerned with equipping the people of God for mission in the world. They are committed to identifying, training, granting peer support to and mentoring their fellow leaders. They empower emerging leaders and are ambitious for them. Leaders of new paradigm churches are accessible and vulnerable, and they have earned the authority that they exercise. They minister on the frontline alongside their people. They are aware of cultural values and trends, and relate the gospel to the community outside their walls.

EDDIE GIBBS, *CHURCHNEXT*

A postmodern leader needs to be less a supervisor and more a mentor. When I interview a candidate for the position of area director, the first question I ask myself is *Can this person pastor or mentor people?*

Whether in the business world or in the church, leaders in the postmodern world will need to get involved in the lives of the people they work with.

They cannot pretend that people's personal lives do not exist. People in the emerging culture are not as good as Boomers at separating their personal from their professional lives. Perhaps they are more honest than my generation. As I was having lunch with the vice president of a large firm, I asked him if he ever got involved in the personal lives of his employees. His answer did not surprise me. He responded immediately, "With my younger employees I have had to be more involved in their personal lives." We might have to get more involved in the lives of emerging-culture people because of their dysfunctional youth. But as we care for them as people, they become committed to the mission before them.

In regard to the mission or the task, a leader needs to emphasize the process, not just the product or result. People in the younger generations need to see the value of what they are doing. Most of them are not particularly motivated by monetary compensation or upward mobility. Many of them see their parents swimming in money and climbing up the ladder of success but stressed out and neglectful of their families. They do not want to end up like their parents. These generations are motivated to commitment by the caring leader who demonstrates a willingness to give people tasks that are meaningful.

It seemed that we were freer than generations before us from ego-dampening hierarchies. I had never walked into a job where I felt it necessary to hold my tongue or give concerted respect or reverence to those older or higher up the food chain. Of course, I sometimes did give such respect, but it seemed voluntary on my part. This led us to the belief that we could walk into any situation and assume that our opinions were probably valuable as, if not more so than, the opinions of anyone else in the room.

ETHAN WATTERS, *URBAN TRIBES*

Emerging-culture people also derive motivation from participating in a team-leadership ministry rather than functioning as the sole leader. Many of them have a difficult time assuming sole responsibility. That should not be surprising. As we make the transition into a postmodern culture, we are moving from the autonomous self to community. In this context the leader's role, according to William Berquist in *The Postmodern Organization,* is to "perform this integrative role through the creation and sustenance of community and through acting in the role of servant to those with whom they work."[27]

In a team-leadership context, decision making needs to be participatory rather than dictatorial. As much as possible decisions should be reached by consensus, thus encouraging more group ownership of the decision and more commitment to the implementation of the decision. Let me give you an example.

Summer camp is a critical component of our campus ministry. It is also a time when our region's entire sixty-five-person staff comes together for two weeks of team ministry with over eight hundred students. For a number of years we went to Windy Gap, a beautiful Young Life camp nestled in the mountains of North Carolina. During the last few years we were at Windy Gap, the camp functioned at capacity, with us needing to turn students away. As camp director, I had the prerogative of choosing either to add a second camp (thus splitting our staff into two groups) or to move away from Windy Gap, a place we had been going for twenty years. However, I recognized the need for a consensus decision that would give all the staff ownership in the decision and a correspondingly stronger commitment to its implementation. We went through a long process that allowed everyone to give input. Although it took much longer to go through the consensus process, the result was that we now have a staff more committed to each other and more committed to the task.

The notion of leadership is an uncomfortable one for people in the emerging culture, and fewer of them are aspiring to be leaders. They need to be inspired by a leader they respect and trust. There are a number of reasons for this resistance to being a leader. They are dealing with lots of internal issues that can cripple them or at least preoccupy them. Many of them have never been affirmed for what they can do and so have a tendency toward low self-esteem. As we will see in more depth in the next chapter, they need a person or a community of people who can help them grow spiritually and work on some of these personal issues. They also need a leader they trust to believe in them by affirming the gifts they possess and encouraging them to develop their gifts.

A number of years ago our summer camp lost two worship leaders. I called two of our younger staff, Susan and Ashlee, to ask them to lead worship for our eight hundred students at camp. Both initially hesitated at such a large undertaking. However, in the past I had encouraged and affirmed them in other areas. They knew I cared for them personally. I was not just trying to use them to perform a task. I told both of them that I believed in them and was confident that they could lead worship. I also said I would be there for them, encouraging them along the way and giving helpful suggestions if needed. They finally said yes. In the end they were great worship leaders. The key was that they knew I cared for them, believed in them and would be there if they needed me.

To help the younger generations grow into leadership, we need to empower them in their tasks, not control them. The key is instilling within them a sense of trust and confidence. Their confidence grows as they are given responsibility for tasks as well as assurance that they can accomplish the task. As we empower them in these tasks, they are able to assume leadership of small-group communities and other responsibilities.

IMPLICATIONS FOR MINISTRY

While Boomers may stand anonymously on the fringes of a church, people in the emerging culture want to become involved. While Boomers have a hard time sharing with a group, the younger generations want to dialogue. The kinds of ministries that we have established for the Boomer generation are not as effective with people in the emerging culture. One example is the seeker service. Boomers, who are more self-assured and autonomous, want to be left alone to observe and then decide for themselves when to get involved. Emerging-culture people need to be invited in, because they are not as self-assured. Once they are inside the door, they want to become part of the community, not remain aloof from the community.

While the seeker service may provide an initial introduction to the church or Christian fellowship, people in the emerging culture need to be invited into a close community almost immediately. Otherwise they will drift away. We need to establish an effective method of drawing them into community as soon as possible once they express interest in our church or Christian fellowship. When I was on campus staff at UNC-Chapel Hill with

InterVarsity Christian Fellowship, we held a picnic for new students before classes began in the fall. At the picnic we had the new students break up into small groups to meet their small-group leaders if they chose to remain involved with InterVarsity. In this way they became involved in a small group from the very beginning of college. In our churches, likewise, we need to think through the best means for inviting people into community.

We also need to consider what type of community is best for the emerging culture. I think a small-group community is critical because it is a place for developing close friends and for sharing pain and joy. It is also a place to find nurture in the faith, since it provides a context where true dialogue can

---

In meeting after meeting, leaders say to one another, "If people were only more committed . . ." "If they would just rise to the challenge . . ." The leaders are broadcasting on the frequencies of challenge and commitment, but few in the grassroots are tuned in. The appeal goes unheard, so the same few people end up receptive and responding year after year. Most people today are tuned elsewhere: to compassion and community. . . . Jesus does not say to Peter, "Will you make the commitment?" His final question is not "Will you rise to the challenge?" Christ says, "Peter do you love me?" "Yes, Lord." "Then feed my sheep." Jesus appeals to compassion and community. So, too, must today's leader.

The phrase "Mary, will you be willing to teach third grade Sunday school next year?" is an invitation to commitment. Mary may do her duty, take her turn, but she will likely never fall in love with her class. You can say, "Mary we invite you to fall in love with this group of kids and give them the privilege of falling in love with you." She is more likely to rise to the opportunity.

KEN CALLAHAN, *LEADERSHIP*

---

take place. What places for close community does your church provide?

We need to reconsider our church leadership structure to see if we have created an environment for the younger generations to grow into leadership within the church. If we retain the modern leadership structure, few emerging-culture people will desire to become involved in leadership. We need to change our leadership structure so they are interested in leadership positions within the church. In the years to come, it will be the leaders from Generation X and the Millennial generation who will equip us to minister effectively while remaining faithful to the gospel. Are we providing spaces for them to be in leadership now?

9

Our Spiritual Journey in Community

In the fall of 1995 Alanis Morissette, a twenty-year-old Generation Xer, burst onto the music scene. Thousands of teenagers resonated with her songs. Her lyrics seemed to express what many young people were feeling. In one song, "Perfect," she describes what it is like to relate to parents who demand perfection. The demands are so numerous and unrealistic that the child soon has little or no self-worth.[1]

Morissette's words reflect the experiences of many people living in the emerging culture. How can they be reached with the gospel, and how can they be assisted along their spiritual journey once they become followers of Jesus Christ? In chapter ten we will look at how to bring the gospel to them. In this chapter we will focus on the Christian's spiritual journey. As Morissette's song indicates, and as we saw in chapter five, we are living in a world that is shame based, not guilt based. How did it get this way? What new concepts do we need to help people in the emerging culture in their spiritual formation?

Many people afflicted by shame need to restore their relationship with their parents, who may have burdened their child with expectations the child could not meet. That is certainly true for the child in the Morissette song cited at the beginning of the chapter. "That simply wasn't good enough, you've gotta try a little harder."

BREAKING THE BOND OF SHAME

Breaking the bond of shame is never easy. Breaking the bond of shame "is a spiritual journey of overcoming the losses, hindrances, and problems that we suffer, to becoming the person we were created to be: spiritual healing begins with the recovery of hope."[2] Do you remember Jerry from chapter five? Jerry's recovery was certainly a spiritual journey. Jerry had a few close friends to journey alongside him. And whether he realized it or not, Jerry had another companion—God—guiding him along the way.

More than anything else in our spiritual journey, we need to know and feel that God is with us. The Israelites maintained a sense of God's presence by recounting God's past faithfulness (Josh 24:2-13). It is amazing how many times in the Old Testament stories the author interrupts the narrative to recite a litany of God's faithful actions in the past. Like the Israelites, we need to remember God's past faithfulness to us. This pause to remember is critical for us, since life for many people today is like trying to stand in a fast-moving, crowded train with no strap to hold onto. We can be thankful that we do have someone to guide us.

Have you ever wondered why the angel gave Jesus two different names? Jesus, the first name, means "Savior." The second name, Immanuel, means "God with us." In his book *Yearning* Craig Barnes describes the significance of these two names to a troubled and confused world:

> The pairing of these names signals a reversal in our typical under-standing of salvation. We don't usually think of salvation as having God with us. We would rather think of it as our being with God, and as being saved from how it is. We would rather think of "the victorious Christian life." But in Jesus Christ, God is revealed as the Savior Immanuel, which means that salvation is not our ascent out of the hard, pain-filled, compromised conditions of this world. Salvation is God's descent down to the lost world that he loves. Becoming a Christian doesn't save us from a blessed thing on earth. Jesus doesn't save us from grief or heartache or injustice. But he does enter every one of these life threatening situations, that he might find us there. Perhaps that is really the only blessed thing after all.[3]

God does promise to be with us in those times of crisis that occur on our spiritual journey. God does not promise to take us out of those situations; God only promises to save us. God was with Jerry during those months of struggle. However, God never promised to help Jerry perform better so that he would not feel shame. Barnes describes how God acts in such situations. "In the moment in which we feel abandoned by both our dreams and the God we thought would save them for us—in precisely that moment we are ready to receive God's true salvation. It is then we discover that God wants to save us, not our dreams."[4] At those times we see God's unfathomably deep love for us.

Love of God. People who are confused, marginalized and torn want more than anything else to be loved and to feel hope. They desperately need to experience God's love. Yet the postmodern generations feel too much shame to allow themselves to be known. Jerry, the student I mentioned earlier in the chapter, wanted to be loved but felt that if people got to know the real Jerry, they would not have anything to do with him. The good news is that God, who knows the real us even better than we know ourselves, still loves us! True intimacy means being really known and really loved. Jerry's fear is that either he can really be known or he can really be loved, but certainly not both. Ironically, we cannot really be loved unless we are really known, because true love is being known. To love and to know are synonymous. Until we come to grips with the fact that God really loves and really knows us, we will never be able to truly love others or be known by them.

Love of others. Experiencing God's love enables us to love and be loved by others in the way that God created us to relate to each other. Much of the shame that many people need to be healed of relates to sexuality. In fact, there is no other area that needs more healing in the emerging culture. This is hardly surprising, since the secular media, the entertainment world, many parents and many of our leaders have supplied such poor role models. Past generations received mixed messages about sex, and sadly, today most of the messages are the same. Sex is understood as an act or a commodity rather than as a committed relationship within certain boundaries, namely marriage.

From the beginning of creation, sexual intercourse has been part of a larger commitment. In the Hebrew language, to have sexual intercourse is to "know" someone. That knowing occurs within the broader context of marriage. As we have observed, to be known is very important for this generation. For many within this emerging culture, however, sex is only a momentary, selfish pleasure having nothing to do with the selfless love of a long-term commitment in marriage.

Many people in the emerging culture who were sexually active before they became Christians feel ashamed and alone in their struggles and fear being ostracized by other Christians. We in the church need to create a community in which these personal struggles can be shared. We need to accept the person without condoning the behavior. Sometimes, if a trusting relationship has already been established, we might need to take initiative and ask questions.

As I meet with students on campus on a regular basis, I ask about sexual struggles or temptations they might be dealing with. We cannot assume that our friends or the people we minister to are not struggling in this area. Many people are trying to deal with pornography, masturbation, homosexuality or sexual intercourse on their own. After students discuss areas of concern with me, I ask them if they want me to hold them accountable as they try to change their behavior. Then whenever I see those students I ask, "How are you doing?" Others think I am just making polite conversation, but I am really following up on the student's area of struggle.

When I began practicing this accountability procedure, I thought people would jump into the bushes or run around the corner when they saw me coming. To my astonishment, they gladly entered into an accountability relationship with me. They knew I deeply cared for them despite their struggles.

Hope from God. God gives us hope in the midst of our suffering. In chapter seven we examined the theological foundation for hope. In chapter ten we will discover the eschatological and existential significance of hope in evangelism. However, in the midst of our spiritual journey we also need to experience the hope that keeps us moving along on our journey. Glimpses of hope along the way reassure us that the end is in sight and that God will stay with us on our spiritual journey until we reach the end of it. Let me tell you a story that illustrates this point.

Betsy and I once had an opportunity to spend ten days hiking in the Swiss Alps. One day we took a thirty-minute gondola ride up First, a mountain above Grindelwald. Then we hiked along a ridge for over an hour and started our descent to Grindelwald. But we had not realized how steep or how long the descent would be. About two hours into it, my legs began to get wobbly, even though we were tacking along the trail to ease our descent. What gave me hope and enabled me to continue was an occasional glimpse of the town. I knew that, although the journey was difficult, the end was in sight. Finally, after a four-hour descent, we arrived at the train station in Grindelwald, exhilarated to have reached our destination.

For many emerging-culture people, all of life is like the steep descent from First. The pain and suffering do not go away. Christians, however, catch brief glimpses of heaven during the times when the path of life emerges from the trees into a clearing. Then hope bursts forth. Craig Barnes reminds us of this hope. "Hope arises out of the hard truth of how things are. Christians will always live carrying in one hand the promises of how it will be and in the other hand reality of how it is. To deny either is to hold only half the truth of the gospel."[5] Often we find hope, not in our moments of reflection, but in our times of pain. Ray Anderson depicts hope as emerging "when the broken edge of life becomes the growing edge of faith: growth begins with openness to the Spirit as the source of change."[6]

In the Gospels we see people coming to Jesus in times of need. Many of them had lost all hope. God gave them hope in the midst of their suffering. God does provide, not necessarily by doing what we want him to do, but by giving himself in the midst of our everyday life. "Hope is found in the time in between Good Friday and Easter—on Just Plain Saturday. All of creation finds itself there, as we continue to wait between the death of our expectations of what God would do and fulfillment of his true promises."[7]

Reality of God. Besides love and hope, people in the emerging culture demand honesty and reality. They are well acquainted with the harsh realities of life. Battle tested, they are able to take the truth. Promise lines like "God loves you and has a wonderful plan for your life" or "ten steps to basic maturity" just do not cut it with these generations. They are ready for us to tell it like it is. Lynne Hybels tells a story about the work of Willow Creek Community Church. She depicts life as it is today:

> The reality, for most of us, is that life is hard. And the sad truth is that

it might not get any easier. So what do we do? Pretend that the inevitable disappointments, losses and heartaches of life don't really hurt that much, and live with a buried despair that forces us into a state of emotional deadness? Or acknowledge the difficulty of life and find acceptable and spiritually sound ways to compensate for the sadness? Far better, I think, is the second option which allows us to experience life authentically and to discover joy in the midst of pain.[8]

Community among God's children. To be able to work through their shame and cope with the harsh realities of life, people today need the support of a Christian community that invites them in and allows them to share themselves. Remembering that shamed people tend to isolate themselves, small-group communities need to be open and supportive. Being able to put our shame feelings into words is a critical first step along the spiritual journey.[9] The acceptance we sense in that community can allow us to trust others in the community and can make us willing to be ministered to by the community.

One form that ministry can take is touch. Patting someone on the back, touching them on the shoulder or giving them a hug can show that we care. I realize the need for sensitivity in this area. However, touch can be a means to experience "the grace of God's acceptance and acceptance by other human beings."[10] As we read through the Gospels, we see Jesus exercising a ministry of touch (Mt 8:3, 15; 9:20, 29).

The Christian community is a new family as well as a safe haven. In this new family we can discover hope in the midst of broken relationships. We probably will not discover perfect people or even improved relationships. But then perfection is not the goal in this life. The goal might be the serenity prayer.

> God, grant me the serenity to accept the things I cannot change,
> Courage to change the things I can, and
> Wisdom to know the difference.

Our hope is not found in the community but in the King of the community—Jesus Christ. God meets us in the Christian community in the midst of our dysfunctional relationships.[11]

The Christian community plays a role in the healing process through its worship, fellowship, teaching and prayers. People can cope with their pain and suffering if they are being loved and cared for. Part of that caring can be the power of touch. Not only can they cope in community, but the community experience can be a healing force, creating faith and love in the midst of the journey. As people begin to feel cared for and trust those in their community or small group, they can begin to share their personal stories. The community becomes part of each person's story and begins to influence each person's values and outlook on life. The community helps put each individual story into the larger context of God's story. Each personal story begins to make sense as it is placed within God's transcendent story of creation, redemption and eschatological hope.

THE JOURNEY OF FAITH

As we have observed before, the younger generations are leery of spiritual facades that rely on image. They are sensitive to pretense, having grown up on TV commercials. What they are looking for has to be real and authentic. When they look at Christianity, they are turned off by images and false promises of the "good life." They know that reality is not easy and are turned off by anything that seems too easy. David Wells describes this type of church as a church where "[God's] truth is too distant, his grace is too ordinary, his judgment is too benign, his gospel is too easy, and his Christ is too common."[12] We cannot rely on programmatic faith models from the past to reach this generation.

John Westfall, in his book *Coloring Outside the Lines,* describes three models of discipleship that would not be effective with people living in a postmodern framework. The first model is the "older saint" model, which encourages people to become more like Christian saints of old by withdrawing from everyday life and finally withdrawing from the world altogether. This model advocates maturity by withdrawal. Emerging-culture people care too much about the world to go along with this model. While giving the appearance of saintly spirituality, this model actually goes against God's desire for followers of Christ to be active in the world.[13]

The second model is the "workbook" model. It focuses on a set of principles for living instead of a personal relationship with Jesus Christ. People who follow this model believe that spiritual maturity is a matter of following some basic principles. People who follow these principles achieve spiritual maturity, and all of their relationships just fall into place. Anyone who does not achieve spiritual maturity simply does not have enough faith. This model is discipleship by law. It produces rigidity in beliefs and relationships.[14] People in the emerging culture are streetwise enough to know that life is not neat and easy. This model lies when it asserts that we can change our being by changing what we do.[15] In fact, being determines doing. Only after we have a real understanding of who we are can we know what to do with life.

Westfall's third model is the "military" model. It is characterized by a clear hierarchy of structure and power. Everyone is under the authority of someone else. While this model is supposed to promote accountability, it actually promotes irresponsibility and dependence. People are not responsible for their own actions.[16] According to Westfall, all of these models replace freedom with guilt, rebellion or blind obedience and thus keep people in bondage.[17] The attempts at maturity focus on external changes only. These generations will see through the facade of these superficial attempts at change.

> *The first emphasis of Celtic Christians is on life as a journey. Emphasis is placed on the going rather than on arriving at one's destination. Celtic spirituality also nurtures a life of prayer recognizing God's presence in all of life. . . . On account of the atoning sacrifice of Christ, there is now hope for humankind, consisting not only of life after death but of life before death. . . . A genuine spiritual journey is not characterized by self-preoccupation but must be lived out in community and love for one's neighbors.*
>
> EDDIE GIBBS, *CHURCHNEXT*

Our companion on the journey: Jesus.
People in the emerging culture need and desire internal transformation within a context of community. They need a companion or a guide for their spiritual journey, not a map. The spiritual journey begins with a relationship

with Christ that permeates every area of life. As the apostle Paul says, "I no longer live, but Christ lives in me" (Gal 2:20). This means more than just trying harder to act like a Christian. Our strategy should be to remove anything in our lives that keeps "the living Christ from expressing Himself through us."[18] The emphasis is on being, not doing. Westfall describes this emphasis on being as unconventional spirituality. Actually, the spirituality he describes is similar to Celtic spirituality lived out in the sixth century in Ireland.

Westfall goes on to say, "It is no longer measured by our performance, and it isn't overly concerned with a destination. What does matter is that we begin to live from the inside out, being women and men who dare to live transparently in a world that knows only superficial imaging."[19] We begin this process in community by sharing our struggles and joys. Sharing our problems with others sets us free from the shame that we have been hiding inside. As we share our struggles or sins, they begin to lose their grip on us. As we become more vulnerable in our sharing, we are set free to move ahead in a relationship of faith with God and others.

Our journey's destination: shalom. According to Cornelius Plantinga, Christians are to be people who live in a state of *shalom,* the Hebrew word for peace. In the Bible shalom is a state of universal flourishing, wholeness and delight. It inspires "joyful wonder." Shalom is the way things ought to be.[20] It is God's design for creation and recreation. Sin breaks shalom by interfering with the way things are supposed to be. Before the Fall, Adam and Eve existed in a state of shalom. After the Fall, things were different. Their sin caused a break in shalom and sadness within God. God hates sin because it disrupts the state of shalom in which people were created to live. God sent Jesus to earth to restore us to shalom.

The restoration to shalom is a faith journey. Faith is simply "the process by which we let God direct our lives or let God be God."[21] It is a journey that involves movement and change. Movement can be in a variety of directions. In the past we usually saw the faith journey as linear. I once was immature, but now I am mature. I doubt that faith development was ever linear. If it was, it no longer is in this postmodern world. Our faith development is a journey, not an upward line on a graph. Whereas a trip focuses on the destination, a journey focuses on the process. In a journey there are side trips and possible returns to past stops as well as incursions into the unknown.[22]

While the journey is different for everyone, there are enough similarities in the journey for people in the emerging culture that we can provide some road signs along the way.

ROAD SIGNS ALONG THE JOURNEY

Running the hundred-meter sprint differs from running a marathon. The primary strategy in the former is to start as fast as possible and to run as hard as possible for the entire race. Obviously, that strategy would be disastrous in a marathon. Marathoners need to pace themselves to go the distance. They need to replace fluids at certain critical points along the way. They catch their breath by slowing their pace for a mile or two. Furthermore, every marathon course has different levels of difficulty. The Pikes Peak Marathon, with its run straight up to the top of Pikes Peak and back down again, differs vastly from the New York Marathon, run primarily along the flat streets of New York City. Each individual runner has a different makeup and requires a different running strategy.

Christians in the past treated the spiritual journey like a hundred-meter sprint. The one who pursued a strategy of doing the right things, such as studying the Bible, praying, reading Christian literature, attending church services and participating in a small group, and who continued doing all these things at the same pace throughout life, would complete the race as a mature Christian. Anyone who stumbled along the way would try to correct it by doing even more of the above activities. This strategy does not work anymore, if it ever did. It is based on *doing* (certain activities) versus *being*. It is based on external activities, not internal transformation. It is also based on a linear view of sanctification that presupposes an ever-upward growth pattern moving from immaturity to maturity with little or no deviation from the norm.

In the last ten years I have seen a number of former students and even a few staff members crash and burn in their spiritual journey. I could identify certain patterns or issues in the lives of some that caused them to crash. Others, however, seemed to be keeping up the right activities (Scripture study, prayer and the like), which should have kept them going on the journey, according to traditional teaching. But they just could not keep going, even after redoubling their efforts. Some sought counseling. Others sought new ex periences with God—spiritual healing or speaking in tongues. Nothing seemed to help until they realized that maybe they were pursuing the wrong strategy in their spiritual journey. They needed to see their spiritual journey as a marathon rather than a sprint. Instead of redoubling their efforts or trying spiritual adrenaline shots to keep them going when they stumbled, they needed to look at the road signs along the way that told them where they were in the spiritual journey. Then they needed to make appropriate changes as they moved along to the next road sign.

Janet Hagberg and Robert Guelich have written a book entitled *The Critical Journey: Stages in the Life of Faith,* which can help us identify the various road signs along our spiritual journey. I have adapted the authors' six stages to fit a postmodern context. Before beginning this discussion, let me make some preliminary comments. First, no one can make this spiritual journey alone, since God created us to live in community. Our spiritual journey needs the help of others, and its destination is shalom—community with God and other Christians. Hagberg and Guelich remind us that moving from one stage to another stage always causes confusion. We may find the transition exhilarating or exhausting. Nothing seems certain.[23] Movement from one stage to the next is usually precipitated by an event over which we have no control, such as a move, a health crisis, deep questions about life or experiencing God in a new way.[24] Such events, which may be crises in our lives, provide the impetus for movement along the spiritual journey. We should not see all crises as bad or continually strive to avoid them. These stages, or road signs, are not necessarily linear. There is usually some movement back and forth between stages.

First road sign: experiencing God. Usually the first road sign along our spiritual journey occurs when we experience God. During the modern era, the first road sign might have been thinking about God. However, people in the emerging culture live life more from the heart than from the head, so the first road sign is likely to be experiencing God. The catalyst for this experience might be a need for someone to "soothe us, love and care for us, and encourage us to go on living."[25] Many postmoderns have had no previous faith experience. At this road sign they might not be exactly sure what they are experiencing, but it gives them greater meaning in life. At this road sign there is a "sense of innocence . . . a ready acceptance of anything to do with God."[26]

Sometimes we experience a roadblock instead of the first road sign. Instead of feeling God's love, we feel shame—a sense of worthlessness—because we feel that God and others have expectations of us that we cannot meet. Jerry experienced shame in his relationship with his earthly father, and he carried it over into his relationship with God. This shame is isolating and keeps us on the fringes of the Christian community, from which we may drift away entirely. Support from others, usually in the form of a small-group community, enables us to move along to the second road sign. Remember Jenny's small group? It enabled her to continue her spiritual journey by helping her feel a sense of belonging.

Second road sign: belonging to a community. This road sign provides an opportunity to learn and belong in an environment that loves us as we are. Many people today need love and acceptance. Too many of them were "loved as long as they were perfect." Many Christian fellowships insist on so many guidelines that newcomers do not feel loved as they are. Being accepted into the community makes people feel free "to explore, to learn, to quest, to absorb, to put into place our set of beliefs or faith principles."[27]

Earlier we considered the tribal group, which defines truth for its members. It is no different in the Christian community. Many people in the emerging culture come into the group with few steadfast values, having grown up in the era in which preferences have supplanted truth. At this road sign on the journey the group helps form our concept of God. We look to the group leaders and other members of the group to give us answers to the questions we are asking. As we find answers, our confidence grows and we are able to make it through the hard times because either we have the answers or we know who can help us get the answers.

We need to be careful at this point in the journey to not confuse entering into the life of the community with making a commitment to Christ. Some may enter the community saying the right words but not living out their faith on a daily basis. Tim Keller, pastor of Redeemer Presbyterian Church in New York City, describes this stage as follows:

> Many people who say "I've come to Christ" are so deeply soaked in secularism and individualism that their lives will show a lot of inconsistency. They require far more extensive and deep instruction and

personal transformation. A lot of people who look converted will lapse, and in many cases, it could be part of their long pre-conversion experience.[28]

One roadblock possible at this point is the development of an "us versus them" mentality stemming from the strong sense of belonging to one's own community. We can feel that our community has all the answers, which can lead to arrogance. Many emerging-culture people may switch to different groups at this point because of their difficulty in making a commitment to any one group. They also switch because they are searching for the right answer or they desire to be a part of a group that is going somewhere. While at the first road sign we feel that we are weak and wrong and that others are right and strong, at this road sign we feel like we are right and strong and everyone else is weak and wrong.[29] All this switching amounts only to circular movement. We may need help in committing ourselves to one group because we can only visit, not belong to, multiple groups. It is important to become full participants, not just spectators, so that we can continue along our journey of faith. If we do not commit to one group, our journey will be blocked.

Third road sign: contributing in community. As we recognize the gifts God has given us, we see that we have something to contribute to others in the community. It is our turn to give. This contribution may take the form of a specific leadership responsibility in the community. Because we may be tentative at first, we need regular encouragement and affirmation from others. Many people in the emerging culture deeply desire to contribute, but they have always been told they are not good enough. They desire to be involved in all types of volunteer work. However, because they are not sure of themselves, they need to hear a commendation such as "Good job." One motive for contributing is that as others have given to us, so we want to give something in return.

A roadblock at this stage may be weariness. Sometimes the weariness comes from doing too much. We need help in knowing when to rest. Like marathoners, we need help pacing ourselves so that we do not hit the wall and crash. Another type of weariness is a sense of disappointment at our coworkers' response to us. We cannot expect everyone to be at the same road sign with us. When they are not, we should not lose patience with them. Another roadblock is that our outward contributions and level of responsibility have moved ahead of our inward development. Many people in the emerging culture are placed in positions of leadership prematurely or without enough support. Some have the skills necessary for leadership but not the emotional or spiritual maturity. We must avoid putting people in leadership positions before they are mature, or we must mentor them along the way so that they are developing as they take on more responsibility. New InterVarsity staff members in our region must complete a one-year internship with more mature staff before they take on major ministry responsibilities. The more mature staff member mentors the younger person's personal life, ministry responsibilities and learning program.

Most emerging-culture people are willing to admit their need for help. For some others, having to ask for help could signify weakness or loss of control. They have learned to be survivors. For me to admit weakness is to admit that I am not surviving on my own, and my facade becomes more rigidly set in place.[30] Twinges of uncertainty may begin to cloud our journey.

Fourth road sign: the tunnel. The fourth road sign is clouded by uncertainty and unanswerable questions. Movement toward the fourth road sign may be precipitated by some crisis of faith. Entering the tunnel makes us feel angry at God and at others for not telling us about this part of the journey. Answers have been displaced by new questions. We have doubts. It is important to realize, though, that doubt is an element of faith, not the opposite of faith. One person describes this process as changing from a person who has "been living in doubt and visiting your faith to living in your faith and visiting your doubts."[31] It is better to deal with our doubts inside the faith and looking out than outside the faith and looking in. According to Frederick Buechner, "At least doubts prove that we are in touch with reality, with the things that threaten faith as well as with the things that nourish it. If we are not in touch with reality, then our faith is apt to be blind, fragile and irrelevant."[32]

We may feel abandoned during this period of doubt. This sense of abandonment may be especially troubling for the younger generations, who have felt abandoned throughout their lives. Hagberg and Guelich describe this point in the journey as a "mode of questioning, exploring, falling apart, doubting, dancing around the real issues, sinking in uncertainty, and indulging in self-centeredness."[33] To those close to us we may look like a hopeless cause.

The key to moving through the tunnel is to search for direction, not answers. That direction is a turning to God. We need to release God from the box we put him in as we discover that God is not who we thought him to be.[34] It is okay to ask questions again. Our companion at this stage of the journey is doubt. We invite God to give us direction.

> Search me, O God, and know my heart;
> > test me and know my anxious thoughts.
> See if there is any offensive way in me,
> > and lead me in the way everlasting. (Ps 139:23-24)

The tunnel road sign can easily become a roadblock if we become consumed with ourselves and if our search ends with ourselves, not faith. We also hit the roadblock if those closest to us in the community of faith lose patience with our questions and abandon us. Some leave the journey at this point.

Fifth road sign: the wall of surrender. Every marathoner goes through it. Some find it relatively easy. For most it is the defining moment in the race. What every marathon runner has to go through is the wall, that invisible barrier that lurks some nineteen or twenty miles into the race and where everything within the runner cries out to abandon the race. The Boston Marathon is so difficult because the wall usually sits along the uphill stretch near Newton. Those who make it through the wall almost always finish the remaining five to six miles of the race. Just as some marathon runners never make it through the wall, though, some Christians never make it through the wall of their spiritual journey.

Going through the wall is characterized by a sense of yielding. Earlier in our journey we had confidence in our own ability to make the journey. Now we are becoming more confident of God's ability to take care of us totally.[35] Ultimately the wall is a meeting of the wills, ours and God's. Our initial Christian commitment marks the decision to follow Jesus on the journey. Here at the wall we have to decide to surrender ourselves totally to Jesus. It does not mean that Christ has not been Lord before now. It is a movement toward allowing Christ to be in total control. I heard one Christian leader describe this experience as jumping off a cliff and waiting for Jesus to catch you before you hit the bottom of the canyon. We are at the mercy of our faithful guide.

Sixth road sign: freedom in community. Although we do not know what lies ahead on the journey, we do know that we have a faithful guide— God. We are at peace, or shalom, under God's guidance, which gives us a freedom to serve in the community. Our primary motivation in life is to love others honestly and to follow God faithfully. We reach out to others "from a sense of fullness, of being loved by God and being asked to love others in return."[36] We are at God's calling to live out God's purposes for us in the world. Winning, losing and accomplishing tasks are secondary to being faithful and available to God. While the fourth road sign could be called the "dark night of the soul," the sixth road sign might be called the "still morning of the soul."

Seventh road sign: loving in community. At this stage in the journey we have truly become God's representatives. We reflect God to others in ways we never imagined possible. We can give to others beyond our capacity because we know that everyone comes from God and is loved by God. We give without any sense that we are making a sacrifice. Christ's life is a model for us, not just an example. We are able to give Christ's wisdom to others. While we still get angry and still feel pain, we can sense God's grace and comfort in the midst of all the confusion around us. We have a sense of peace and can experience the taste of sabbath rest that God desires for all his people. Finally, at this point in the journey we "become aware that the more of God we have, the less of anything else we need."[37]

REORIENTATION OF THE JOURNEY

How do we assist people in their spiritual journey? How does the church need to change the way it fosters community, communication, worship and preaching? As we saw in the last chapter, community is the foundation of the spiritual journey. Our journey is not just our own personal, isolated journey but a communal journey, in which we as a whole community are in the journey together. How do we help the church community in its journey?

As we have had to reorient our foundations from the self to community, so we will need to reorient our communication with God, each other and the world from primarily a detached, word-dominated communication to a participatory communication based on word and image.

Communication reorientation. As we continue to move into the emerging culture, our communication patterns will need to change. Are we willing to adapt our communication patterns? Let us look at some of the changes that might need to be made from a modern to postmodern pattern.

One of these dramatic changes in our culture is the shift from words to images. To do church in a way that is entirely text-driven is the kiss of death. People simply do not read, they observe. We have a culture raised in watching. . . . We need to adapt to capturing images that communicate truth and to move from static to dynamic communication systems.

ERWIN MCMANUS, *THE UNSTOPPABLE FORCE*

MOVING FROM MODERN TO POSTMODERN

From Word to Image
Image has become a powerful tool within our culture. Our first response to this change may be to think that this is a negative change. However, as we will see, God continually uses images to communicate with us. We need to be sure we use both word and image in our communication so we can connect with all the God-given senses each person possesses.

From Detached to Participant
In modern culture we were taught to be objective and thus remain detached from what we were studying. We were taught to use reason and not to use passion. While we still need to use our mind, we also need to recognize that none of us can be totally objective. We bring our own past understanding and thus should feel free to fully participate in the learning experience with both our mind and heart.

From Didactic to Narrative

As we were previously taught to be detached in communication, so we were also taught that the didactic portions of Scripture, worship or preaching were preferred over the narrative portions. However, we are now discovering that Scripture is one big narrative of God's kingdom story. The Scripture, our spiritual lives and our learning experience need to be couched in the narrative, God's kingdom story and how our story fits into God's larger story.

From Knowledge to Transformation

In the past we too often thought that the goal of communication was more knowledge. If we had more knowledge in our minds, we would use that knowledge for good. However, we have seen that knowledge by itself is not enough. In the emerging culture, hopefully we as Christians are learning that the true goal is not more knowledge but transformation. We need our hearts changed, not just our minds filled.

From Inward Focused to Outward Focused

Communication, in modern culture, mostly centered on the self. We would almost always ask the question "What about me?" We are beginning to see that in the emerging culture communication does not center on the individual person but on the community. Hopefully, in the Christian community we are beginning to see that it does not center upon us but upon God and what he wants to accomplish in us and through us in our surrounding communities.

What impact do these communication changes have on worship and preaching?

Worship reorientation. Worship is described in Romans as presenting our whole beings as living sacrifices to God because of his mercy. These living sacrifices are a spiritual act of worship (Rom 12:1). Sally Morgenthaler describes worship as follows:

> Worship is a two-way communication between believers and God, a dialogue of response involving both actions and speech. God reveals His presence; our need for intimacy is met and we respond in thanksgiving and praise. God speaks through the Word; we are convicted and repent. God extends mercy through Jesus Christ; we respond with

adoration. In other words, real worship provides opportunities for
God and God's people to express their love for each other.[38]

God speaks to us in the language of picture images: shepherd,
divine warrior, father, mother, spouse. Why are we so quick to sap
these powerful pictures by reducing them to the abstract concepts of
a systematic theology? If anything, an evangelical postmodern
reading of the Bible can instill in our hearts a sense of mystery that
bows before a God we can know.

TREMPER LONGMAN, *MARS HILL REVIEW*

I do not think many of us (modern or postmodern) would disagree with
this definition of worship. So why all the fuss? Part of our worship battles
are due to a lack of understanding of worship idioms in the past. Changes
in worship were part of the radical change of the Reformation. People like
Martin Luther freely used "secular" melodies in his religious songs. "The
style of worship songs that Martin Luther introduced was radical for his day.
Luther made use of melodies from popular folk songs which were seen as
irreverent by established church authorities. Generations later they are considered a traditional, standardized form of conservative evangelical
worship."[39]

While people like Luther were borrowing from the culture, other Re-
formers were trying to stamp out the idols and corruption they saw in the
Catholic Church. Kathi Allen describes this action.

> During the Reformation, the link between artistic and sacred was sev-
> ered in the Protestant church. Overzealous reformers, attempting to
> purge the church of idols and corrupt practices, destroyed centuries
> of religious art. . . . Singing and instrumentation nearly ceased. While
> singing and limited instrumentation returned fairly quickly, other art
> forms were suspect and scorned.[40]

In the early 1800s Charles Finney began to Americanize Protestant worship in the United States. His motivation was one of pragmatism—whatever is needed to save souls. He was trying to meet people where they were in their culture. "Choirs and organs appeared in churches whose Reformed and Puritan ancestors had once banished them. Pulpits were whittled down in size to simple lecterns for holding a Bible and the preacher's notes. The sacramental furniture was almost hidden from view."[41]

Today, like during the Reformation and during the frontier days of the early 1800s, worship is at the forefront of many battles over how the church should relate to the surrounding culture. Many people, like Rick Warren, are asking which of our cherished worship traditions we should retain. "We invite the unchurched to come and sit on 17th century chairs (which we call pews), sing 18th century songs (which we call hymns) and listen to a 19th century instrument (a pipe organ)."[42] One could also add "and hear a twentieth-century reasoned argument (which we call a sermon)."

An emerging-culture worship service may diverge from a traditional service. But remember that in Bach's day some of his works were not traditional enough for many people. Some worship styles that speak to people in the emerging culture will probably cause ripples in many Christian communities. Steve Hayner describes some of these possible changes.

As for worship, this is a generation raised on MTV, fast-moving, visually oriented, media excellence. We don't need to provide this kind of experience, but there is a need to recognize new forms, new instrumentation (organs have given way to synthesizers, and guitars have given way to instrumental ensembles), and new music styles. The traditional hymns don't have to be abandoned, but for this generation, "Holy, Holy, Holy" may need an African drum accompaniment or a reggae beat. It is also key in worship to recognize [young people's] need for personal connection, personal healing, and personal experience. The facades of another generation's Sunday morning ritual exercises will not do. Worship must touch the heart as well as the head.[43]

As we will see more fully in the next chapter, worship today is a critical factor for many people along their spiritual journey in becoming a Christian. For most people in the emerging culture, *experience or belonging* comes before *believing* in their journey to becoming a Christian. They need to experience community and God. What better place to do both than in Christian worship? Andy Park expresses his excitement about the role worship has in the conversion process:

> I see worship as a major factor in bringing people along this continuum from unbelief toward knowing God. With the added factors of hearing biblical truth and having friends who can personally interact with them, worship is a powerful tool for convincing and convicting

---

You can't legislate a change in attitude. So to walk into a church on a Sunday morning, where people (from different ethnic groupings) are trying to live harmoniously draws people. For many of the African Americans they walk in and see that white people are on our turf. It is (white) people coming to the south side of Madison, into a predominantly African American church saying "we want to understand you better." I think what is unique about our worship experience is that in Christian circles, when we talk about multi-ethnicity, it's mainly white Christians talking about bringing others in. It's a lot different when you have someone who is from an ethnic minority culture, in my case African American, saying "we want to be more inclusive." It does have a different flavor because we have firsthand experience in what it feels like to not be appreciated and not be included. So we are wanting to be more sensitive in making others feel included. I think that adds another twist, for people to walk in and to hear someone of another culture say "we value you."

ALEX GEE, PASTOR OF FOUNTAIN OF LIFE

people of God's existence and his love for them. Many people have told me that their crucial turning point of becoming Christians has been during worship times.[44]

For a number of people, it is not embracing new forms of worship but recapturing ancient elements of worship—the sacraments of baptism and Communion—that cause excitement. These two sacraments embody the gospel message and create a captivating image of the gospel. Andy Crouch describes the crucial nature of the sacraments as follows:

> The sacraments answer the postmodern hunger for a true story after modernity's impoverished recital of facts and figures. Week after week, they allow us to revisit the story of the Christian gospel—another's death for the sake of our life. But they do so in a uniquely comprehensive way, bringing us the words, images, sounds, tastes, and smells of that story—the splashing of water, the sound of a breaking loaf of matzo, the pouring of wine.[45]

While some people will be drawn to the forms of worship in the emerging culture, many others will be drawn to the ethnic diversity of many churches in the emerging culture, such as Mosaic in Los Angeles. Worship is the primary activity of many of the multiethnic and multigenerational churches in the emerging culture.

Worship is what can bring multiethnic communities together. As Matt Redman explains,

> Worship creates community and outreach, not the other way around. It is the core ministry of the church out of which all others flow. . . . Without a compelling awareness in worship of the presence of the God who draws all nations to himself, there is not enough motivation to form a lasting and meaningful multi-ethnic Christian community.[46]

As we have seen, worship is a critical element of the church in the emerging culture. Here are some of the key characteristics of worship in the emerging culture.

IMAGINATIVE WORSHIP: EMERGING CHARACTERISTICS

GOD FOCUSED
In a culture that is still focused upon ourselves, we need to make sure our focus is centered on God. We are called to worship God with our whole beings.

COMMUNITY BASED
Our worship is not primarily based upon our own individual identity but rather on our community identity as a church.

AUTHENTIC
While excellence in our worship may be helpful, authenticity is much more important to God and to seekers in our midst. We need to be real people who are able to share all our emotions.

PARTICIPATION BY ALL
In worship our purpose is not centered on performance by a few but participation by all. We are all to present our bodies as living sacrifices.

USE OF ALL OUR SENSES AND TRADITIONS
We need to make sure we are open to the use of all our senses in worship and open to other traditions with which we might not at first feel comfortable.

CHANGING OUR HEART
Worship should change our heart as well as our mind. Our different traditions tend to emphasize one over the other. God calls us to emphasize both heart and mind.

WITNESS TO THE SURROUNDING COMMUNITIES
Worship can be a powerful witness in the emerging culture with its desire to belong, openness to spirituality and need to experience God. As we consider the forms of our worship, we should not primarily consider our own interests but rather what forms of worship would connect with the surrounding communities.

The communication task is more than the mere use of words. Communication is the reception of words and perceptions by the listener in a cognitive, intuitive and emotional level.

Aristotle spoke of the *"logos"*—the words, *"ethos"*—the motive of the speaker and *"pathos"*—an emotional appeal to the audience. For modern listeners, preaching was the age of the logos, the words. For 21st century listeners preaching must value the ethos and pathos as well.

Any hope for involvement must start with the attitude (ethos) of the preacher. No one cares how much we know until he knows how much we care.

The sermon creates a clash of cultures: the culture of Christ with its norms and values and the postmodern culture with its own norms and values. (Let us make sure we don't have a clash with a 3rd culture, modern culture.) For the logos of the Christian Message to connect with the contemporary listener, the preacher must first enter the listener's sphere of postmodern understanding.

Before we can begin to bring meaning and relevance to the listener, the preacher must gain entry into his or her sphere of understanding. This speaks of the incarnational ministry of Christ, who first entered our realm so that we might enter His realm. Listeners become involved as they sense the speaker's involvement in their lives.

GRAHAM JOHNSTON, *PREACHING IN A POSTMODERN WORLD*

PREACHING REORIENTATION

As we have needed to think about new forms of worship in the emerging culture, so also we need to think about a reorientation of new forms or methods of preaching. Preaching in the emerging culture will need to take into account that we are living more and more in a world that starts with subjective truth (preferences), not objective truth, as its beginning. People in the emerging culture are at the same time committed to community and suspicious of people in authority. Furthermore, it is a culture that resonates with image more than word. It is composed of a people who see the world more from a cynical (despairing) viewpoint than a progressive (optimistic) viewpoint. With these cultural characteristics, how do we as Christians speak into this context?

Instead of an exercise in transferring information so that people have a coherent well-informed worldview or belief system, preaching in the emerging culture aims at inspiring transformation. . . . Preaching becomes less and less a well reasoned argument, and more and more a shared practice among preacher and hearers. The preacher becomes less scholar and more sage, less lecturer and more poet plus prophet.

BRIAN McLAREN, *LEADERSHIP,* SUMMER 2003

In the past, homiletical theory started with the assumption that there should be a gap between the preacher and the congregation. This distance symbolized the gap between God and his people. The preacher was charged with speaking the truth from God. He (usually not she) was God's representative to the people. It is intriguing to me that this tradition of setting apart of the preacher from the congregation in the Protestant tradition originated during the Reformation, because the Reformation was primarily about lessening the distance between God and his people. David Lose challenges us to have a new paradigm of preaching as conversation.

By envisioning preaching as a conversation we hope to eliminate this gap. Both the preacher and hearer are members of one body of faith, the same priesthood of all believers. . . . Conversational preaching is more like a conversation among friends, more representative of the diversity of those gathered together and more inviting of their response. Noting that homily is derived from the Greek word for conversation, preaching should nurture the community's conversation about meaning in light of their life together and shared tradition.[47]

Story becomes an important vehicle to communicate the Scriptures. While in the modern world we in the church concentrated more on the letters of Paul in the New Testament and the prophetical books of the Old Testament, in the emerging culture we will probably need to spend more time in the Gospels and the historical books of the Old Testament. Preachers need to set the biblical story they are preaching into both the larger context of God's redemptive story and into the congregation's context. Brian McLaren describes what this might look like.

> An effective pastor today must be a teller of The Story—Genesis to Revelation Story—not just a good storyteller. This means that all communication must be done in light of the whole story of what God has promised to do, has done and is doing. . . . A story does something that no abstract proposition can ever do. It stops you in your tracks and makes you think. It catches your attention and won't let you go. . . . When pastors preach narrative passages from the Bible, they are not doing it to illustrate a point. The story is the point.[48]

Not only do people need to hear the stories—and the Story—of the Bible, they also need to hear the hope that is imbedded in the gospel story. They live in a world without hope. Graham Johnston expresses the hope this way.

> Today's preaching must hold our hope in Christ, a hope that can satisfy people's longing for certainty and shatter their cynicism. The tension for postmodern listeners lies between the heart and the mind. The mind tells them that nothing is real or trustworthy; but the heart still longs for the clarity of meaning and purpose.[49]

Preachers need also to demonstrate that hope in their own life. The preachers need to be honest and appropriately vulnerable in their public and private conversations in the church. We need to demonstrate that we are human. We need to share our own joys and suffering in our spiritual journey. We need to share that we are fellow travelers with others in the congregation. We are on a spiritual journey together as a community.

Here is a summary of some of the foundational characteristics of preaching in an emerging culture context.

NARRATIVE PREACHING: EMERGING CHARACTERISTICS

PART OF A LARGER WORSHIP EXPERIENCE

Instead of being the primary attraction in our worship services today, preaching (though still important) should be a part of the larger worship experience.

MULTIPLE PREACHING VOICES

To recognize that it is God's Word, not the preacher, that is authoritative and to recognize that God has gifted multiple people with the gift of preaching/teaching, we need multiple preaching voices in our congregation.

DEVELOPMENT OF TRUST WITH AUDIENCE

Since positional authority is less important in the emerging culture, the preacher needs to develop trust with the audience over time to be effective. The preacher needs to share stories from his or her own life journey so that the congregation can identify with the messenger and the message.

CONVERSATIONAL STYLE

So that people can identify with the speaker and be willing to respond to the message, the speaker needs to emphasize a more conversational than oratory style of preaching.

USE OF WORD AND IMAGE

As we move more and more to an image-based culture, we need to recognize that image is a critical way that God has communicated since the beginning of time. As communicators of God's Word, we need to make sure we also make use of image to not only meet people where they are but also to communicate God's story.

CONNECT AUDIENCE'S STORY WITH GOD'S KINGDOM STORY
People today need to see both that God is relevant to their own life situation and that their life is part of a much bigger picture. They need a vision of God's kingdom story.

MISSIONALLY FOCUSED
A large part of God's kingdom story is God's mission. In our preaching we need to make sure we do not only immerse ourselves in either our individual or our church's life. We need to make sure we focus on God's mission and God's role for us in accomplishing his mission.

SUMMARY
If we are going to assist emerging-culture people in their spiritual journeys, we need to develop strategies and methodologies specific to them. In some ways Baby Boomers are more like the rich young ruler who found that he overpacked for his journey and needed to jettison some of his gear. Jesus' advice to him was clear. "One thing you lack. . . . Go, sell everything you have and give to the poor, and you will have treasure in heaven. Then come, follow me" (Mk 10:21). Boomers need to jettison many things along their spiritual journey.

People in a postmodern world already feel that they have less of everything. Their problem is not that they have too many possessions. They are running on empty and may not be able to start the trip. They can identify with the prodigal son who feels unworthy to come home: "Father, I have sinned against heaven and against you. I am no longer worthy to be called your son" (Lk 15:21). People in the emerging culture need to hear the father's response time and time again on their journey. "'Let's have a feast and celebrate. For this son of mine was dead and is alive again; he was lost and is found.' So they began to celebrate" (Lk 15:23-24). Emerging-culture people will need to have their gas tanks filled many times along their spiritual journey. They need to hear the message of hope continuously in worship and preaching.

IMPLICATIONS FOR MINISTRY

We need to help those we minister among, especially those of the younger generations, to see the Christian life as a spiritual journey with twists and turns along the way. In the past the church has sometimes understood maturing in the Christian faith as doing certain things and not doing other things. In a postmodern culture the maturing process cannot be contained in a tidy package. The younger generations to follow will have to work through a lot of internal baggage to mature. Outward behavior will carry little validity in the absence of inward change. Therefore, we need to reexamine the discipleship strategies we use to make sure they are suitable for assisting people in their growth as Christians. Cookie-cutter programs will not be of much use to us.

Areas that might need attention include the following:

- overcoming shame through God's love and acceptance

- appreciating family in the light of our new family in Christ

- understanding our sexuality by seeing God's design for us

- accepting our self-image by seeing that we are created in God's image

- obtaining an overview of Scripture to appreciate God's story

- finding opportunities to serve in order to feel a part of the community

- providing eternal hope in the midst of pain and suffering

Our worship and teaching experiences need to assist in these areas.

In the past we have often discipled on a one-to-one basis. Some of my staff have found that a better method of discipling is in clusters of from two to four. A community can form from these clusters that encourage the people to be open and intimidate them less than a one-to-one relationship might. Fellow people in the cluster can hold each other accountable. The structure needs to include more mentoring than teaching. Modeling and dialoguing are key components of mentoring relationships.

We need to warn people in the emerging culture that the spiritual journey will be difficult and frustrating at times. We need to be honest about the ups and downs of the spiritual journey. Patience and hope are key qualities for the mentor as well as for the person being mentored. The journey may be long, but it is rewarding. One of the greatest joys in my life is observing a person who has been struggling suddenly see the light and start to move ahead in the spiritual journey. All of us need to understand that the journey takes a lifetime. However, our destination is secured and our hope is a certainty, not just a wish.

Communities Offering Hope

When I arrived at Chicago's O'Hare Airport for the Trinity Seminary-sponsored conference titled "Telling the Truth," I was picked up in a limousine because of my role as a speaker. I was glad it wasn't a real limousine, because that would have been embarrassing. But it was a nice car with a twenty-five-year-old driver who I will call Jane. I began asking Jane a few questions, and during the twenty-minute drive from O'Hare to Trinity, I listened to her share her life story.

She told me that she was estranged from her family. Her father was both a workaholic and an alcoholic. She had an okay relationship with her mom, but her mom was kind of flighty and really wasn't available for her. Her mom wanted to be her friend and not her mother. For a long time the daughter liked that and then realized that she needed a mom. She needed some guidance. Her father never showed emotion. They never said they loved her, and so she basically didn't connect emotionally with her family. She got involved in a relationship that didn't go well, became pregnant and had a child. Six years later, she was engaged to be married to somebody who was thirty-five and had his own ten-year-old child. She was determined to marry only once.

When Jane dropped me off, she thanked me for listening to her story. She said that she had driven two other groups of people to the conference, and when she got to the point where she mentioned having a six-year-old child without being married, the conversation kind of dried up.

If we are going to work within the emerging culture, we can't be shocked. Jane's is a fairly mild story compared to some of the things you're facing within your church or on your college campus. We need to be people who will listen and allow others to share their story. Then we need to help them place their story into the larger context of God's story. One of my prayers at the end of the conference was that Jane would be my driver back to the airport. And if she was, I think I would have earned the right—her trust—to be able to share God's story with her as we headed back to the airport. If I did not get a chance to do that (which I did not), then hopefully somebody else along the way in her life will. Because I listened to her story, someone will be able to share with her how her story fits into the larger gospel message.

What I have just described to you is narrative evangelism. It was actually over twenty years ago that I first heard a narrative evangelism presentation. At that time I did not have a label for the experience. The year was 1982 and I was helping to lead a campuswide evangelism event with Billy Graham sponsored by InterVarsity Christian Fellowship at UNC-Chapel Hill.

Billy Graham stepped up to the podium to speak and then just stood there for a few seconds, not knowing what to say. All seven thousand students and faculty at UNC-Chapel Hill that Tuesday night in September 1982 sat stunned. It was probably one of the few times that Billy Graham had ever been at a loss for words. Finally he said, "I am not sure there is any more I can say. You have just witnessed one of the most articulate presentations of the gospel you will ever hear." This remarkable presentation had been made by Doris Betts, chairperson of the UNC faculty council, as she shared her Christian story that evening. What follows is an excerpt from her story.

> I am not one of those for whom faith has been easy, or ecstatic; nor one who knows faith through a Damascus experience, but one who has had to work at it, who will probably always have to work at it.
>
> So when at eighteen I went away to college, I was not only ripe to lose my inherited, habitual Christianity—I was dying to get rid of its weight and mental encumbrance. At that time I thought I saw clearly what some of Flannery O'Connor's self-righteous women characters see—I saw that Jesus Christ appealed to the losers, the weak, the

dumb of this world, but not to Miss Pharisee of 1954. Did I lose my faith at college? Lose it! I threw it! I flung it away. I gladly dumped it into two containers: a small wastebasket marked Cultural Anthropology, and a large dumpster called Intellectual Pride. . . .

What changed me is a long, private story. I will only say that it took many years, that it was no sudden mountain-top experience, that it came to a climax at a helpless moment when my intellect alone had tried everything else and had given up.

Do you know the story of the solitary mountain climber whose pitons broke out and left him swinging by a rope alone over a chasm thousands of feet straight down? He tried everything. As a last resort he shouted a prayer for God to save him. From overhead a voice suddenly answered him: "This is God; I have heard you, my son, and will save you; just let go of the rope." The climber hung in astonished silence. Again the commanding voice came from above: "This is God; trust me that your prayer has been heard—just let go of the rope." Finally the climber called uneasily: "Listen, is anybody else up there?"

For me, nobody else was up there, and I let go of the rope. Thus I came back to faith and to the church not from fear and guilt, but in thanksgiving, because my prayers, like the climber's, got answered. At that time I hadn't even settled the question of God's existence yet, much less the Christ and his cross.

God gave to the descendants of the apostle Thomas that worrisome, sensitive, aggravating, questioning and doubting intellect; at its best, it is a part of his image. And to us, too, when we are hanging by a slender thread over the chasm of what we cannot solve and do not understand, to us in our helplessness the good news of God's love in Christ comes down and speaks to the strongest, most intricate, most prideful intellect.

The amazing thing is that for everyone, of whatever IQ, whatever gift, whatever income or sex or class or race or station—for all of us there is a moment when God offers us his love one more time.

At the moment when we accept that love with thanks, when we can let go of the rope, then, for the first time, we are really free to fly.[1]

NARRATIVE EVANGELISM

Although none of us fully understood what we were hearing at the time, I am convinced that the conversion story Doris was sharing with us occurred in the transition between the Enlightenment/modern era and the emerging/ postmodern culture. She had grown up and rejected the Christ of the rational Enlightenment era. But then she came to accept Christ in the meaninglessness of the postmodern era. The idiom she was using to share her story was what we then called a testimony; now we call it narrative evangelism. Doris was placing her story in the context of God's story. She was providing plausibility for the Christian faith, not defending its credibility. She shared in a context that allowed faculty and many students to see the authenticity of the Christian faith lived out in everyday life.

> *Beginning in the 1990s people have instinctively come to distrust universal claims and are longing for more visible evidence of truth. In other words, they long for plausibility. It is not that people are disinterested in what is true. It is just that they are more interested in what is believable.*
>
> WILLIAM DYRNESS, "WHAT IS GOD'S TRUTH?"

The church in the postmodern era must continue to tell the "old, old story" of the gospel. However, the church needs to start telling the story by helping others to consider the plausibility and authenticity of the gospel, not by making a rational defense of its credibility. Narrative evangelism merges "our story" with "God's story" through sharing it with others. Narrative evangelism is preferred in a postmodern context. Since it is more personal, the story invites others to enter into it.[2] Today many people make commitments to Christ based on stories that seem coherent and ring true to them.[3]

Stories are an important postmodern method of communication.[4] Remember that the postmodern era includes no commitment to absolute truth. Truth is established through the tribal groups to which one belongs. In ancient times the essence of a tribe was communicated by a story form that was handed down from generation to generation within the community. What held a community together was the shared story. The Israelites shared that tradition as they handed down their story from generation to generation to encourage the community to remain faithful to God. Time and time again in the Old Testament, "Yahweh's people's story" is handed down. Joshua said to all the people,

> This is what the LORD, the God of Israel, says: "Long ago your forefathers, including Terah the father of Abraham and Nahor, lived beyond the River and worshiped other gods. But I took your father Abraham from the land beyond the River and led him throughout Canaan and gave him many descendants." . . .
>
> Then the people answered, "Far be it from us to forsake the LORD to serve other gods!" (Josh 24:2-3, 16)

Conflict came into the community when the people's account of the story differed from God's account. That conflict is illustrated in the book of Habakkuk. The Israelites were convinced that part of God's story was that Jerusalem would never be defeated, since the temple in Jerusalem was the seat of God's throne. However, Habakkuk (around 600 B.C.) could see the handwriting on the wall. Barring some miraculous intervention, Jerusalem was going to fall to the Babylonians. Habakkuk cried out to God continually as he tried to make sense of God's actions. At one point Habakkuk became so frustrated that he exclaimed to God,

> I will stand at my watch
>   and station myself on the ramparts;
> I will look to see what he will say to me,
>   and what answer I am to give to this complaint. (Hab 2:1)

Eventually Habakkuk had to adapt his understanding of the story to God's account of the story concerning Jerusalem.

The goal of narrative evangelism is similar to the dialogue between God and Habakkuk: to help the people you are talking with adapt their life stories to be more in line with God's story. The story that the Christian community adopts is Jesus' story—Jesus' life. Thus to become a Christian (to convert) is to adopt the story of Christ so that we become part of the story line.[5] Our story becomes a part of Jesus' story. As Leighton Ford describes the process, "The Story that there is a God who cares about the individual human being is an old message—but it has been given a new attractiveness, a new plausibility in our time. Our Postmodern generations are more ready than ever to hear this Story with new ears—Why? Because of the emptiness and brokenness of Postmodern life."[6]

The conversion process in narrative evangelism can be called a "collision of narratives."[7] When God's story touches our story, a collision takes place. When we encounter a story that calls into question part of our story, we need to reconsider our story. We may not like the process, because it can shake our equilibrium. That certainly happened to Habakkuk. Doris Betts's story disturbed the equilibrium of a number of her colleagues because through Doris God's story had collided with their story. One of my friends on the faculty, who is not a Christian, had his story shaken that night. He told me afterward that if they had asked for people willing to make a commitment to Christ following Doris's story, he would have "signed up." In the emerging culture, where absolute truth is not a given and is rarely considered as an option, our evangelism and apologetics will need to take a different direction.

EMBODIED APOLOGETICS

Since we are entering (or have already arrived in) this postmodern culture, the ground rules for engaging our culture with the gospel of Jesus Christ need to change. The gospel—the good news about Jesus Christ—is changeless and eternal. However, the way we go about proclaiming the gospel and defending it does need to change. Strategies for evangelism that were successful ten years ago are no longer as effective, with a few isolated exceptions.

In 1982, when the InterVarsity Christian Fellowship student group at UNC-Chapel Hill sponsored the weeklong evangelistic outreach with Billy Graham, over three-quarters of the undergraduate student body (ten thousand students) attended at least one event. In many ways it was a highly successful week. But if we were to undertake a similar outreach now, we would probably make many changes. The size of the event would probably need to be scaled back. The theme, "A Reason to Live," would also need to be changed. The theme was appropriate for a student generation (Baby Boomers) that grappled with truth questions and desired a rational presentation of the gospel. Today I would probably call the outreach "An Offering of Hope." Why change the theme?

Up until the last fifteen years, Christian apologists successfully employed a rational defense of Christian truths to defend the faith against Enlightenment attacks. Enlightenment thinkers might not agree that there was universal truth, but they did agree that there was truth. Our approach to apologetics assumed that we were dealing with individuals who had a cohesive view of truth. So the two sides in the debate could engage each other using objective truth as common ground. Evangelism then was concerned with persuading people of the cognitive truth of the gospel. Truth in this paradigm was understood as propositional correctness, with a call for acceptance (exemplified by the title of the book *Evidence That Demands a Verdict*).[8]

Some in the Christian household of faith do not seem to realize that a major cultural paradigm shift is taking place. However, such changes are not always easy to recognize as they are occurring. George Hunter helps us with this lagging recognition when he states, "The pillars of 'modern' western civilization erected during the Enlightenment are now crumbling. . . . We are now in a period of culture lag—in which most people in the western world are not yet as aware as scientists and philosophers that the Enlightenment is over."[9]

But nobody can live in the past. If we do not engage the changes that are taking place, our chances of reaching the emerging culture with the gospel of Jesus Christ will be greatly diminished. George Barna predicted, "Our projections are that unless things change significantly in the church and the culture, people in the emerging culture are less likely to accept Christ as their savior than prior generations. . . . These are the first generations raised without the assumption that Christ is the starting place for religious expectations."[10]

Postmodern culture has discarded any notion of universal truth and recognizes only preferences. All claims to universal truth are equally valid. Alister McGrath writes, "There is no universal or privileged vantage points that allow anyone to decide what is right and what is wrong. . . . All belief systems are to be regarded as equally plausible."[11] Many evangelicals are in a quandary. We have been taught to follow the apologetic path set forth in 1 Peter 3:15, "Always be prepared to give an answer to everyone who asks you to give the reason for the hope that you have." Today we need to emphasize the hope within us more than the reason.

Many evangelicals are poised to give an answer even though no one is asking the question.[12] Some people are trying to hold on to the Enlightenment era. Ravi Zacharias, a leading evangelical apologist, states that "postmodernism is dangerous not because of what it has done to the secular person, but because it destroys our apologetic, our methods for determining truth."[13] If it is true that our past apologetic methods have been destroyed or severely hampered, is it good to keep holding to the past? Isn't it better to adopt new apologetic methods for a new era, a new emerging culture?

In postmodern times what people hear will be drowned out by what they see in the lives of Christians. People today are weary of words. . . . The focus needs to move from the credibility of the faith, that something is claimed true intellectually speaking, to the plausibility of the faith, that something is experienced as true in the way we live. This is where postmodern people live and this emphasis cannot be understated. . . . We need to indwell the ministry rather than looking at it from the outside. But for this to happen it is clear that this "indwelling" must mean being part of the community whose life is shaped by the story which the Bible tells.

GRAHAM JOHNSTON, *PREACHING IN A POSTMODERN WORLD*

Pastors, campus workers and youth workers who deal with people under the age of forty are seeing a need to adapt. Jeffery Dietrich, a pastor in New Hampshire who works with young seekers, described difficulties in evangelism today:

> One of the problems I have with the Four Spiritual Laws is that it makes the assumption that people believe in absolutes, and they don't. The presupposition is that they're going to accept truth, and they don't. We've had a seekers group in our home. When we open the Scriptures, these people don't accept the Scripture. They think my sermons are wonderful, but if I say something they disagree with they say "well that's his opinion." . . . They want to dialogue about things. They want a relationship.[14]

Over three-quarters of all young people reject any notion of absolute moral truth, favoring a relative view of right and wrong.[15] Therefore we need to lead people to discover the truth for themselves instead of telling them what to believe. People in the emerging culture do not like being told anything. However, they are willing to discuss things. They are suspicious of people who arrogantly claim to know the truth.

> *In the movie The Matrix Neo wanted to learn the secret of the matrix, he was told you have to experience it to know it. This represents a significant shift from modernity which suggested that one's subjective feelings were fallible and unreliable in discerning truth.*
>
> CHUCK SMITH, *THE END OF THE WORLD . . . AS WE KNOW IT*

The Socratic method of evangelism represents an inductive approach. Postmodern people take delight in dialogue and discussion. They take joy in the process of discovering truth for themselves with the assistance of others in community. In the Socratic method of evangelism, the discussion leader poses a question and then allows people to explain what they think the answer is. The leader continues to ask questions, probing for deeper meaning of the idea or the passage the group is discussing. The Socratic method works best when the leader has a thorough grasp of the material and is able to ask probing and directive questions while fielding questions from the group. It is also important that the leader has already established a trust relationship with the people in the group.[16] The Socratic method is not a hit-and-run evangelistic technique but a long-term conversation in which all participants, including the leader, are stretched.[17]

Most people under thirty rarely ask, "What do you think?" They ask instead, "How do you feel?" Thus this is the question that our apologetics needs to answer. Some evangelicals are so steeped in the rational apologetic mindset that they consider any alternative to be heretical. However, we need to remember that apologetics is a defense of the faith that is appropriate for the contemporary secular mindset. For some people a rational apologetic is still needed. However, we should not hold on to a rational apologetic only because many of us are comfortable with it.

Examining the first-century Hebrew and Greek mindset might help us in our quandary. Have you ever wondered why Jesus primarily used stories while Paul primarily used rational arguments? The answer lies in the difference between Hebrew and Greek thought. Greek thought was static, emphasizing contemplation or thinking, while Hebrew thought was dynamic, emphasizing action. Greek thought was more abstract, while Hebrew thought was more concrete. Greek thought looked at the individual component, thereby splitting heart and mind, while Hebrew thought looked at the totality of the whole, thereby combining the heart and mind.[18] Jesus spoke in story form because it captured the imagination of Hebrew people. Paul, on the other hand, spoke in abstractions that engaged the Greek mind. Also, the Greeks emphasized the individual, while the Hebrews emphasized community.

It would not be inaccurate to compare the Enlightenment with Greek thought while comparing postmodernism with Hebrew thought. If this assumption is correct, evangelists desiring to reach postmodern generations may need to spend more time in the Gospels and in those Old Testament narratives that the postmodern mindset can more easily identify with.

Like the Hebrews of old, whose hearts Jesus tried to reach through storytelling, postmodernists will be reached primarily through the heart rather than the mind. Even Ravi Zacharias admits that the intellectual questions eventually turn to questions of the heart at the universities where he lectures. The intellect of the average college student today is intertwined with the heart.[19] That is consistent with Hebrew thought, which connects the intellect and the heart. As Philip Kenneson states,

> *In a postmodern world the most effective witness to a world of disconnected people is the church that forms community and embodies the reality of the new society. People in a postmodern world are not persuaded to faith by reason as much as they are moved to faith by participation in God's earthly community.*
>
> ROBERT WEBBER, *ANCIENT-FUTURE FAITH*

If we could unequivocally prove to people that the proposition that God exists is objectively true, the inhabitants of our culture would yawn [Xers and Millennials would say, "So what?" or, "Why ask why?"] and return to their pagan slumbers. What our world is waiting for, and what the church seems reluctant to offer, is not more incessant talk about objective truth, but an embodied witness that clearly demonstrates why anyone should care about any of this in the first place. . . . Our non-Christian neighbors are right in refusing to accept what we say we believe but which our lives make a lie. If the claim Jesus is Lord of the Universe is true, one must have a concrete historical community who by their words and deeds narrate the story in a way that gives some substance to it.[20]

The most urgent apologetic task before us is to live our lives in community in such a way that those around us will come and ask, "Why are you different? What keeps you going? What is the hope in your heart?" We still have to be "prepared to give an answer to everyone who asks you to give the reason for the hope that you have" (1 Pet 3:15). But as I have said, now we emphasize the hope that resides in the heart rather than reasoning.

We need to provide entrances for those who are not yet Christians to inquire without feeling threatened. One way to do this is through "porch evangelism." "Porches" are transitional spaces where we invite friends to observe and participate without becoming too involved. Remember from chapter eight that Myers describes the "porch" as the significant social space in the community. The "porches" can be open dinners, social events or sporting events.

Although these postmodern generations might not be looking for the truth, they are looking for what is real. One reason for the popularity of the MTV shows *Real World* and *Road Rules* as well as CBS's *Survivor* is that they attempt to portray real life as it is, including the good, the bad and the ugly. Our apologetic to the emerging culture world needs to emphasize an inclusive community that welcomes others so that they can observe the reality of the Christian faith. A postmodern apologetic also needs to emphasize a loving community that reaches out to the needy and the hurting. Last, a postmodern apologetic needs to emphasize the hope we have—that God will prevail and that there will be a new heaven and a new earth.

The Great Commission was a biblical mandate that resonated in the modern era. "Jesus came to them and said, 'All authority in heaven and on earth has been given to me. Therefore go and make disciples of all nations, baptizing them in the name of the Father and of the Son and of the Holy Spirit, and teaching them to obey everything I have commanded you. And surely I am with you always, to the very end of the age' " (Mt 28:18-20). The Great Commission is centered upon truth (teaching) and self (disciples), and it implies a view of human progress.

However, a new mandate might be needed for the postmodern era, possibly the Great Commandment: " 'Love the Lord your God with all your heart and with all your soul and with all your mind.' This is the first and greatest commandment. And the second is like it: 'Love your neighbor as yourself.' All the Law and the Prophets hang on these two commandments" (Mt 22:37-40). The Great Commandment focuses on relationships (neighbor) and community. It implies human frailty or misery, which need a loving environment. It also implies the presence of God in the process. Humankind is not left to its own initiative.

> *The church must pray for us to see ourselves as the whole body and escape the self-centered, needs-based Christianity that asks questions like, "Am I being fed?" or "Are my spiritual needs being met?" Let us ask instead, "Are we loving God and our neighbor?" We must become immersed in the culture without caving into it.*
>
> CHRIS SEAY, "EAST MEETS WEST"

The apologetic to the emerging culture needs to be one that is lived out in a faithful community, demonstrates an active love and offers eternal hope. This embodied apologetic finds its theme in Colossians 1:4-5: "We have heard of your *faith* in Christ Jesus and of the *love* you have for all the saints—the faith and love that spring from the *hope* that is stored up for you in heaven" (emphasis added). Let us look more closely at each of these three components.

FAITHFUL COMMUNITY

The community of faith is the basis of Christian apologetics today. Even the most intellectually convincing rational apologetic may receive a response of "So what?" The church today must establish its plausibility before it even begins to talk about the credibility of the Christian faith. Its plausibility is established as it puts faith into action. "Postmoderns can best understand a holy, loving, just, forgiving, life-giving God of grace when they see a holy, just, forgiving, life-giving community founded on the grace of God. . . . The church becomes the plausibility structure of the Christian world."[21] People in the emerging culture cannot be convinced by rational argument, because they do not believe in absolute truth. However, because of their commitment to community, they are impressed with the truth lived out in community. This demonstration of the truth in community is convincing to a postmodern mindset. Therefore, evangelism is only possible when the community doing the evangelism lives out the Christian message. The medium is the message.

> *One of the common terms to label non-Christians is "lost people." Sometimes I wonder if we would be wiser to apply the term lost to ourselves. God has sent us into the world as ambassadors and agents of God's love. Yet many of us have never really arrived in the world—our destination. So in that light who is lost, them or us?*
>
> BRIAN McLAREN, *MORE READY THAN YOU REALIZE*

Eddie was the major dorm drug pusher, the leader of a gang made up of some of the rougher guys in the dorm. Almost everyone in the dorm, except probably Mary and Andy, knew about Eddie. Then Mary and Andy, who were part of an InterVarsity small group in Eddie's dorm, decided to befriend him. They were influenced to do this by their group study of Luke 15, which describes God's concern for the lost. Eddie had thought that anyone who befriended him wanted drugs, yet Mary and Andy did not seem to want anything other than friendship.

After a while Mary and Andy invited Eddie to a few outings with their small group. Eddie recognized most of the members of the small group, since they lived in his dorm. Eddie knew that the members of this group were Christians, but he did not make a connection between their kindness toward him and their Christian faith. The group members related to each other in a caring, even loving way that he had not seen before. They welcomed Eddie into their midst for what they could give to him, not what they could get from him. As Eddie continued to see the love of this group in action, he was drawn into it and away from his rough friends. Eventually Eddie

---

A highly individualized approach to evangelism separated evangelism from the church. Enlightenment evangelism centers almost exclusively on the change accomplished in the individual. You are saved. You are a new person. You have been born again. Consequently it does not adequately stress the role of the church in the nurturing process of salvation. At conversion a convert has only begun the process of being saved. The church is the community in which the process is encouraged and brought to completion.

ROBERT WEBBER, *ANCIENT-FUTURE FAITH*

---

became a committed follower of Christ. He maintained contact with his old group, trying to share with them what had happened to him. They did not understand the changes in Eddie. What changed Eddie was seeing a community of people caring for each other and then caring for him. That small-group community was the gospel message for Eddie.

The church community was a powerful apologetic for the gospel in first-century Jerusalem. As the onlookers observed the character of the early church community (Acts 2:42-47; 4:32-35), the Lord "added to their number daily those who were being saved" (Acts 2:47). The community of Christ's followers demonstrated a caring for each other that was something new. Families in that era cared exclusively for their own family members. Yet in the church, groups of unrelated followers of Jesus Christ were forming intimate, caring communities. According to Stanley Hauerwas, "The church's most important social task is nothing less than to be a community capable of hearing the story of God we find in the Scripture and living in a manner that is faithful to that story . . . a community capable of forming people with virtues sufficient to witness to God as truth in the world."[22] These small-group communities were visible witnesses of what it means to be a part of the body of Christ, which loves all of its members and loves Christ and demonstrates that love for the triune God through worship.

> As a church we're trying to recover the biblical motif of the suffering body of Christ in order to minister to the suffering body of a postmodern culture. . . . In part this means making a concerted effort to connect with people—the lonely child, the single mom, the prostitute, the drug dealer. Remembering the suffering Christ moves us to embrace the suffering ones among us.
>
> SOONG-CHAN RAH, *LEADERSHIP*, FALL 2000

Jesus stated that the early Christian community was to be characterized by worshiping him and loving each other. For people in the emerging culture, which is open to the supernatural and the transcendent, a dynamic worshiping community is a powerful apologetic for the gospel. Our communities of faith can worship God boldly with glad and sincere hearts because they are assured of the future, even in the midst of present pain and suffering. Dynamic worship services demonstrate the interaction that exists between God and the people of God. Attending a worship service may not be helpful to members of the Boomer generation, who tend to be closed to the supernatural. For emerging-culture people, however, who tend to be fascinated by the supernatural, a dynamic worship service could be a powerful message of the reality of God. The Duke InterVarsity large-group meeting has traditionally been a place where many students who were not yet Christians came to observe and experience dynamic worship. While for some the life of the community is the message, for others the worship of the community is the message.

Whether it likes to or not, the church has always presented itself as a messenger of the gospel. At its worst it presents itself as a community mirroring the disunity of the world by distancing itself from Christians of different racial, cultural or socioeconomic groups. At its best it presents itself as a sign to the world acknowledging the lordship of Christ and seeking to model what it means to live under the guidelines of the divine reign characterized by peace, justice, righteousness and love. By living as a faithful community of followers of Christ, we indicate what the reign of God is like: a community of love.[23]

LOVING COMMUNITY

Jesus did not propose theological knowledge, prayer life, Bible study or leadership responsibilities as the identifying marks of his followers. They would be known by their love. According to Kevin Offner, "the greatest apologetic for Christianity is not a well-reasoned argument but a wildly loving community. Our Lord did not say that they will know us by our truth—as important as this is—but by our love. At the very heart of the gospel is not a proposition but a person, Jesus Christ, who is made manifest in and through his called-out ones in their life together."[24]

> *Community is the lightning rod that attracts postmoderns to participation in the metanarrative. Community is the living, breathing answer to the question of "Is this real?" Through community seekers will be able to ask questions in a safe place.*
>
> ED STETZER, *PLANTING NEW CHURCHES IN A POSTMODERN AGE*

As long as we Christians try to debate postmodern generations from the position that we are right and they are wrong, we will merely turn them off and drive them away. As long as we treat them as souls to be won for our side rather than as human beings who need a touch and a listening ear, we build walls between us. However, if we can weep for the vast majority of emerging-culture people who are experiencing deep pain, and if we can demonstrate compassion to those around us, then we can build bridges.

I like to do my writing in the Davis Library on the UNC-Chapel Hill campus. I sit at a table next to a window overlooking one of the main pathways on campus. I catch myself now and then looking down at the students as they walk to and from classes. I often wonder about their struggles and their pain, sometimes weeping about it. Twenty-five years of campus ministry has not desensitized me to their hurts. We need to demonstrate Jesus' compassion to these postmodern generations—the compassion that Jesus felt for the Israelite people as he stood over Jerusalem and wept for the people in the city below.

God calls us to demonstrate our compassion through performing deeds of love as God's community. Deanne Trollinger, an InterVarsity staff member, tells of an act of kindness that she and some of her students at Salem College have performed on campus.

> Celeste and I headed for Gramley Dorm, along with the others. We had all that we needed: a tall bottle of Dow bubble cleaner, sponges, rags and Drano. We approached a door on the first floor with a bit of apprehension—what would the person behind the door think? We knocked anyway, and as a freshman answered the door, we introduced ourselves and told her that we were a part of Salem's InterVarsity small group. We asked her if we could clean her sink to demonstrate God's love in a practical way. She was apologetic about the filth on her sink and welcomed our scrubbing of it.
>
> Celeste and I scrubbed several more sinks that evening, as did the rest of the women who attended the small group. The sinks were indeed filthy, and the women who had dirtied them asked questions about our group and the reason why we were serving them in such a way. We look forward to cleaning sinks on campus each month in hopes that every student at Salem College can come into contact with the love of Christ.

Little deeds of kindness that lead to deeper compassion are a great apologetic for the gospel in a postmodern world. Those deeds of love at Salem probably did more than any evangelistic talk to open those students' hearts to hear the gospel.

A small group at UNC-Greensboro came up with a similar idea. Mitch White tells the following story:

> "Can I have your trash?" was the sound you heard throughout the dorm one Tuesday night. It was the sound of an all-male InterVarsity

small group in Bailey Dorm going door to door emptying the trash cans of the guys in that dorm. This group had been studying James and had a big discussion about living out their faith. One guy made the statement "This is a great discussion, but what are we going to do about it?" Right then they decided to get up and go serve the guys in the dorm in order to show them God's love in a practical way.

Boy, did they get a response! Many of the guys wouldn't let them touch their trash; many asked, "What are you doing?"

The small group replied honestly, "We've been studying James and decided that we didn't want to just learn but to live out our faith. So we want to serve you by taking out your trash."

This has opened up many doors for this group. As they live in their dorm now, there are doors opened for them to be a part of people's lives. They will physically take out students' trash, but it will lead to opportunities for Christ to take their other garbage.

To gain a hearing in the postmodern world, the gospel must be demonstrated in acts of love as well as being proclaimed through a variety of means. Leighton Ford describes this type of evangelism as follows:

> The Story of God's grace must not only be told in words. We must model an evangelism of grace. We must communicate not only with a clear voice, but with the authentic touch of grace. Our evangelism must be a hands-on evangelism, in which we roll up our sleeves and dare to touch human lives. Our voice must be clear and our touch must be real.[25]

A great way to touch others with God's grace is by participating in volunteer opportunities. No matter what people say about the younger generations, they cannot say these generations are not willing to serve. While Boomers wanted to save the world, these generations want to make a difference in the neighborhood around them. They are doing so in record numbers. Nationally, over two-thirds of American teens did some type of volunteer work in the space of one year.[26] Over 25 percent of all college students now volunteer on the average of five hours a week in community service projects. These percentages have risen significantly in recent years.[27]

When we participate in someone else's community through volunteer programs on campus or in the community, we meet new people. Volunteer projects also afford us an opportunity to give touches of grace to other volunteers. Many people in the emerging culture will not be able to hear the gospel unless they can see and experience the touch of the gospel. Our acts of kindness provide that touch and arouse curiosity about our Christian faith. Trust inevitably develops as they see us loving and caring for them. As we listen to them share about themselves, they are willing and sometimes eager to hear what we have to say. Let me share with you an e-mail from one of my InterVarsity staff that demonstrates how service projects with non-Christians can be springboards for evangelism.

> I am finally recovering from our week in New Orleans and wanted to let you know how our evangelism trip went. It's so funny because when we first started planning this trip, we wanted to take five believers and five of their nonbelieving friends. We ended up taking only one girl who wasn't a Christian, and I wondered how the trip was going to be an evangelism project.
>
> But when our team came down to New Orleans and met thirty nonbelieving students from UVA and SWU, things exploded! After one day on the site, almost everyone had had a significant conversation with one of these students. It was as if sharing in their lives and the gospel with these guys was not optional.
>
> By the middle of the week, after we had eaten, slept, worked and even shared a unisex bathroom, played ultimate Frisbee with a bunch from UVA and went to a karaoke bar with the girls from SWU, we were pretty deep into relationships with them. Wednesday night, after going to dinner at a local church, we went back to the convent where we stayed for quiet times and worship. One girl, Alex, came in right as we were getting ready to sing, and we asked her to join us. She went and got twenty of her friends, and they all joined us for worship. It was so powerful! We sang "Show Your Power," and when it came to "and our inheritance give us the lost," the lost were in the room with us! And then we all went out and had a great time Cajun dancing at a bowling alley—it's a New Orleans thing.
>
> The deal was that they were drawn to our community. They liked

the way we cared for each other, the way we didn't slam on each other, the way we cared for them and pursued them and included them in our group. They knew we were Christians. They knew there was something about us that they didn't have and that they wanted. And we talked about it with them. We talked about our group and about Jesus and how he has worked in our lives. I was so proud of our team.

Our deeds and words should tell the postmodern generations that they matter to us and to God. Leith Anderson, a pastor in Minnesota, was once asked what he would communicate to secular people if he had only one sentence. He replied, "I'd say, you matter to God."[28] Postmodern people today need to know that God created them, loves them and offers hope to them. They also need to see the church to be a diverse community, drawing all ethnic groups together in unity.

Our generation without necessarily knowing it, is calling the church back to what the church has always been called to be—a multi-generational, multi-cultural, open, orthodox and culturally engaged body of believers. This is what the church will need to be in order to speak to the postmodern culture with any legitimacy.

DIETER AND VALERIE ZANDER, "THE EVOLUTION OF GEN X,"
RE:GENERATION QUARTERLY

MULTIETHNIC COMMUNITY

We are in the midst of one of the greatest migrations in history. People from the Middle East are migrating to parts of Europe. A vast migration from parts of South and Central America is headed to the United States. There is also a large migration from Asia to parts of Canada and the United States. Many countries are experiencing a large influx of people who are very different from the present ethnic groups in the country. The United States's ethnic makeup is rapidly changing. That change will continue to occur for the foreseeable future.

Table 5.

1960		2000		2040 (projected)	
White	89%	White	69%	White	56%
Black	10%	Black	12%	Black	12%
Latino	<1%	Latino	12%	Latino	22%
Asian	<1%	Asian	4%	Asian	8%
Multiracial	——	Multiracial	2%	Multiracial	2%

All these changes should impact the way churches are thinking about how to do ministry in the coming years.

The love of Christ is the basis behind the desire to see the kingdom of God established in the world among God's people. God's love extends to all races and ethnic groups, so God's people are called to love not only all individuals but also all races and nations. God's ultimate goal is not just for racial reconciliation to occur but for all races and nations to worship and glorify him.

The love of God requires justice for all ethnic groups and nations. This drives us to fight against forces of evil that seek to destroy races of people. Each racial and ethnic group that experiences oppression wrestles with God over the fight against evil and the historical reality of racism in this country. Not only is each racial and ethnic group called to work out what faithfulness to God looks like within the context of its own history, but also it needs to move toward understanding what that faithfulness looks like in a multiethnic context.

As we have already seen, people in the emerging culture need to see the gospel lived out in order for them to be drawn to truth of the gospel. Steve Hayner describes people's reactions when they see this phenomenon in person.

> When people walk into a multi-ethnic church, the first thing that happens is surprise; surprised to see all of those people together. The next question that occurs to them is, does this really work? Is this authentic? When they begin to see people caring about one another; when they begin to see people appreciating each other's culture, yet honoring the individual cultures; that is a surprising and attractive thing.

True community involves living lives of repentance before each other. Individuals must learn to ask for—and receive—forgiveness. God's love for all peoples permeates Scripture and is central to God's story of redemption. At the end, each tribe and nation will worship the Lamb—as a member of their particular tribe and nation!

COMMUNITIES OFFERING HOPE

At the entrance to Dante's hell there is a sign that says, "Abandon hope, all you who enter here."[29] This sign could also describe the postmodern generations as they struggle to find meaning and hope for the future. Many have lost all hope in finding meaning. Suicide seems like a viable option to some. Others find hope in worshiping rock stars. When singer Kurt Cobain, a hero to many younger people, committed suicide, he took a sense of hope with him.

Kurt Cobain was a model for many teens in the decade of the 1990s. He grew up an average teen in the 1980s. His younger years had been very happy; he was usually the center of attention—singing, drawing and acting out skits with his family. Just before his eighth birthday, however, his mother filed for divorce. Kurt, like many youngsters experiencing the divorce of their parents, withdrew into his own private world. The divorce devastated him. His mother thinks he felt shame about it. Between 1975 and 1984, Kurt shuttled among parents, maternal grandparents and three sets of aunts and uncles.

Kurt was like many young people in the emerging culture. They have been exposed to drugs and violence. Many, like Kurt, had absent or abusive parents. Donna Gaines, a writer for *Rolling Stone,* depicts the generation as follows:

Many kids feel trapped in a cycle of futility and despair. Adults have abandoned an entire generation by failing to provide for or protect them or prepare them for independent living. Yet when young people began to exhibit symptoms of neglect reflected in their rates of suicide, homicide, substance abuse, school failure, recklessness and general misery, adults condemned them as a group of apathetic, illiterate, amoral losers.[30]

In some ways Kurt tried to be the savior of this generation. "But he wasn't Jesus and he couldn't save us. . . . From Jesus to Cobain in 2,000 years. There is no Mommy and Daddy, no great savior coming down to walk us through the millennium."[31] Kurt did not have the answers to all of life's struggles. He did not even have the answer to his own struggles. Ultimately the pain was too much to bear. Kurt Cobain committed suicide. The "savior" was gone.

As Christians, we have to empathize with the pain and suffering of postmodern people. In our words of compassion and deeds of caring, we can show them that although Kurt Cobain was not the emerging culture's savior, it has one in Jesus Christ. He *does* have all the answers, and he can take on all our pain. People in the emerging culture may have come to a place where they are willing to receive Christ's hope. Many of them have given up on growth and prosperity, and societal progress has hit a brick wall. As Robert Jensen exclaimed, "When hope in progress has been discredited, modernity has no resource either for renewing it or acquiring any sort of hope. . . . Hopelessness is the very definition of Postmodernism."[32]

Yet our communities and individuals continue to search for purpose, meaning and hope. Although people no longer have a sense of being in control of their lives, they still seek meaning, personal empowerment and inner direction. We as a church community cannot give people an earthly hope, but we are called to offer a heavenly hope. We should point people to the new reality, an eschatological reality where tears and pain will not exist.

> Then I saw a new heaven and a new earth, for the first heaven and the first earth had passed away, and there was no longer any sea. I saw the Holy City, the new Jerusalem, coming down out of heaven from God, prepared as a bride beautifully dressed for her husband. And I heard a loud voice from the throne saying, "Now the dwelling of God is with men, and he will live with them. They will be his people, and God himself will be with them and be their God. He will wipe every tear from their eyes. There will be no more death or mourning or crying or pain, for the old order of things has passed away."
>
> He who was seated on the throne said, "I am making everything new!" Then he said, "Write this down, for these words are trustworthy and true." (Rev 21:1-5)

The purpose of the community of faith is to point people in this direction. As a community of faith, love and hope, we are God's instrument for transmitting the gospel. What kind of process is this in a postmodern context?

WITNESSING COMMUNITY

The people of God have been called to be active witnesses in every age. This calling is not a choice. Even in the Old Testament, God prepared the way for his community to be a witness.

> "You are my witnesses," declares the LORD,
>   "and my servant whom I have chosen,
> so that you may know and believe me
>   and understand that I am he." (Is 43:10)

Being a witness is not about doing but about being. A witness is someone who has seen and experienced something and then proclaims it to others. A witnessing community demonstrates the gospel through good deeds and also proclaims to others what it has experienced firsthand.

Many Christians are afraid to be witnesses because they have been told that to speak out for what they believe demonstrates intolerance. But respecting the beliefs of others does not require us to keep silent about our beliefs. According to Don Posterski, "Rather than taking people seriously, tolerance treats people superficially. Instead of conveying 'Who you are and what you believe is to be valued,' tolerance says, 'I will endure you.'. . . The [implied] message is 'I do not take you seriously.' "[33] If tolerance means simply looking past people, allowing them to have their beliefs, "it may be good enough, legally and politically, for the pluralistic society; but it is not good enough . . . for the one who did not say, 'Tolerate your neighbor,' but 'Love your neighbor.' "[34]

As communities witnessing to Christ, we are called to go boldly into the world, loving our neighbors and pointing them to Christ. How do we accomplish that task?

A POSTMODERN CONVERSION PROCESS

I have identified six steps in the postmodern conversion process. These steps are not necessarily sequential, nor does everyone go through all of them. The purpose of identifying these steps is to help guide both the Christian and the one seeking Christ along the journey to faith. The six steps are (1) discontentment with life, (2) confusion over meaning, (3) contact with Christians, (4) conversion to community, (5) commitment to Christ and (6) a calling to a transformed life.

Discontentment with life. People who are content with their lives are usually not open to the gospel. A sense of discontentment with life can be a good thing if it leads to people finding Christ. The postmodern outlook on life is pessimistic. Many Boomers, on the other hand, are content with life and thus are not open to the gospel. But the postmodern generations' lack of contentment can lead them to seek new meaning in life.

Confusion over meaning. Since there are no absolutes in the postmodern era, meaning is an elusive pursuit. Meaninglessness runs rampant in a postmodern world. Even TV commercials discourage the search for meaning. "Why ask why?" and "Just do it" are two favorite commercial lines that discourage any search for ultimate meaning in life. Some people have given up the search for meaning in life because they have been frustrated in their past pursuits of meaning. The search for meaning has led others in many different directions, from rock stars to the New Age and from self-help groups to environmental causes. However, many searchers are dissatisfied with the answers they have found. There is much fluidity from tribal group to tribal group. This fluidity potentially bodes well for the gospel.

Contact with Christians. This stage is critical. Unfortunately, many seekers do not have a high opinion of Christians. They may have had negative encounters with Christians in the past, or they may have political disagreements with the Christian Right. They may have stereotypes about how Christians act or what Christians believe. On the other hand, many Christians, even those who are young enough to be part of the postmodern generation, do not understand or desire to understand this postmodern generation. They yearn for the relative certainty of the Enlightenment era.

To demonstrate the tension that exists between what is needed from Christians by people in the emerging culture who are not Christians and the misunderstanding by many Christians of how they should relate to the culture, let me share two e-mails with you. After speaking to a group of students from a religion class one evening, I received these e-mails in the space of ten minutes.

Dear Jimmy,

I just wanted to thank you again for coming to talk to our religion class tonight. I especially enjoyed your very gentle manner, and wish all Christians exhibited such patience and friendliness. I am not a Christian, although (and perhaps even because!) I was raised in a household headed by my very Southern Baptist father. But I have rediscovered an interest in faith since my best friend began to challenge me. It's slow going (I am now a junior in college), but I want you to know that you are one of a very few people who has made a difference in this search of mine, which I think is of central importance in my life. I hope I figure it out soon. This has turned into a lengthier message than I originally imagined, but as you see, I just wanted to express my gratitude and let you know that you have made an impact on my life.

Sincerely,

M.

Jimmy,

Thanks so much for coming to talk to us tonight. It was such a wonderful discussion. I do have some issues in what you are saying. I am concerned about Christians working in the culture. I don't think we can be 100% immersed in culture because we need, like you said, accountability, support and a family to return home to. So it seems to me that a successful Christian lifestyle is more like a bubble that we live in and bounce into the secular world to share Christ. While that is a very simplified outlook, I think this is what we should do. I'd like to meet with you, or if your schedule is super busy, then we could talk about this over e-mail.

In Christ's love,

A.

M. definitely needs Christians to reach out to her and spend time with her. On the other hand, A. is too concerned as a Christian about being tempted or tainted by the secular culture. Herein lie the tensions between the needs of the people in the emerging culture and the fears of many Christians if they enter that world. For people like M. to become a Christian, people like A. will need to go into M.'s world, befriend her and invite her into her Christian community.

Conversion to community. People living in a postmodern world will view life from a communal perspective, not from the Enlightenment perspective of the autonomous self. Becoming a Christian means leaving one community for a new community. Therefore, it is imperative that individuals become involved in the Christian community as part of their decision-making process. Entry into the Christian community may occur through a small group, a seeker service, a regular worship service or a social outing of the small group.

Whereas Boomers prefer anonymity as they make their initial forays into the Christian community, the younger generations will probably like to participate as much as possible. Many Boomers arrive at a rational, carefully thought-through decision after gathering all the evidence. Emerging-culture people make their decisions more spontaneously, from the heart and based on their experience within the community. Therefore it is important to allow these postmodern generations plenty of time to experience the community and to get to know as many people in the community as possible. The evangelistic process becomes a community affair more than a one-to-one encounter. If the community is narrowly defined, such as a formal or informal small group, the seeker can get to know people in some depth.

Many people with a postmodern mindset experience a two-stage conversion. First, the person becomes converted to the community, which may be a small group or a larger community. Over a period of time, the seeker begins to identify with the community and feels a sense of belonging. At this point the seeker may be a member of the community without having made a commitment to Christ.

Commitment to Christ. The seeker identifies with the community but may not be aware of the need to make a commitment to Christ. That commitment may form over a period of time or may take place at a specific moment. Past evangelistic efforts centered primarily on a "point-in-time" conversion process. In the postmodern world more people commit to Christ over a period of time. However, that commitment to Christ needs to happen.

In the Enlightenment era, many people made intellectual decisions regarding Christ but never committed their lives to him. In the postmodern era we need to take deliberate steps, or else many will become converted to the community but not to Christ, the King of the community.

A calling to a transformed life. People in the emerging culture will not be satisfied with a nominal Christian life. If they become Christians, they will want to be serious about their faith. They will, with help from the Christian community, want to be transformed to be like Jesus. We need to make sure that we create an environment where that transformation can take place. We need to be patient with them. It will be a lifelong process.

IMPLICATIONS FOR MINISTRY

We need to take careful stock of our evangelistic strategies to make sure that we are being faithful to God and working effectively in this postmodern context. We cannot rely on strategies that were effective years ago or that we feel most comfortable with. For a number of years in the 1980s I would debate the authority of the Scriptures with a religion professor in his class. Gradually I began to see that students were not interested in that question. So our last exchange consisted of dialoguing with the students about how Jesus was portrayed in movies. Students seemed much more interested in discussing the story of Jesus than in debating the authority of Scripture. The gospel story is a key element in evangelism within this postmodern generation.

The key question for emerging-culture people today is not "Is it true?" but "Is it real?" Their lives are more likely to be changed through the heart than through the mind. They need to see the incarnation of the gospel in people's lives more than to hear the proclamation of the gospel through our words. Do we have places where seekers can see the gospel in action? Do we invite them into our community? They need to experience the love of Jesus more than they need to be informed that Jesus is love.

As well as inviting seekers into our communities, we need to enter their communities. People in the postmodern world are increasingly separated into tribal groups. We need to think about the different tribal groups in our community or on our campus. Which ones do members of our church or fellowship already have contact with? We need to begin our efforts with those groups. The message we take to them is a message of hope.

SUMMARY

God is calling us to be a people of hope who offer the gospel of hope to an emerging culture without hope. We begin by *caring* for these postmodern people as real people with real hurts. We need to meet them where they are and listen to their stories. Next we must be *praying* that God will give us wisdom to know how to demonstrate God's love by word and deed and that God will draw these people to himself. Finally, we must be *sharing* ourselves and the hope of the gospel with them so that they will begin to understand that God loves them and desires to give them a home that they have never had, a place to belong. They also need to understand that it is only God who can provide this hope for discovering life's meaning, purpose and direction.

Many Christians see the emerging culture as a hopeless cause. But I think that the opportunity for revival is greater today than it has been in the last forty years. In the recent past, people have looked to the stable family of the 1950s, societal changes in the 1960s, the "me generation" of the 1970s and the good life of the 1980s for hope. In the 1990s and beyond, people are struggling to survive the confusing changes that surround them. They feel hopeless. Are we ready to offer them God's hope?

Notes

Chapter 1: A Simple Question, a Complex Journey

[1] Frederick Buechner, *The Longing for Home* (San Francisco: Harper, 1996), p. 135.

[2] Dennis Okholm. "I Don't Think We're in Kansas Anymore, Toto! Postmodernism in Our Everyday Lives," *Theology Matters,* July/August 1999, p. 1.

[3] H. Richard Niebuhr, *Christ and Culture* (New York: Harper & Row, 1951), p. vii.

[4] Stanley Menking, "Preparing for the Future: A Report, Generation X," summary of Consultation for Generation X Pastors, Perkins School of Theology, February 15-20, 1996.

[5] James Davison Hunter, "Before the Shooting Begins," *Columbia Journalism Review,* August 1993, pp. 29-32.

[6] Charles Colson, *Against the Night: Living in the New Dark Ages* (Ann Arbor, Mich.: Servant, 1989), p. 23.

[7] Carl F. H. Henry, *Gods of This Age or God of the Ages* (Nashville: Broadman, 1994), p. 6.

[8] Laurermar I. Barrett, "The Religious Right and the Pagan Press," *Columbia Journalism Review,* August 1993, p. 34.

[9] Alasdair MacIntyre, *After Virtue* (Notre Dame, Ind.: University of Notre Dame Press, 1981), p. 22.

[10] Ibid.

[11] Ibid., p. 231.

[12] Ibid., p. 165.

[13] Michael Horton, *Beyond Culture Wars* (Chicago: Moody Press, 1994), p. 91.

[14] Kenneth A. Myers, *All God's Children and Blue Suede Shoes* (Wheaton, Ill.: Crossway, 1989), p. 88.

[15] James Davison Hunter, *Culture Wars: The Struggle to Define America* (New York: HarperCollins, 1991), p. 42.

[16] James Dobson, "Why I Use 'Fighting Words,' " *Christianity Today,* June 19, 1995, pp. 27-30.

[17] James Woodbridge, "Culture War Casualties," *Christianity Today,* March 8, 1995, p. 26.

[18] Dobson, "Why I Use," p. 18.

[19] Tom Sine, *Cease Fire: Searching for Sanity in America's Culture Wars* (Grand Rapids: Eerdmans, 1995), p. 211.

[20] Woodbridge, "Culture War Casualties," p. 25.

[21] James Boice, *Two Cities, Two Loves* (Downers Grove, Ill.: InterVarsity Press, 1996), p. 152.

[22] Sine, *Cease Fire,* p. 286.

Chapter 2: The Adaptive Generations
[1]Robert Bellah, *The Good Society* (New York: Vintage, 1991), pp. 43-44.
[2]R. J. Matson, cartoon in Neil Howe and William Strauss, *13th Gen* (New York: Vintage, 1993), p. 193.
[3]Jeffrey Bantz, "Generation X: Implications," paper for Latin American Mission, 1995, p. 33.
[4]George Barna, *The Invisible Generation* (Glendale, Calif.: Barna Research Group, 1992), p. 44.
[5]Robert Coles, "Idealism in Today's Students," *Change,* September/October 1993, p. 19.
[6]Barna, *Invisible Generation,* p. 44.
[7]Robert Webber, *The Younger Evangelicals* (Grand Rapids: Baker, 2002), p. 47.
[8]Tim Celek and Dieter Zander, *Inside the Soul of a New Generation* (Grand Rapids: Zondervan, 1996), p. 31.
[9]Alan Deutschman, "The Upbeat Generation," *Fortune,* July 13, 1992, p. 48.
[10]Arthur Levine, *When Dreams and Heroes Died* (San Francisco: Jossey-Bass, 1980), p. 105.
[11]Howe and Strauss, *13th Gen,* p. 5.
[12]Edith Hill Updike, "The Dashed Dreams of Generation X," *Business Week,* August 7, 1995.
[13]David Gross and Sophfronica Scott, quoted in Dan Cray, "Twentysomething," *Time,* July 16, 1990, p. 57.
[14]Paul Rogat Loeb, *Generation at the Crossroads* (New Brunswick, N.J.: Rutgers University Press, 1994), p. 41.
[15]Steve Hayner, "The Church and Generational Diversity," unpublished paper, InterVarsity Christian Fellowship, Madison, Wis., 1994.
[16]Loeb, *Generation at the Crossroads,* p. 53.
[17]Neil Howe and William Strauss, *Millennials Rising: The Next Great Generation* (New York: Vintage, 2000), p. 128.
[18]David Lipsky and Alexander Abrams, *Late Bloomers* (New York: Random House, 1994), p. 87.
[19]Quoted in Jeff Shriver, "Bridging the Gap: Generation X Challenges the Church," *Prism,* May 1994, p. 9.
[20]Judith Wallerstein, *The Unexpected Legacy of Divorce* (New York: Hyperion, 2000), p. 298.
[21]Ibid., p. 295.
[22]Quoted in Mary Crystal Cage, "The Post-Baby Boomers Arrive on Campus," *The Chronicle of Higher Education,* June 30, 1993, sec. A, p. 28.
[23]Mark Judge, "The Indigent and the Odyssey: Back to Mom and Dad's—A Generation X Journey into Heroism," *Washington Post,* August 13, 1994, p. 3C.
[24]Levine, *When Dreams and Heroes Died,* p. 21.
[25]Gross and Scott, quoted in Cray, "Twentysomething," p. 57.
[26]J. Walker Smith, *American Demographics,* September 2001, p. 48.
[27]Howe and Strauss, *Millennials Rising,* p. 16.
[28]Ibid., p. 86.
[29]Smith, *American Demographics,* p. 48.
[30]Jack Wheat, "Zapping Old Schools of Thought," *News and Observer,* October 16, 1994, pp. 22-23A.
[31]William Dunn, *The Baby Bust* (Ithaca, N.Y. : American Demographic Books, 1993), p. 127.
[32]Deborah J. Hirsch, "Politics Through Action: Student Service and Activism in the 90's," *Change,* September/October 1993, pp. 32-35.
[33]Elijah Anderson, "The Code of the Streets," *Atlantic Monthly,* May 1994, p. 88.
[34]Geoffrey T. Holtz, *Welcome to the Jungle: The Why Behind Generation X* (New York: St. Martin's Press, 1995), p. 73.
[35]Loeb, *Generations at the Crossroads,* p. 68.

[36]Quoted in Rebecca Haas, "Introducing Those of Generation X," *Boston Globe*, December 29, 1991, pp. NH 1, 16.

[37]Andrew Smith, "Talking About My Generation," *The Face*, July 1994, p. 82.

[38]William Mahedy and Janet Bernadi, *A Generation Alone* (Downers Grove, Ill.: InterVarsity Press, 1994), p. 31.

[39]Ibid., p. 21.

[40]William Willimon, "Reaching and Teaching the Abandoned Generation," *Christian Century*, October 20, 1993, pp. 116-19.

[41]Dennis Atwood, "Jesus and Generation X," *Ivy Jungle Report*, summer 1995, p. 7.

[42]Douglas Coupland, *Life After God* (New York: Pocket Books, 1994), p. 359.

[43]Joel Deanne, "A Brief History of Generation X," *On Being*, October 1994, p. 26.

[44]Craig Barnes, *Yearning: Living Between How It Is and How It Ought to Be* (Downers Grove, Ill.: InterVarsity Press, 1991), p. 17.

[45]Mahedy and Bernardi, *Generation Alone*, p. 70.

Chapter 3: Emerging Postmodern Culture

[1]This story was first given by three major league umpires to Peter Kaufman in an interview in the 1960s. Later Walter Truett Anderson shared the story in a book titled *Reality Isn't What It Used to Be* (San Francisco: Harper & Row, 1990), p. 75.

[2]J. Richard Middleton and Brian J. Walsh, *Truth Is Stranger Than It Used to Be* (Downers Grove, Ill.: InterVarsity Press, 1995), p. 31.

[3]Diogenes Allen, "Christian Values in a Post-Christian Context," in *Postmodern Theology* (San Francisco: HarperCollins, 1989), p. 21.

[4]Mike Regele, *Death of the Church* (Grand Rapids: Zondervan, 1996), p. 76.

[5]Os Guinness, *The American Hour* (New York: Free Press, 1993), p. 316.

[6]Albert Borgmann, *Crossing the Postmodern Divide* (Chicago: University of Chicago Press, 1992), p. 22.

[7]Ibid., p. 25.

[8]Thomas Oden and David Dockery, ed., *The Challenge of Postmodernism* (Wheaton, Ill.: Victor, 1995), p. 28.

[9]Borgmann, *Crossing the Postmodern Divide*, p. 25.

[10]Ibid., p. 142.

[11]Carl F. H. Henry, *Twilight of a Great Civilization* (Westchester, Ill.: Crossway, 1988), pp. 36-37.

[12]David Walsh, *After Ideology* (San Francisco: HarperCollins, 1990), p. 139.

[13]David Wells, *No Place for Truth* (Grand Rapids: Eerdmans, 1993), p. 286.

[14]Robert Ellwood, *The Sixties Spiritual Awakening* (New Brunswick, N.J.: Rutgers University Press, 1994).

[15]Michael Sandel, "America's Search for a New Public Philosophy," *Atlantic Monthly*, March 1996, p. 66.

[16]Lance Morrow, "1968," *Time*, January 11, 1988, pp. 23-24.

[17]Ibid., p. 19.

[18]Hans Bertens, *The Idea of the Postmodern* (London: Routledge, 1995), p. 221.

[19]George Hunsberger and Craig Van Gelder, ed., *The Church Between Gospel and Culture* (Grand Rapids: Eerdmans, 1995), p. 127.

[20]Thomas Kuhn, *The Structure of Scientific Revolutions* (Chicago: University of Chicago Press, 1962), pp. 84-85.

[21]Gene Edward Veith, *Postmodern Times* (Wheaton, Ill.: Crossway, 1994), p. 21.

[22]Václav Havel, "Adrift in the Post-Modern World," *Charlotte (N.C.) Observer*, July 24, 1994, p. 1C.

[23]David Bosch, *Transforming Mission* (Maryknoll, N.Y.: Orbis, 1993), p. 349.

[24]Aleksandr Solzhenitsyn, "A World Split Apart," commencement address, Harvard University, Cambridge, Mass., June 8, 1978.

[25]San Stiver, "Much Ado About Athens and Jerusalem: The Implications of Postmodernism for Faith," *Review and Expositor* 91 (1994): 415.

[26]Walter Brueggemann, *Texts Under Negotiation* (Minneapolis: Fortress, 1993), p. 8.

[27]Holly Ryan, editorial, *University of North Carolina Daily Tar Heel*, November 11, 1994.

[28]Kenneth J. Gergen, *The Saturated Self* (New York: Basic Books, 1991), p. 133.

[29]Charles MacKenzie, "Facing the Challenge of Postmodernism," *RTS Ministry*, spring 1995, p. 9.

[30]Veith, *Postmodern Times*, p. 16.

[31]Wells, *No Place for Truth*, p. 86.

[32]Stanley Grenz, *A Primer on Postmodernism* (Grand Rapids: Eerdmans, 1995), p. 15.

[33]Veith, *Postmodern Times*, p. 86.

[34]Middleton and Walsh, *Truth Is Stranger Than It Used to Be*, p. 155.

[35]Stanley Menking, "Preparing for the Future: A Report, Generation X," summary of Consultation for Generation X Pastors, Perkins School of Theology, February 15-20, 1996, p. 4.

[36] Os Guinness, *Fit Bodies, Fat Minds* (Grand Rapids: Baker, 1994), p. 128.

[37]Richard Lints, *The Fabric of Theology* (Grand Rapids: Eerdmans, 1993), p. 216.

[38]Ibid., p. 48.

[39]Ibid., p. 216.

[40]Andrés Tapia, "Missed the Point," *Re:Generation Quarterly*, summer 1995, p. 3.

Chapter 4: Created for Community

[1]Stanley Grenz, *Theology for the Community of God* (Nashville: Broadman & Holman, 1994), p. 233.

[2]Mark Schwehn, *Exiles from Eden* (New York: Oxford University Press, 1993), p. 131.

[3]Grenz, *Theology*, p. 269.

[4]J. Richard Middleton and Brian J. Walsh, *Truth Is Stranger Than It Used to Be* (Downers Grove, Ill.: InterVarsity Press, 1995), p. 188.

[5]Paul Hanson, *The People Called* (San Francisco: Harper & Row, 1986), p. 469.

[6]Ibid., p. 28.

[7]Gareth Icenogle, *Biblical Foundations for Small Group Ministry* (Downers Grove, Ill.: InterVarsity Press, 1994), p. 118.

[8]David Bosch, *Transforming Mission* (Maryknoll, N.Y.: Orbis, 1993), p. 166.

[9]Grenz, *Theology*, p. 629.

[10]Robert Banks, *Paul's Idea of Community* (Peabody, Mass.: Hendrickson, 1994), p. 108.

[11]Stanley Grenz, *The Social God and the Relational Self* (Louisville, Ky.: Westminster John Knox, 2001), p. 281.

[12]John Wesley, *The Journal of John Wesley* (London: Capricorn, 1963), pp. 210-13 (December 10, 1734).

[13]Patrick Mays, "Reaching Baby Busters," *Evangelism*, November 1994, p. 5.

[14]D. Elton Trueblood, *The Incendiary Fellowship* (New York: Harper & Row, 1967), p. 31.

Chapter 5: Freed from Guilt and Shame

[1]Rodney Clapp, "Shame Crucified," *Christianity Today*, March 11, 1991, p. 26.

[2]James Boice, *Genesis* (Grand Rapids: Zondervan, 1982), p. 118.

[3]Dietrich Bonhoeffer, *Ethics* (New York: Macmillan, 1955), pp. 144-45.

[4]Donald Capps, *The Depleted Self* (Minneapolis: Fortress, 1993), p. 83.

[5]James Whitehead and Evelyn Whitehead, *Shadows of the Heart* (New York: Crossroad, 1994), p. 95.

[6]Boice, *Genesis*, p. 146.

[7]Ibid., p. 121.

[8]Ibid., p. 28.

[9]C. Norman Kraus, *Jesus Christ Our Lord* (Scottsdale, Penn.: Herald, 1990), p. 216.

[10]Robert Albers, *Shame: A Faith Perspective* (New York: Haworth, 1975), p. 103.

[11]Capps, *Depleted Self*, p. 28.

[12]David deSilva, "Despising Shame: A Cultural-Anthropological Investigation of the Epistle to the Hebrews," *Journal of Biblical Literature*, summer 1994, p. 446.

[13]Rodney Clapp, "Shame Crucified," *Christianity Today*, March 11, 1991, p. 26.

[14]Capps, *Depleted Self*, p. 28.

[15]Robert Webb, *The Reformed Doctrine of Adoption* (Grand Rapids: Eerdmans, 1947), p. 179.

[16]Quoted in James W. Fowler, *Weaving the New Creation* (San Francisco: HarperCollins, 1991), p. 13.

[17]Steve Hayner, "The Church and Generational Diversity," unpublished paper, InterVarsity Christian Fellowship, Madison, Wis., 1994, p. 8.

[18]Julie A. Gorman, *Community That Is Christian: A Handbook on Small Groups* (Wheaton, Ill.: Victor, 1993), p. 32.

[19]Ray Anderson, *Self Care: A Theology of Personal Empowerment and Spiritual Healing* (Wheaton, Ill.: Victor, 1995), p. 151.

[20]Ibid., p. 153.

[21]Robert Karen, "Shame," *Atlantic Monthly*, February 1992, p. 40.

[22]Gershen Kaufman, *Shame: The Power of Caring* (Cambridge, Mass.: Schenkman, 1980), p. 9.

[23]Millard J. Erickson, *Christian Theology* (Grand Rapids: Baker, 1985), p. 962.

[24]David Anderson, "When God Adopts," *Christianity Today*, July 19, 1993, pp. 37-39.

[25]Donald Guthrie, *New Testament Theology* (Downers Grove, Ill.: InterVarsity Press, 1981), p. 555.

[26]Rudolf Bultmann, "Pisteuo," in *Theological Dictionary of the New Testament*, ed. Gerhard Kittel and Gerhard Friedrich, abridged ed., ed. Geoffrey W. Bromiley (Grand Rapids: Eerdmans, 1985), p. 853.

[27]Eddie Gibbs, *In Name Only* (Wheaton, Ill.: Victor, 1994), p. 13.

[28]Ibid., p. 15.

[29]Ibid., p. 21.

[30]Anderson, *Self Care*, p. 25.

[31]Ibid.

[32]Ibid., p. 56.

[33]Ibid., p. 55.

[34]Fowler, *Weaving*, p. 13.

Chapter 6: From Lonely Orphan to God's Adopted Child

[1]Derek R. Moore-Crispan, "Galatians 4:1-9: The Use and Abuse of Parallels," *Evangelical Quarterly* 60 (1989): 114.

[2]Robert Webb, *The Reformed Doctrine of Adoption* (Grand Rapids: Eerdmans, 1947), p. 179.

[3]Francis Lyall, "Roman Law in the Writings of Paul—Adoption," *Journal of Biblical Literature* 88 (1969): 458-66.

[4]Webb, *Reformed Doctrine,* p. 171.

[5]Ibid., p. 20.

[6]Frank Thielman, *Paul and the Law* (Downers Grove, Ill.: InterVarsity Press, 1994), p. 136.

[7]James M. Scott, "Adoption," in *Dictionary of Paul and His Letters,* ed. Gerald Hawthorne et al. (Downers Grove, Ill.: InterVarsity Press, 1993), p. 15.

[8]Webb, *Reformed Doctrine,* p. 17.

[9]Martin W. Schoenberg, "*Huiothesia:* The Adoptive Sonship of the Israelites," *Ecclesiastical Review* (1962): 61.

[10]Scott, "Adoption," p. 16.

[11]David Anderson, "When God Adopts," *Christianity Today,* July 19, 1993, pp. 37-39; Moore-Crispin, "Galatians 4:1-9," p. 115.

[12]Webb, *Reformed Doctrine,* p. 18.

[13]Millard J. Erickson, *Christian Theology* (Grand Rapids: Baker, 1985), p. 962.

[14]Anderson, "When God Adopts," p. 37.

[15]Donald Guthrie, *New Testament Theology* (Downers Grove, Ill.: InterVarsity Press, 1981), p. 555.

Chapter 7: Hope in the Midst of Suffering

[1]Jürgen Moltmann, *Theology of Hope* (Minneapolis: Fortress, 1993), p. 32.

[2]William Mahedy and Janet Bernadi, *A Generation Alone* (Downers Grove, Ill.: InterVarsity Press, 1994), p. 82.

[3]Moltmann, *Theology of Hope,* p. 15.

[4]S. M. Smith, "Theology of Hope," in *Evangelical Dictionary of Theology,* ed. Walter Elwell (Grand Rapids: Baker, 1984), p. 523.

[5]Moltmann, *Theology of Hope,* p. 15.

[6]E. Hoffman, "Hope," in *Dictionary of New Testament Theology,* ed. Colin Brown (Grand Rapids: Zondervan, 1981), 2:243.

[7]Ibid., p. 242.

[8]Walter Zimmerli, *Man and His Hope in the Old Testament* (Naperville, Ill.: Alec R. Allenson, 1968), pp. 24-25.

[9]Ibid., p. 5.

[10]Tom Sine, *Cease Fire: Searching for Sanity in America's Culture Wars* (Grand Rapids: Eerdmans, 1995), p. 251.

[11]J. M. Everts, "Hope," in *Dictionary of Paul and His Letters,* ed. Gerald Hawthorne, Ralph P. Martin and Daniel Reid (Downers Grove, Ill.: InterVarsity Press, 1993), p. 415.

[12]Stephen H. Travis, *I Believe in the Second Coming of Jesus* (London: Hodder & Stoughton, 1982), p. 12.

[13]Walter Brueggemann, *Hopeful Imagination: Prophetic Voices in Exile* (Philadelphia: Fortress, 1986), pp. 3-4.

[14]Ibid., p. 30.

[15]Travis, *I Believe,* pp. 20-21.

[16]Stanley Grenz, "Withering Flowers in the Garden of Hope," *Christianity Today,* April 6, 1992, p. 21.

[17]Sine, *Cease Fire,* p. 244.

[18]Everts, "Hope," p. 416.

[19]A. J. Conyers, *The Eclipse of Heaven* (Downers Grove, Ill.: InterVarsity Press, 1992), p. 69.

[20]Brian Hebblethwaite, *The Christian Hope* (Grand Rapids: Eerdmans, 1975), p. 248.

[21]Ibid., p. 57.

[22]Ibid., p. 67.

[23]Ibid., p. 94.

[24]Ibid., p. 114.

[25]Conyers, *Eclipse of Heaven*, p. 175.

[26]Jean Bethke Elshtain, *Democracy on Trial* (New York: BasicBooks, 1995), p. 11.

[27]Ibid., p. 66.

[28]David Bosch, *Transforming Mission* (Maryknoll, N.Y.: Orbis, 1993), p. 361.

[29]Herman Ridderbos, *Paul: An Outline of His Theology* (Grand Rapids: Eerdmans, 1975), p. 248.

[30]Everts, "Hope," p. 417.

[31]Edmund Clowney, *The Message of 1 Peter* (Downers Grove, Ill.: InterVarsity Press, 1988), p. 44.

[32]Ibid.

Chapter 8: Communities of Belonging

[1]Robert Wuthnow, *I Came Away Stronger* (Grand Rapids: Eerdmans, 1994), p. 21.

[2]Robert Wuthnow, *Loose Connections: Joining Together in America's Fragmented Communities* (Cambridge, Mass.: Harvard University Press, 1998), p. 124.

[3]Joseph R. Myers, *The Search to Belong: Rethinking Intimacy, Community and Small Groups* (Grand Rapids: Zondervan, 2003), p. 20.

[4]Robert Wuthnow, *Sharing the Journey* (New York: Free Press, 1994), p. 36.

[5]Douglas Coupland, *Microserfs* (New York: HarperCollins, 1995), p. 335.

[6]Ibid., p. 371.

[7]Ibid., p. 5.

[8]Wuthnow, *I Came Away Stronger*, pp. 342-43.

[9]Wuthnow, *Sharing the Journey*, p. 31.

[10]Ibid., p. ix.

[11]Tim Celek and Dieter Zander, *Inside the Soul of a New Generation* (Grand Rapids: Zondervan, 1996), p. 114.

[12]Carl George, *Prepare Your Church for the Future* (Grand Rapids: Revell, 1991), p. 41.

[13]Long, *Small Group Handbook*, p. 32.

[14]S. D. Gaede, *Belonging* (Grand Rapids: Zondervan, 1985), p. 46.

[15]Carl R. George, *The Coming Church Revolution* (Grand Rapids: Revell, 1994), p. 69.

[16]Ibid., p. 71.

[17]Wuthnow, *I Came Away Stronger*, p. 346.

[18]George, *Prepare Your Church*, p. 99.

[19]Gorman, *Community That Is Christian*, p. 92.

[20]Douglas Hyde, *Dedication and Leadership* (Notre Dame, Ind.: University of Notre Dame Press, 1966), p. 48.

[21]Gaede, *Belonging*, p. 219.

[22]Richard Lamb, *Following Jesus in the Real World* (Downers Grove, Ill.: InterVarsity Press, 1995), p. 95.

[23]Richard Peace, "Reaching X-Generation Through Small Groups," lecture presented at the National Small Group Conference at Eastern College, St. Davids, Pennsylvania, May 1995.

[24]This Bible study method was developed by InterVarsity's National Bible Study Task Force under the leadership of Bob Grahman and Lindsay Olesberg.

[25]Coupland, *Microserfs*, p. 360.

[26]David Prior, *Creating Community* (Colorado Springs: NavPress, 1992), p. 123.

[27]William Berquist, *The Postmodern Organization* (San Francisco: Jossey-Bass, 1993), p. 13.

Chapter 9: Our Spiritual Journey in Community

[1]Alanis Morissette, "Perfect," on *Jagged Little Pill,* Maverick 4-45901.

[2]Ray Anderson, *Self Care: A Theology of Personal Empowerment and Spiritual Healing* (Wheaton, Ill.: Victor Books, 1995), p. 59.

[3]M. Craig Barnes, *Yearning: Living Between How It Is and How It Ought to Be* (Downers Grove, Ill.: InterVarsity Press, 1991), p. 142.

[4]Ibid., p. 21.

[5]Ibid., p. 16.

[6]Anderson, *Self Care,* p. 237.

[7]Barnes, *Yearning,* p. 166.

[8]Lynne Hybels and Bill Hybels, *Rediscovering Church* (Grand Rapids: Zondervan, 1995), p. 166.

[9]Karen, "Shame," p. 46.

[10]Robert Albers, *Shame: A Faith Perspective* (New York: Haworth, 1995), p. 126.

[11]Barnes, *Yearning,* p. 145.

[12]David Wells, *God in the Wasteland* (Grand Rapids: Eerdmans, 1994), p. 30.

[13]John Westfall, *Coloring Outside the Lines* (San Francisco: Harper Collins, 1991), p. 10.

[14]Ibid., p. 13.

[15]Barnes, *Yearning,* p. 166.

[16]Westfall, *Coloring,* p. 14.

[17]Ibid., p. 15.

[18]Ibid., p. 21.

[19]Ibid., p. 25.

[20]Cornelius Plantinga Jr., *Not the Way It's Supposed to Be* (Grand Rapids: Eerdmans, 1995), p. 10.

[21]Janet O. Hagberg and Robert A. Guelich, *The Critical Journey: Stages in the Life of Faith* (Dallas: Word, 1989), p. 4.

[22]Ibid., p. 5.

[23]Ibid., p. 14.

[24]Ibid., p. 15.

[25]Ibid., pp. 36-37.

[26]Ibid., pp. 39-40.

[27]Ibid., p. 53.

[28]Tim Keller, "Reaching the Secular Person," paper presented at Presbyterian Church of America's Church Planting Conference, 1996, p. 7.

[29]Hagberg and Guelich, *Critical Journey,* p. 93.

[30]Ibid., pp. 82-83.

[31]Carmen Renee Berry, "In Search of Spiritual Community," *Leadership,* fall 2003, p. 12.

[32]Frederick Buechner, *The Longing for Home* (San Francisco: Harper, 1996), p. 168.

[33]Hagberg and Guelich, *Critical Journey,* p. 93.

[34]Ibid., p. 98.

[35]Ibid., p. 107.

[36]Ibid., pp. 136-37.

[37]Ibid., p. 154.

[38]Sally Morgenthaler, *Worship Evangelism* (Grand Rapids: Zondervan, 1995), p. 48.

[39]Andy Park, *To Know You More* (Downers Grove, Ill.: InterVarsity Press, 2002), p. 242.

[40]Kathi Allen, "Blessing the Arts," *Next* 5, no. 3: 1-3.

[41]Frank C. Senn, "Orthodixia, Orthopraxis and Seekers," in *The Strange New World of the Gospel: Re-evangelizing in the Postmodern World,* ed. Carl E. Braaten and Robert W. Jenson (Grand Rap-

ids: Eerdmans, 2002), p. 145.
[42]Robert Putnam, *Better Together: Restoring the American Community* (New York: Simon & Schuster, 2003), p. 125.
[43]Steve Hayner, "Evangelism, Worship and Generational Diversity," paper presented to a pastor's conference in California, January 1995.
[44]Park, *To Know You More*, p. 94.
[45]Andy Crouch, "Life After Modernity," in *The Church in Emerging Culture*, ed. Leonard Sweet (Grand Rapids: Zondervan, 2003), p. 85.
[46]Robb Redman, *The Great Worship Awakening: Singing a New Song in the Postmodern Church* (San Francisco: Jossey-Bass, 2002), p. 113.
[47]David Lose, *Confessing Jesus Christ: Preaching in a Postmodern World* (Grand Rapids: Eerdmans, 2003), pp. 127-29.
[48]Brian McLaren, interview in Jimmy Long's *Emerging Culture: Ministry Resources in a Changing World* (Downers Grove, Ill.: InterVarsity Press, 2004), section 3.
[49]Graham Johnston, *Preaching to a Postmodern World* (Grand Rapids: Baker, 2001), p. 136.

Chapter 10: Communities Offering Hope
[1]Doris Betts, "Slow-Change Artist," *His*, April 1983, pp. 4-6.
[2]John Sims, "Postmodernism: The Apologetic Imperative," in *The Challenge of Postmodernism*, ed. David Dockery (Wheaton, Ill.: Victor, 1995), p. 332.
[3]Leighton Ford, *The Power of Story* (Colorado Springs: NavPress, 1994), pp. 76-77.
[4]James W. Sire, "On Being a Fool for Christ and an Idiot for Nobody," in *Christian Apologetics in a Postmodern World*, ed. Timothy R. Phillips and Dennis L. Okholm (Downers Grove, Ill.: InterVarsity Press, 1995), p. 112.
[5]Brad Kallenberg, "Conversion Converted: A Postmodern Formulation of the Doctrine of Conversion," *Evangelical Quarterly* 67 (1999): 347.
[6]Ford, *Power of Story*, pp. 67-68.
[7]Ibid., p. 14.
[8]Kallenberg, "Conversion Converted," p. 347.
[9]George Hunter, *How to Reach Secular People* (Nashville: Abingdon, 1992), p. 38.
[10]Quoted in Deborah Caldwell, "Questions of Faith," *Dallas Morning News*, January 25, 1995, p. 1G.
[11]Alister McGrath, *Intellectuals Don't Need God and Other Modern Myths* (Grand Rapids: Zondervan, 1993), p. 177.
[12]Philip Kenneson, "There's No Such Thing as Objective Truth, and It's a Good Thing Too," in *Christian Apologetics in the Postmodern World*, ed. Timothy R. Phillips and Dennis Okholm (Downers Grove, Ill.: InterVarsity Press, 1995), p. 169.
[13]Ravi Zacharias, "Reaching the Happy Thinking Pagan," *Leadership*, spring 1995, p. 23.
[14]Jack Lindberg, "Evangelism and the Local Church," *Context*, winter 1995, p. 9.
[15]Kevin Graham Ford, *Jesus for a New Generation* (Downers Grove, Ill.: InterVarsity Press, 1995), p. 173.
[16]For a fuller discussion of Socratic evangelism, see George Barna, *Evangelism That Works* (Ventura, Calif.: Regal, 1995), pp. 107-25.
[17]Ford, *Power of Story*, p. 117.
[18]James Barr, *The Semantics of Biblical Language* (Glasgow: Oxford University Press, 1961), p. 10.
[19]Zacharias, "Reaching the Happy Thinking Pagan," p. 20.
[20]Kenneson, "There's No Such Thing," p. 166.

[21]Dennis Hollinger, "The Church as Apologetic," in *Christian Apologetics in a Postmodern World,* ed. Timothy R. Phillips and Dennis L. Okholm (Downers Grove, Ill.: InterVarsity Press, 1995), p. 191.

[22]Stanley Hauerwas, *A Community of Character* (Nashville: Abingdon, 1991), pp. 1, 3.

[23]Stanley Grenz, *Theology for the Community of God* (Nashville: Broadman & Holman, 1994), p. 655.

[24]Kevin Offner, "American Evangelicalsim: Adrift with Amnesia," *Re:Generation Quarterly,* winter 1995, p. 9.

[25]Ford, *Power of Story,* p. 122.

[26]Robert Wuthnow, *Learning to Care* (New York: Oxford University Press, 1995), p. 6.

[27]William Willimon and Thomas Naylor, *The Abandoned Generation* (Grand Rapids: Eerdmans, 1995), p. 158.

[28]Ford, *Power of Story,* p. 73.

[29]Quoted in Jürgen Moltmann, *Theology of Hope* (Minneapolis: Fortress, 1993), p. 6.

[30]Donna Gaines, "Suicidal Tendencies: Kurt Did Not Die for You," *Rolling Stone,* June 2, 1994.

[31]Ibid., p. 61.

[32]Robert Jenson, "How the World Lost Its Story," *First Things,* October 1993, pp. 19-24.

[33]Donald Posterski, *True to You* (Winfield, B.C.: Wood Lake Books, 1995), p. 139.

[34]Ibid.

Bibliography

Chapter 1: A Simple Question, a Complex Journey

Anderson, Leith. *Winning the Value War.* Minneapolis: Bethany House, 1994.

Baron, Michael. "America's Culture Wars Tradition." *U.S. News & World Report,* September 21, 1992, p. 24.

Barrett, Lauremar I. "The Religious Right and the Pagan Press." *Columbia Journalism Review,* August 1993, pp. 33-36.

Berger, Allen. "Calling a Cease Fire in Culture Wars." *Chicago Tribune,* August 3, 1993, sec. 1, p. 17.

Boice, James. *Two Cities, Two Loves.* Downers Grove, Ill.: InterVarsity Press, 1996.

Cantor, Norman F. *Medieval History: The Life and Death of a Civilization.* London: Macmillan, 1969.

Colson, Charles. *Against the Night: Living in the New Dark Ages.* Ann Arbor, Mich.: Servant, 1989.

Decter, Midge. "Ronald Reagan and the Culture War." *Commentary,* March 1991, pp. 43-46.

Dobson, James. "Why I Use 'Fighting Words.'" *Christianity Today,* June 19, 1995, pp. 27-30.

Ehrenhalt, Alan. "Learning from the Fifties." *Wilson Quarterly,* summer 1995, pp. 3-29.

Frank, Douglas. *Less than Conquerors: How Evangelicals Entered the Twentieth Century.* Grand Rapids: Eerdmans, 1986.

Guinness, Os, and John Seel. *No God but God.* Chicago: Moody Press, 1992.

Henry, Carl F. H. *Gods of This Age or God of the Ages.* Nashville: Broadman, 1994.

Horton, Michael S. *Beyond Culture Wars.* Chicago: Moody Press, 1994.

Hunter, James Davison. "Before the Shooting Begins." *Columbia Journalism Review,* August 1993, pp. 29-32.

————. *Culture Wars: The Struggle to Define America.* New York: HarperCollins, 1991.

Huntington, Samuel P. "The Clash of Civilizations?" *Foreign Affairs,* summer 1993, pp. 22-49.

Kaufman, Leslie. "Life Beyond God." *New York Times Magazine,* November 16, 1994, pp. 46-50.

Klein, Joe. "Whose Values?" *Newsweek,* June 8, 1992, pp. 19-22.

MacIntyre, Alasdair. *After Virtue.* Notre Dame, Ind.: University of Notre Dame Press, 1981.

Myers, Kenneth A. *All God's Children and Blue Suede Shoes.* Wheaton, Ill.: Crossway, 1989.

Okholm, Dennis. "I Don't Think We're in Kansas Anymore, Toto! Postmodernism in Our Everyday Lives." *Theology Matters,* July/August 1999, pp. 1-6.

Reed, Eric. "Leading into the Unknown." *Leadership,* fall 1999, pp. 58-64.

Regele, Mike. *Death of the Church.* Grand Rapids: Zondervan, 1995.

Robertson, Pat. *The Turning Tide.* Dallas: Word, 1993.

Sine, Tom. *Cease Fire: Searching for Sanity in America's Culture Wars.* Grand Rapids: Eerdmans, 1995.

Sweet, Leonard. "What the World Needs Now." *Leadership,* spring 1993, pp. 20-28.

Sweet, Leonard, ed. *Church in the Emerging Culture.* Grand Rapids: Zondervan, 2003.

Woodbridge, John D. "Culture War Casualties." *Christianity Today,* March 1995, pp. 20-26.

Chapter 2: The Adaptive Generations

Aeschliman, Gordon. "Generation X: Will the Church Be in Their Future?" *Prism,* May 1994, pp. 12-16.

Anderson, Elijah. "The Code of the Streets." *Atlantic Monthly,* May 1994, pp. 81-94.

Atwood, Dennis. "Jesus and Generation X." *The Ivy Jungle Report,* summer 1995, p. 7.

Bantz, Jeffrey. "Generation X: Implications." Latin American Mission, 1995.

Barna, George. "George Barna on Busters." *The Ivy Jungle Report,* summer 1996, pp. 1, 11.

————. *The Invisible Generation.* Glendale, Calif.: Barna Research Group, 1992.

————. "The Twentysomething Crowd: Baby Busters." *Ministry Current,* July/September 1993, pp. 5-8.

Bibby, Reginald, and Donald C. Posterski. *Teen Trends: A Nation in Motion.* Toronto: Stoddard, 1992.

Breitenbach, Gene. "Tracking with Generation X." *The Ivy Jungle Report,* fall 1994, pp. 5, 17-18.

Bruni, Frank. "Generation X." *Boston Globe,* November 21, 1993, p. 1G.

Cage, Mary Crystal. "The Post-Baby Boomers Arrive on Campus." *Chronicle of Higher Education,* June 30, 1993, p. 27A.

Caldwell, Deborah. "Questions of Faith: Generation X." *Dallas Morning News,* January 25, 1995, p. 1(G).

Celek, Tim, and Dieter Zander. *Inside the Soul of a New Generation.* Grand Rapids: Zondervan, 1996.

Cohen, Jason, and Michael Krugman. *Generation Ecch.* New York: Simon & Schuster, 1994.

Coles, Robert. "Idealism in Today's Students." *Change,* September/October 1993, pp. 16-20.

Coupland, Douglas. *Life After God.* New York: Pocket Books, 1994.

Cray, Dan. "Twentysomething." *Time,* July 16, 1990, pp. 55-62.

Deanne, Joel. "A Brief History of Generation X." *On Being,* October 1994, pp. 22-27.

Deutschman, Alan. "The Upbeat Generation." *Fortune,* July 13, 1992, pp. 42-54.

Dunn, William. *The Baby Bust.* Ithaca, N.Y.: American Demographic Books, 1993.

Ford, Kevin Graham. *Jesus for a New Generation.* Downers Grove, Ill.: InterVarsity Press, 1995.

Greller, Martin M. *From Baby Boom to Baby Bust.* Reading, Mass.: Addison-Wesley, 1989.

Haas, Rebecca. "Introducing Those of Generation X." *Boston Globe,* December 29, 1991, p. 1NH.

Hahn, Todd, and David Verhaagen, *Gen Xers After God.* Grand Rapids: Baker, 1998.

Hayner, Steve. "The Church and Generational Diversity." Unpublished paper, InterVarsity Christian Fellowship, Madison, Wis., January 1994.

Hirsch, Deborah J. "Politics Through Action: Student Service and Activism in the 90s." *Change,* September/October 1993, pp. 32-35.

Holtz, Geoffrey T. *Welcome to the Jungle: The Why Behind Generation X.* New York: St. Martin's Press, 1995.

Hornblower, Margot. "Great Xpectations." *Time,* June 9, 1997, pp. 58-68.

Howe, Neil, and William Strauss. *13th Gen.* New York: Vintage, 1993.

———. *Millennials Rising: The Next Great Generation.* New York: Vintage, 2000.

Judge, Mark. "The Indigent and the Odyssey: Back to Mom and Dad's—A Generation X Journey into Heroism." *Washington Post,* August 31, 1994, sec. 4, p. 3.

Kelly, Gerard. *Retrofuture.* Downers Grove, Ill.: InterVarsity Press, 1999.

Ladd, Everett C. "Exposing the Myth of the Generation Gap." *Reader's Digest,* January 1995, pp. 49-54.

Lancaster, Lynne, and David Stillman. *When Generations Collide.* New York: Harper Business, 2002.

Levine, Arthur. "The Making of a Generation." *Change,* September/October 1993, pp. 8-14.

Lipsky, David, and Alexander Abrams. *Late Bloomers.* New York: Random House, 1994.

Liu, Eric, ed. *NEXT—Young American Writers on the New Generation.* New York: W. W. Norton, 1994.

Loeb, Paul Rogat. *Generation at the Crossroads.* New Brunswick, N.J.: Rutgers University Press, 1994.

Mahedy, William, and Janet Bernardi. *A Generation Alone.* Downers Grove, Ill.: InterVarsity Press, 1994.

Martin, David. "The Whiny Generation." *Newsweek,* November 1, 1993, p. 10.

Mays, Patrick. "Reaching Baby Busters." *Evangelism,* November 1994, pp. 1-11.

Menking, Stanley. "Preparing for the Future: A Report, Generation X." Summary of Consultation for Generation X Pastors, Perkins School of Theology, February 15-20, 1996.

Mills, D. Quinn. *Not Like Our Parents: How the Baby Boom Generation Is Changing America.* New York: Morrow, 1987.

Nelson, Rob, and John Cowan. *Revolution X: A Survival Guide for Our Generation.* New York: Penguin, 1994.

Paul, Pamela. "Getting Inside Gen Y." *American Demographics,* September 2001, pp. 43-49.

————. "Millennial Myths." *American Demographics,* December 2001, p. 20.

Potts, Kris. "Generation X: Face to Face with Boomers—An Interview with George Barna." *InterVarsity Magazine,* winter 1994-1995, pp. 7-8.

Rainer, Thom. *The Bridger Generation.* Nashville: Broadman & Holman, 1997.

Reed, Eric. "Ministering with My Generation," *Leadership,* fall 2000, pp. 49-54.

Regele, Mike. *Death of the Church.* Grand Rapids: Zondervan, 1996.

Ritchie, Karen. *Marketing to Generation X.* New York: Lexington Books, 1995.

Rushkoff, Douglas. *The Gen X Reader.* New York: Ballantine, 1994.

Sacks, Peter. *Generation X Goes to College: An Eye-Opening Account of Teaching in Postmodern America.* Chicago: Open Court, 1996.

Sciacca, Fran. *Generation at Risk.* Chicago: Moody Press, 1990.

Shapiro, Joseph. "Just Fix It." *U.S. News & World Report,* February 22, 1993, pp. 50-57.

Tittley, Mark. "Ministry and the Millennial Generation." *NextWave,* May 1999.

Updike, Edith Hill. "The Dashed Dreams of Generation X." *Business Week,* August 7, 1995, pp. 38-39.

Wallerstein, Judith. *The Unexpected Legacy of Divorce.* New York: Hyperion, 2000.

Wee, Eric L. "The Death of the Date." *Washington Post,* January 8, 1995, p. 1B.

White, James Emery, and Garth Bolinder. "Should We Target Generations?" *Leadership,* spring 1999, pp. 104-6.

Zander, Dieter, and Valerie Zander. "The Evolution of Gen X Ministry," *Re:Generation Quarterly,* fall 1999, pp. 16-19.

Zoba, Wendy Murray. *Generation 2K.* Downers Grove, Ill.: InterVarsity Press, 1999.

Chapter 3: Emerging Postmodern Culture

Allen, Diogenes. "Christian Values in a Post-Christian Context." In *Postmodern Theology.* San Francisco: HarperCollins, 1989.

Anderson, Leith. "The Church at History's Hinge." *Bibliotheca,* January-March 1994, pp. 3-10.

Anderson, Walter Truett. *Reality Isn't What It Used to Be.* San Francisco: Harper & Row, 1990.

Barna, George. "Americans Are Most Likely to Base Truth on Feelings." *Barna Research Online,* February 12, 2002.

Benne, Robert. *The Paradoxical Vision.* Minneapolis: Fortress, 1995.

Bertens, Hans. *The Idea of the Postmodern.* London: Routledge, 1995.

Borgmann, Albert. *Crossing the Postmodern Divide.* Chicago: University of Chicago Press, 1992.

Bosch, David J. *Transforming Mission.* Maryknoll, N.Y.: Orbis, 1993.

Braaten, Carl E., and Robert W. Jenson. *Either/Or: The Gospel or Neopaganism.* Grand Rapids: Eerdmans, 1995.

Brockelman, Paul. *The Inside Story: A Narrative Approach to Religious Understanding and Truth.* Albany: State University of New York Press, 1992.

Brueggemann, Walter. *Texts Under Negotiation.* Minneapolis: Fortress, 1993.

Colson, Charles. "Postmodern Power Grab." *Christianity Today,* January 20, 1994, p. 80.

Cowlet, Geoffrey, and Karen Springen. "Rewriting Life Stories." *Newsweek,* April 17, 1995, pp. 70-71.

Dockery, David S., ed. *The Challenge of Postmodernism.* Wheaton, Ill.: Victor, 1995.

Ellwood, Robert S. *The Sixties Spiritual Awakening.* New Brunswick, N.J.: Rutgers University Press, 1994.

Erickson, Millard J. *Truth or Consequences.* Downers Grove, Ill.: InterVarsity Press, 2001.

Gatlin, Todd. "Postmodernism Defined at Last." *Utne Reader,* July/August 1989, pp. 52-61.

Gibbs, Eddie. *ChurchNext.* Downers Grove, Ill.: InterVarsity Press, 2000.

Gergen, Kenneth J. *The Saturated Self.* New York: BasicBooks, 1991.

Goetz, David. "The Riddle of Postmodern Culture." *Leadership,* winter 1997, pp. 52-56.

Grenz, Stanley. *A Primer on Postmodernism.* Grand Rapids: Eerdmans, 1995.

———. "Twentieth-Century Theology: The Quest for Balance in a Transitional Age." *Perspectives,* June 1993, pp. 10-13.

Grenz, Stanley, and John Franke. *Beyond Foundationalism.* Louisville, Ky.: Westminster John Knox, 2001.

Grenz, Stanley J., and Roger E. Olson. *Twentieth-Century Theology.* Downers Grove, Ill.: InterVarsity Press, 1992.

Griffin, David Ray. *God and Religion in the Postmodern World.* Albany: State University of New York Press, 1989.

Guinness, Os. *The American Hour.* New York: Free Press, 1993.

———. *Fit Bodies, Fat Minds.* Grand Rapids: Baker, 1994.

Havel, Václav. "Adrift in the Post-modern World." *Charlotte Observer,* July 24, 1994, p. 1C.

Hunsberger, George, and Craig Van Gelder, ed. *The Church Between Gospel and Culture.* Grand Rapids: Eerdmans, 1995.

Hutchins, Kim. "The Dance of Truth." *Mars Hill Review,* fall 1998, pp. 9-11.

L'Engle, Madeleine. "Story as the Search for Truth." *Radix* 22, no. 2 (1994): 10-13.

Lints, Richard. *The Fabric of Theology.* Grand Rapids: Eerdmans, 1993.

Lundin, Roger. *The Culture of Interpretation.* Grand Rapids: Eerdmans, 1993.

MacKenzie, Charles. "Facing the Challenge of Postmodernism." *RTS Ministry,* spring 1995, p. 8.

McGrath, Alister. *Christian Theology: An Introduction.* Oxford: Blackwell, 1994.

Middleton, J. Richard, and Brian J. Walsh. *Truth Is Stranger Than It Used to Be.* Downers Grove, Ill.: InterVarsity Press, 1995.

Morrow, Lance. "1968." *Time,* January 11, 1988, pp. 16-27.

Murphy, Nancey, and James McClendon. "Distinguishing Modern and Postmodern Theologies." *Modern Theology,* April 1989, pp. 191-213.

Newbigin, Lesslie. *Foolishness to the Greeks.* Grand Rapids: Eerdmans, 1986.

———. *The Gospel in a Pluralist Society.* Grand Rapids: Eerdmans, 1990.

Oden, Thomas. *After Modernity.* Grand Rapids: Zondervan, 1990.

———. *Two Worlds: Notes on the Death of Modernity in America and Russia.* Downers

Grove, Ill.: InterVarsity Press, 1992.

Phillips, Timothy, and Dennis Okholm, ed. *Christian Apologetics in the Postmodern World.* Downers Grove, Ill.: InterVarsity Press, 1995.

Rieff, Philip. *The Triumph of the Therapeutic.* New York: Harper & Row, 1966.

Rue, Loyal. *By the Grace of Guile.* New York: Oxford University Press, 1994.

Sandel, Michael. "America's Search for a New Public Philosophy." *Atlantic Monthly,* March 1996, pp. 57-74.

Schreiter, Robert. *Constructing Local Theologies.* Maryknoll, N.Y.: Orbis, 1985.

Schwehn, Mark. *Exiles from Eden.* New York: Oxford University Press, 1993.

Sheler, Jeffrey L. "Spiritual America." *U.S. News & World Report,* April 4, 1994, pp. 48-59.

Soong-Chan, Rah. "Navigating Cultural Currents." *Leadership,* fall 2000, pp. 38-42.

Steigerwald, David. *The Sixties and the End of Modern America.* New York: St. Martin's Press, 1995.

Stiver, Dan. "Much Ado About Athens and Jerusalem: The Implications of Postmodernism for Faith." *Review and Expositor* 91 (1994).

Sweet, Leonard. *Postmodern Pilgrims.* Nashville: Broadman & Holman, 2000.

———. *SoulTsunami.* Grand Rapids: Zondervan, 1999.

Tanner, Kenneth, and Christopher A. Hall. *Ancient and Postmodern Christianity.* Downers Grove, Ill.: InterVarsity Press, 2002.

Thiselton, Anthony C. *Interpreting God and the Postmodern Self.* Grand Rapids: Eerdmans, 1996.

Tilley, Terrence W. *Postmodern Theologies.* Maryknoll, N.Y.: Orbis, 1995.

Towns, Elmer, and Warren Bird. *Into the Future.* Grand Rapids: Revell, 2000.

Turner, James. *Without God, Without Creed.* Baltimore: Johns Hopkins University Press, 1985.

Van Gelder, Craig. "Scholia: Postmodernism as an Emerging Worldview." *Calvin Theological Journal* 26 (1991): 412-17.

Veith, Gene Edward. *Postmodern Times.* Wheaton, Ill.: Crossway, 1994.

Walsh, David. *After Ideology: Recovering the Spiritual Foundations of Freedom.* San Francisco: HarperCollins, 1990.

Webber, Robert. *Ancient-Future Faith.* Grand Rapids: Baker, 1999.

Wells, David F. *God in the Wasteland.* Grand Rapids: Eerdmans, 1994.

———. *No Place for Truth.* Grand Rapids: Eerdmans, 1993.

Chapter 4: Created for Community

Banks, Robert. *Paul's Idea of Community.* Peabody, Mass.: Hendrickson, 1994.

Clapp, Rodney. *Families at the Crossroads.* Downers Grove, Ill.: InterVarsity Press, 1993.

Grenz, Stanley. *The Social God and the Relational Self.* Louisville, Ky.: Westminster John Knox, 2000.

————. *Theology for the Community of God.* Nashville: Broadman & Holman, 1994.

Hanson, Paul. *The People Called.* San Francisco: Harper & Row, 1986.

Icenogle, Gareth. *Biblical Foundations for Small Group Ministry.* Downers Grove, Ill.: InterVarsity Press, 1994.

Lohfink, Gerhard. *Jesus and Community.* Philadelphia: Fortress, 1982.

Chapter 5: Freed from Guilt and Shame

Albers, Robert. *Shame: A Faith Perspective.* New York: Haworth, 1995.

Alter, Jonathan, and Pat Wingert. "The Return of Shame." *Newsweek,* February 6, 1995, pp. 21-25.

Boice, James. *Genesis.* Grand Rapids: Zondervan, 1982.

Bonhoeffer, Dietrich. *Ethics.* New York: Macmillan, 1955.

Capps, Donald. *The Depleted Self.* Minneapolis: Fortress, 1993.

Clapp, Rodney. "Shame Crucified." *Christianity Today,* March 11, 1991, pp. 26-28.

deSilva, David. "Despising Shame: A Cultural-Anthropological Investigation of the Epistle to the Hebrews." *Journal of Biblical Literature,* summer 1994, pp. 439-61.

Fowler, James W. "Shame: Toward a Practical Theological Understanding." *Christian Century,* August 25-September 1, 1993, pp. 816-19.

Fryling, Robert. "Campus Ministry Memo." Madison, Wis.: InterVarsity Christian Fellowship, February 4, 1993.

Hugen, Melvin, and Cornelius Plantinga Jr. "Naked and Exposed." *Books & Culture,* March/April 1996, pp. 3, 27-29.

Kaufman, Gershen. *The Psychology of Shame.* New York: Springer, 1989.

Lasch, Christopher. "For Shame." *New Republic,* August 10, 1992, pp. 29-34.

Lewis, Michael. *Shame: The Exposed Self.* New York: Free Press, 1995.

Neidenthal, Paula. " 'If Only I Weren't' Versus 'If Only I Hadn't': Distinguishing Shame and Guilt in Counterfactual Thinking." *Journal of Personality and Social Psychology* 67, no. 4 (1994): 585-95.

Ryan, Dale, and Juanita Ryan. *Recovery from Shame.* Downers Grove, Ill.: InterVarsity Press, 1990.

Whitehead, James, and Evelyn Whitehead. *Shadows of the Heart.* New York: Crossroad, 1994.

Chapter 6: From Lonely Orphan to God's Adopted Child

Andersen, David. "When God Adopts." *Christianity Today,* July 19, 1993, pp. 37-39.

Barth, Markus. "Conversion and Conversations: Israel and the Church in Paul's Epistle to the Ephesians." *Interpretation* 17 (1963): 3-24.

Boice, James. *Foundations of the Christian Faith.* Downers Grove, Ill.: InterVarsity Press, 1986.

Capaldi, Gerard. "In the Fulness of Time." *Scottish Journal of Theology* 25 (1972): 197-216.

Erickson, Millard J. *Christian Theology.* Grand Rapids: Baker, 1985.

Grudem, Wayne. *Systematic Theology.* Grand Rapids: Zondervan, 1994.

Guthrie, Donald. *New Testament Theology.* Downers Grove, Ill.: InterVarsity Press, 1981.

Kelly, Doug. "Adoption: An Underdeveloped Heritage of the Westminster Standards." *The Reformed Theological Review* 52 (September-December 1993): 110-20.

Kirby, Gilbert W. "God's Adoption Procedure." *Christianity Today,* June 22, 1973, pp. 14-15.

Lyall, Francis. "Roman Law in the Writings of Paul—Adoption." *Journal of Biblical Literature* 88 (1969): 458-66.

Moore-Crispin, Derek R. "Galatians 4:1-9: The Use and Abuse of Parables." *The Evangelical Quarterly* 60 (1989): 203-23.

Moule, C. F. D. "Adoption." In *The Interpreter's Dictionary of the Bible,* 1:48. Nashville: Abingdon, 1962.

Palmer, F. H. "Adoption." In *The Illustrated Bible Dictionary,* 1:17. Wheaton, Ill.: Tyndale House, 1980.

Rosnell, William H. "New Testament Adoption—Graeco-Roman or Semitic?" *Journal of Biblical Literature* 71 (1952): 233.

Schoenberg, Martin W. "Hyiothesia: The Adoptive Sonship of the Israelites." *Ecclesiastical Review,* fall 1962, pp. 261-73.

Schweizer, Eduard. "Hyiothesia." In *Theological Dictionary of the New Testament.* Abridged ed. Edited by Geoffrey W. Bromiley. Grand Rapids: Eerdmans, 1985.

Scott, James M. "Adoption." In *Dictionary of Paul and His Letters,* pp. 15-18. Edited by Gerald Hawthorne, Ralph P. Martin and Daniel Reid. Downers Grove, Ill.: InterVarsity Press, 1993.

Thielman, Frank. *Paul and the Law.* Downers Grove, Ill.: InterVarsity Press, 1994.

Webb, Robert Alexander. *The Reformed Doctrine of Adoption.* Grand Rapids: Eerdmans, 1947.

Chapter 7: Hope in the Midst of Suffering

Bauckham, Richard. "Moltmann's Theology of Hope Revisited." *Scottish Journal of Theology* 42 (1989): 199-214.

Beker, J. Christiaan. *Suffering and Hope.* Grand Rapids: Eerdmans, 1987.

Brueggemann, Walter. *Hopeful Imagination: Prophetic Voices in Exile.* Philadelphia: Fortress, 1986.

Buechner, Frederick. *The Longing for Home.* San Francisco: Harper, 1996.

Bultmann, Rudolf. "Hope." In *Theological Dictionary of the New Testament,* pp. 229-32. Abridged ed. Edited by Geoffrey W. Bromiley. Grand Rapids: Eerdmans, 1985.

Conyers, A. J. *The Eclipse of Heaven.* Downers Grove, Ill.: InterVarsity Press, 1992.

Elshtain, Jean Bethke. *Democracy on Trial.* New York: BasicBooks, 1995.

Everts, J. M. "Hope." In *Dictionary of Paul and His Letters,* pp. 415-17. Edited by Gerald Hawthorne, Ralph P. Martin and Daniel Reid. Downers Grove, Ill.: InterVarsity Press, 1993.

Grenz, Stanley J. "Withering Flowers in the Garden of Hope." *Christianity Today,* April 6, 1992, pp. 10-21.

Hebblethwaite, Brian. *The Christian Hope.* Grand Rapids: Eerdmans, 1985.

Hoffman, E. "Hope." In *Dictionary of New Testament Theology,* 2:238-44. Edited by Colin Brown. Grand Rapids: Zondervan, 1981.

Kirkpatrick, William David. "Christian Hope." *Southwestern Journal of Theology,* spring 1994, pp. 33-44.

Minear, P. S. "Hope." In *The Interpreter's Dictionary of the Bible,* pp. 640-43. Edited by George Buttrick. Nashville: Abingdon, 1962.

Moltmann, Jürgen. *Theology of Hope.* Minneapolis: Fortress, 1993.

Neff, David. "Why Hope Is a Virtue." *Christianity Today,* April 3, 1995, pp. 24-25.

Ridderbos, Herman. *Paul: An Outline of His Theology.* Grand Rapids: Eerdmans, 1975.

Smith, S. M. "Theology of Hope." In *Evangelical Dictionary of Theology,* pp. 532-34. Edited by Walter Elwell. Grand Rapids: Baker, 1984.

Tasker, R. V. "Hope." In *The Illustrated Bible Dictionary,* 2:658-59. Edited by J. D. Douglas. Wheaton, Ill.: Tyndale House, 1980.

Travis, Stephen H. *Christian Hope and the Future.* Downers Grove, Ill.: InterVarsity Press, 1980.

———. "Hope." In *New Dictionary of Theology.* Edited by Sinclair Ferguson. Downers Grove, Ill.: InterVarsity Press, 1988.

———. *I Believe in the Second Coming of Jesus.* London: Hodder & Stoughton, 1982.

———. *The Jesus Hope.* Downers Grove, Ill.: InterVarsity Press, 1974.

Zimmerli, Walther. *Man and His Hope in the Old Testament.* Naperville, Ill.: Alec R. Allenson, 1968.

Chapter 8: Communities of Belonging

Amitai, Etzioni. *The Spirit of Community.* New York: Crown, 1993.

Bergquist, William. *The Postmodern Organization.* San Francisco: Jossey-Bass, 1993.

Berry, Carmen Renee. "In Search of Spiritual Community." *Leadership,* spring 2003, p. 12.

Bird, Warren. "The Great Small Group Takeover." *Christianity Today,* February 7, 1994, pp. 25-29.

Collins, Jim. *Good to Great.* New York: Harper Business, 2001.

Coupland, Douglas. *Microserfs.* New York: HarperCollins, 1995.

Ford, Paul. "From My Vision to Our Vision." *Leadership,* summer 2000, pp. 34-38.

Gaede, S. D. *Belonging.* Grand Rapids: Zondervan, 1985.

George, Carl F. *The Coming Church Revolution.* Grand Rapids: Revell, 1994.

————. *Prepare Your Church for the Future.* Grand Rapids: Revell, 1991.

Gorman, Julie A. *Community That Is Christian: A Handbook on Small Groups.* Wheaton, Ill.: Victor, 1993.

Hybels, Lynne, and Bill Hybels. *Rediscovering Church.* Grand Rapids: Zondervan, 1995.

Hyde, Douglas. *Dedication and Leadership.* Notre Dame, Ind.: University of Notre Dame Press, 1966.

Lamb, Richard. *Following Jesus in the Real World.* Downers Grove, Ill.: InterVarsity Press, 1995.

Long, Jimmy, et al. *Small Group Leaders' Handbook: The Next Generation.* Downers Grove, Ill.: InterVarsity Press, 1995.

McLaren, Brian. "Emerging Values." *Leadership,* summer 2003, pp. 34-39.

McManus, Erwin. *An Unstoppable Force.* Loveland, Colo.: Group, 2001.

Murren, Doug. *Leadership.* Ventura, Calif.: Regal, 1994.

Myers, Joseph. *The Search to Belong: Rethinking Intimacy, Community and Small Groups.* Grand Rapids: Zondervan, 2003.

Peace, Richard. "Reaching the X-Generation Through Small Groups." Paper presented at the National Small Group Conference, St. Davids, Pa., May 1995.

Prior, David. *Creating Community.* Colorado Springs: NavPress, 1992.

Putnam, Robert. *Better Together.* New York: Simon & Schuster, 2003.

Snyder, Howard. "Authentic Fellowship." *Christianity Today,* October 2003, p. 102.

Sweet, Leonard. *AquaChurch.* Loveland, Colo.: Group, 1999.

Watters, Ethan. *Urban Tribes.* New York: Bloomsbury, 2003.

Wuthnow, Robert. *I Came Away Stronger.* Grand Rapids: Eerdmans, 1994.

———. *Loose Connections: Joining Together in America's Fragmented Communities.* Cambridge: Harvard University Press, 1998.

———. *Sharing the Journey.* New York: Free Press, 1994.

Zimmerman, John C. "Leadership Across the Gaps Between Generations." *Crux,* June 1995, pp. 42-53.

Chapter 9: Our Spiritual Journey in Community

Allport, Gordon. "The Quest for Religious Maturity." In *Waiting for the Lord: Thirty-Three Meditations on God and Man,* p. 60. Edited by Peter A. Bertocci. New York: Macmillan, 1978.

Anderson, Ray. *Self Care: A Theology of Personal Empowerment and Spiritual Healing.* Wheaton, Ill.: Victor, 1995.

Astin, Alexander W. "Student Values: Knowing More About Where We Are Today." *American Association of Higher Education Bulletin,* May 1984, pp. 10-12.

Barnes, M. Craig. *Yearning: Living Between How It Is and How It Ought to Be.* Downers Grove, Ill.: InterVarsity Press, 1991.

Bascom, Tim. *The Comfort Trap.* Downers Grove, Ill.: InterVarsity Press, 1993.

Capps, Donald. *The Depleted Self.* Minneapolis: Fortress, 1993.

Cox, Harvey. *Fire from Heaven: The Rise of Pentecostal Spirituality and the Reshaping of Religion in the Twenty-First Century.* Reading, Mass.: Addison-Wesley, 1995.

Dunne, John S. *A Search for God in Time and Memory: An Exploration Traced in the Lives of Individuals from Augustine to Sartre.* London: Macmillan, 1969.

Easum, Bill, and Dave Travis. *Beyond the Box.* Loveland, Colo.: Group, 2003.

Fackre, Gabriel. *The Religious Right and the Christian Faith.* Grand Rapids: Eerdmans, 1982.

Foster, Richard. "Becoming Like Christ." *Christianity Today,* February 5, 1996, pp. 26-31.

Fowler, James W. *Weaving the New Creation.* San Francisco: HarperCollins, 1991.

Gergen, Kenneth J. *The Saturated Self.* San Francisco: HarperCollins, 1991.

Gibbs, Eddie. *In Name Only.* Wheaton, Ill.: Victor, 1994.

Hagberg, Janet O., and Robert A. Guelich. *The Critical Journey: Stages in the Life of Faith.* Dallas: Word, 1989.

Johnston, Graham. *Preaching to a Postmodern World.* Grand Rapids: Baker, 2001.

Jones, Tony. *Postmodern Youth Ministry.* Grand Rapids: Zondervan, 2001.

Karen, Robert. "Shame." *Atlantic Monthly,* February 1992.

Kaufman, Gershen. *Shame: The Power of Caring.* Cambridge, Mass.: Schenkman, 1980.

Kierkegaard, Søren. *Journals.* Translated by Alexander Dru. London: Oxford University Press, 1938.

Kimball, Dan. *The Emerging Church.* Grand Rapids: Zondervan, 2003.

Kraus, C. Norman. *Jesus Christ Our Lord: Christology from a Disciple's Perspective.* Scottsdale, Penn.: Herald, 1987.

Lose, David. *Confessing Jesus Christ.* Grand Rapids: Eerdmans, 2003.

McFague, Sallie. *Models of God: Theology for an Ecological, Nuclear Age.* Philadelphia: Fortress, 1987.

McLaren, Brian. *The Church on the Other Side.* Grand Rapids, Mich.: Zondervan, 2000.

———. *A New Kind of Christian.* San Francisco: Jossey-Bass, 2001.

Morgenthaler, Sally. *Worship Evangelism.* Grand Rapids: Zondervan, 1995.

Offner, Kevin F. "Adrift with Amnesia." *Re:Generation Quarterly,* winter 1995, pp. 6-8.

Park, Andy. *To Know You More.* Downers Grove, Ill.: InterVarsity Press, 2002.

Parks, Sharon. *The Critical Years.* San Francisco: Harper & Row, 1986.

Plantinga, Cornelius, Jr. *Not the Way It's Supposed to Be.* Grand Rapids: Eerdmans, 1995.

Redman, Robb. *The Great Worship Awakening.* San Franciso: Jossey-Bass, 2002.

Schreiner, Sally. "Contending with the Powers in the City." *The Gospel and Culture* 5, no. 1 (1995): 5-6.

Sine, Tom. *Live It Up! How to Create a Life You Can Love.* Scottsdale, Penn.: Herald, 1993.

Smith, Chuck. *The End of the World . . . as We Know It.* Colorado Springs: WaterBrook, 2001.

Solzhenitsyn, Aleksandr. *The Gulag Archipelago: An Experiment in Literary Investigation.* Translated by Thomas P. Whitney. New York: Harper & Row, 1975.

Stetzer, Ed. *Planting New Churches in a Postmodern Age.* Nashville: Broadman & Holman, 2003.

Webber, Robert. *The Younger Evangelicals.* Grand Rapids: Baker, 2002.

Westfall, John F. *Coloring Outside the Lines.* San Francisco: HarperCollins, 1991.

Chapter 10: Communities Offering Hope

Abraham, William J. "A Theology of Evangelism." *Interpretation,* summer 1994, pp. 116-29.

Arias, Mortimer. *Announcing the Reign of God.* Philadelphia: Fortress, 1986.

Barna, George. *Evangelism That Works.* Ventura, Calif.: Regal, 1995.

———. *Generation Next.* Ventura, Calif.: Regal, 1995.

Barr, James. *The Semantics of Biblical Language.* Glasgow: Oxford University Press, 1961.

Braaten, Carl, and Robert Jenson. *The Strange New Word of the Gospel.* Grand Rapids: Eerdmans, 2002.

Costas, Orlando. *Liberating News: A Theology of Contextual Evangelization.* Grand Rapids: Eerdmans, 1989.

Edgar, William. "No News Is Good News: Modernity, the Postmodern and Apologetics." *Westminster Theological Journal* 57 (1995): 359-82.

Filiatreau, Mark. "Good News on 'Old News.'" *Re:Generation Quarterly,* winter 1995, pp. 14-18.

Ford, Kevin Graham. *Jesus for a New Generation.* Downers Grove, Ill.: InterVarsity Press, 1995.

Ford, Leighton. *The Power of Story.* Colorado Springs: NavPress, 1994.

Gaines, Donna. "Suicidal Tendencies: Kurt Did Not Die for You." *Rolling Stone,* June 2, 1994, pp. 59-61.

Griffin, Em. *The Mind Changers.* Wheaton, Ill.: Tyndale House, 1981.

Hunsberger, George. "Is There Biblical Warrant for Evangelism?" *Interpretation,* spring 1995.

Hunter, George. *The Celtic Way of Evangelism.* Nashville: Abingdon, 2000.

———. *How to Reach Secular People.* Nashville: Abingdon, 1992.

Jenson, Robert. "How the World Lost Its Story." *First Things,* October 1993, pp. 19-24.

Kallenberg, Brad J. "Conversion Converted: A Postmodern Formulation of the Doctrine of Conversion." *Evangelical Quarterly* 67 (1995): 335-64.

———. *Live to Tell.* Grand Rapids: Brazos, 2002.

Keller, Tim. "Reaching the Secular Person." Unpublished paper, 1995.

Lindberg, Jack. "Evangelism and the Local Church." *Contact,* winter 1995, pp. 7-17.

Long, Jimmy. "Generating Hope." In *Telling the Truth: Evangelizing Postmoderns,* pp. 322-25. Edited by D. A. Carson. Grand Rapids: Zondervan, 2000.

Long, Thomas. "Beavis and Butthead Get Saved." *Theology Today,* July 1994, pp. 199-203.

McGrath, Alister. *Intellectuals Don't Need God and Other Modern Myths.* Grand Rapids: Zondervan, 1993.

———. *A Passion for Truth.* Downers Grove, Ill.: InterVarsity Press, 1996.

McLaren, Brian. *More Ready Than You Realize.* Grand Rapids: Zondervan, 2002.

Mundy, Chris. "The Lost Boy: The Life of Kurt Cobain." *Rolling Stone,* June 2, 1994, pp. 51-53.

Newbigin, Lesslie. *The Gospel in a Pluralist Society.* Grand Rapids: Eerdmans, 1989.

Posterski, Don. *Friendship: A Window on Ministry to Youth.* Scarborough, Ontario: Project Teen Canada, 1985.

————. *True to You.* Winfield, B.C.: Wood Lake Books, 1995.

Richardson, Rick. *Evangelism Outside the Box.* Downers Grove, Ill.: InterVarsity Press, 2000.

Roxburgh, Alan. *Reaching a New Generation.* Downers Grove, Ill.: InterVarsity Press, 1993.

Sider, Ronald J. *One-Sided Christianity?* San Francisco: HarperCollins, 1993.

Sire, James W. *Chris Chrisman Goes to College.* Downers Grove, Ill.: InterVarsity Press, 1993.

Tiplady, Richard, ed. *Postmission.* London: Pasternoster Press, 2002.

White, James Emery. "Gateway Country." *Leadership,* summer 2001, pp. 35-39.

Willimon, William, and Thomas Naylor. *The Abandoned Generation.* Grand Rapids: Eerdmans, 1995.

Wimber, John, with Kevin Springer. *Power Evangelism.* San Francisco: HarperCollins, 1992.

Wuthnow, Robert. *Learning to Care.* New York: Oxford University Press, 1995.

Zacharias, Ravi. "Reaching the Happy Thinking Pagan." *Leadership,* spring 1995, pp. 18-27.

Names Index

Subject Index

Scripture Index